KILLING OTHERS

KILLING OTHERS

A Natural History of Ethnic Violence

Matthew Lange

CORNELL UNIVERSITY PRESS   ITHACA AND LONDON

First published 2017 by Cornell University Press
First printing, Cornell Paperbacks, 2017

Printed in the United States of America

Library of Congress Cataloging-in-Publication Data

Names: Lange, Matthew, author.
Title: Killing others : a natural history of ethnic violence / Matthew Lange.
Description: Ithaca : Cornell University Press, 2017. | Includes bibliographical references and index.
Identifiers: LCCN 2016030015 (print) | LCCN 2016031136 (ebook) | ISBN 9781501704871 (cloth : alk. paper) | ISBN 9781501704888 (pbk. : alk. paper) | ISBN 9781501707766 (Reflowable formats) | ISBN 9781501707773 (PDF ebook)
Subjects: LCSH: Ethnic conflict. | Ethnic conflict—History.
Classification: LCC HM1121 .L37 2017 (print) | LCC HM1121 (ebook) | DDC 305.8—dc23
LC record available at https://lccn.loc.gov/2016030015

Cornell University Press strives to use environmentally responsible suppliers and materials to the fullest extent possible in the publishing of its books. Such materials include vegetable-based, low-VOC inks and acid-free papers that are recycled, totally chlorine-free, or partly composed of nonwood fibers. For further information, visit our website at www.cornellpress.cornell.edu.

To Elias Clayton, Elmer Jackson, Isaac McGhie, and all victims of ethnic violence

Contents

Illustrations

Acknowledgments

Unknowingly, I have been working on *Killing Others* for the past fifteen years, as the book synthesizes, remolds, and extends insight I gained from past projects on colonial state legacies, state formation and transformation, the impact of colonialism on ethnic violence, and the effects of education on ethnic violence. Because my research for this book has been going on for so long, many people and organizations have assisted me with it.

Dietrich Rueschemeyer, James Mahoney, and Patrick Heller have been and continue to be fabulous mentors. My colleagues John A. Hall, Maurice Pinard, Eran Shor, and Thomas Soehl generously commented on different drafts of this book and helped me formulate ideas through frequent discussions. John A. Hall deserves special thanks, as he read and provided insightful comments on three different versions and is an unending source of encouragement. Another colleague, T. V. Paul, provided valuable contacts for my fieldwork in Kerala. A number of talented former students helped me gather data, complete statistical analyses, and edit the manuscript, including Andrew Dawson, Sara Hall, Jason Jensen, and Kalyani Thurairajah. The International Centre for Ethnic Studies at both Colombo and Kandy in Sri Lanka, the Centre for Development Studies in Kerala, the Public Records Office and British Library in the UK, the OKD Institute of Social Change and Development in Assam, the Colorado Historical Society, and the Cornell University Library provided access to valuable documents that informed this study. Several individuals in these organizations offered support, guidance, and friendship, including K. M. de Silva, Indranee Dutta, Sunil Mani, Thambirajah Ponnudurai, and Bhupen Sarmah. Outside of these organizations, Rena Choparou, Gopa Gopa Kumar, Yiannis Papadakis, Alexis Rappas, Michael Tharakan, Jandhyala Tilak, and Michalinos Zembylas generously assisted with my fieldwork and offered valuable advice. My editor at Cornell, Roger Haydon, has also been enormously helpful on the publishing end, and two anonymous reviewers provided constructive recommendations and critiques. Finally, the research for this book has been generously funded by three different grants from the Social Sciences and Humanities Research Council of Canada.

Others have contributed to this book more indirectly. My parents, Eileen and Keith Lange, have been a constant source of support and guidance throughout my life. Last but not least, I owe Clodine, Nicolas, and Anna—my wife and children—for my daily dose of love and inspiration.

KILLING OTHERS

KILLING OTHERS

Like many of their peers, Elias Clayton, Elmer Jackson, and Isaac McGhie left the southern United States in the early 1900s in search of the American dream in the North. Their dream turned into a nightmare. On June 15, 1920, all three young men were falsely accused of raping a young woman and arrested. Despite their innocence, they must have hoped and prayed that their steel prison cells were sturdy because a two-thousand-man mob had stormed the police station, had overpowered the officers, and was trying to extricate the accused. After struggling for quite some time, the mob finally broke the hinges off the doors. Once in possession of the accused, the mob beat and insulted the prisoners before hanging them by their necks from a light pole.[1] Following their deaths, photographers took pictures of the grisly yet carnival-like murder scene. The gut-wrenching photo presented in Figure i.1 captures the utterly horrific character of the violence in a way that a narrative description cannot, with jubilant participants and onlookers surrounding the broken and lifeless bodies of the three young victims.[2] The image

---

1. For a detailed description of the events, see Fedo (2000).
2. Scholars disagree about whether to show photos of the victims of extreme violence. Some argue that such photos should not be shown because they are insensitive and instrumentalize the victims. Others argue that such photos allow readers to understand the horrors and hardships of violence in a way that narrative description cannot. Because the last thing I want to do is show disrespect for Elias, Elmer, and Isaac, I thought long and hard about including the photo of the lynchings, and I discussed the photo with friends, colleagues, and my editor. In the end, I decided to show the photo. In particular, objective empirical analysis of the causes of ethnic violence can render violence

FIGURE i.1. The lynchings of Elias Clayton, Elmer Jackson, and Isaac McGhie

also highlights the ultimate reason why Elias, Elmer, and Isaac were murdered: They were African Americans and their assailants were white. Had Elias, Elmer, and Isaac been white, the residents of Duluth would have let the criminal justice system deal with them. In fact, had Elias, Elmer, and Isaac been white, it is safe to say that they would *not* have been falsely accused of raping a white woman.

The life of Beata Uwazaninka was also brutally altered by her Otherness. As a girl, Beata lived with her grandmother in rural Rwanda. One night, neighbors entered their home while she and her grandmother were sleeping and bludgeoned her grandmother to death with a hammer; Beata was spared because she was only a child. The men killed Beata's grandmother because she was Tutsi, and they were not prosecuted for the murder, in turn, because she was Tutsi. According to Beata, "That was how I found out I am a Tutsi, but to be honest, I had no idea what it meant" (Uwazaninka 2006). Even for a seven-year-old girl, this lack of awareness might seem surprising, but Hutus and Tutsis have the same skin

---

banal, and the photo helps readers to realize and remember the true human cost of ethnic violence. And instead of objectifying the victims, I believe the photo allows people to empathize with Elias, Elmer, and Isaac.

color, practice the same religions, speak the same language, and—for all intents and purposes—share the same culture. As a result, it can be difficult to distinguish between Hutus and Tutsis, and there is considerable disagreement about what actually constitutes "Hutuness" and "Tutsiness." Seven years after Beata's grandmother was butchered for being Tutsi, Beata survived a one-hundred-day genocidal rampage during which Hutus killed two-thirds of all Rwandan Tutsis, including nearly a hundred members of Beata's family. These acts further clarified for Beata the ultimate meaning of being Tutsi in late-twentieth-century Rwanda: It meant many Hutus believed she was an enemy who was better dead than alive.

Beata, Elias, Elmer, and Isaac all suffered at the hands of others because they were "Others." That is, they were victims of ethnic violence. Sadly, there are millions of other stories like theirs, as diverse peoples all around the world have been attacked and murdered because of ethnic difference. Data compiled by the Center for Systemic Peace indicate that three million people died from ethnic violence between 1990 and 2013, and the center claims that this is a conservative estimate (Marshall 2014).[3] And just like Beata and the loved ones of Elias, Elmer, and Isaac, millions more live with the life-changing scars of ethnic violence.

Although all episodes of ethnic violence share basic commonalities, ethnic violence comes in a great variety of forms. Most notably, episodes of ethnic violence differ according to goal, scale, target, level of organization, and degree of state involvement; and variation along these lines promotes different types of ethnic violence, including lynchings, riots, protests, terrorist attacks, civil wars, and genocides.[4] These types are distinct, but many episodes of ethnic violence combine multiple types either because one type transforms into another over time or because ethnic violence takes multiple forms simultaneously.

The deaths of Elias, Elmer, and Isaac exemplify *ethnic lynchings*. These are a unique form of ethnic violence in which people from a dominant ethnic community murder particular members of a subordinate ethnic community as punishment for an alleged crime. In addition to retribution, lynchings help maintain systems of ethnic domination. *Ethnic riots* also seek retribution and to reinforce communal power but are much more indiscriminate than lynchings, with mobs seeking to kill and destroy the property of any member of the

---

3. Beyond taking conservative estimates of deaths, the figure also excludes deaths from several conflicts that clearly had ethnic components. For example, the figure does not include deaths from the civil war in the Democratic Republic of Congo, which killed as many as five million people between 1996 and 2003 and began as a clear case of ethnic violence. The figure also excludes the decade-long ethnic civil war between Hutus and Tutsis in Burundi beginning in 1993, which is estimated to have killed 300,000 people.

4. For a description of different types of ethnic violence, see Horowitz (2001).

target community. Hindu riots against Muslims in India are notable examples. Violent *ethnic protests*, most frequently organized by subordinate communities, raise awareness of ethnic grievances through marches, sit-ins, and acts of symbolic destruction, and such protests usually turn violent when members of the dominant ethnic community—including the police—attack protesters. African National Congress (ANC) protests against the apartheid government of South Africa and the state-led violence against the protesters exemplify this form of ethnic violence. *Ethnic terrorist attacks* purposefully and indiscriminately kill and destroy the property of Others in ways that promote widespread fear. This form of ethnic violence is most common when great disparities in power exist, with members of one ethnic community resorting to terrorist methods when it is unable to use more standard methods of warfare. Palestinian attacks on Israelis offer one notable example. *Ethnic civil war* is one of the most deadly forms of ethnic violence. It involves extended military struggles between organized segments of different ethnic communities, with each side attempting to vanquish the other to either control the state or form an independent ethnic homeland. The Syrian civil war pitting the Alawite-dominated state against Sunni opposition is one example of an ethnic civil war. Finally, *ethnic genocide* is the most deadly form of ethnic violence and involves deliberate attempts to exterminate entire populations of Others. The Rwandan genocide is one atrocious example.

Some scholars of ethnic violence note that such a great variety of forms creates a problem for general analysis, as different types of ethnic violence might have different causes (Brubaker and Laitin 1998; Gilley 2004; Horowitz 2001). There is certainly truth to this warning. Breaking norms of interethnic contact, for instance, might cause a lynching but will have very little impact on genocide, as the latter requires a much greater existential threat. Yet disaggregating ethnic violence also comes at a heavy cost: It overlooks broad similarities that make possible general understandings of ethnic violence. And although general explanations overlook some of the differences between the lynchings of African Americans and the genocidal violence against Tutsis, they help us make sense of most episodes of ethnic violence.

In the pages that follow, this book pursues general understandings and therefore analyzes all types of ethnic violence. The analysis is broad in three additional ways. First, it explores ethnic violence in all regions of the world. Second, it investigates transformations in ethnic violence over time. Finally, believing that the best scientific work integrates a wide variety of evidence, this book merges insight from numerous disciplines. Combining all these elements, *Killing Others* offers a natural history of ethnic violence that considers its origins, causes, transformations, and future.

Studies of ethnic violence must pay attention to Beata, Elias, Elmer, Isaac, and other victims to highlight the sheer inhumanity that is ethnic violence. This is particularly important for causal analyses, which can be so focused on evidence that they trivialize the actual violence. At the same time, special attention must be given to perpetrators. Indeed, any attempt to explore the causes of ethnic violence must consider what pushes people to attack and kill people from other ethnic communities. Common sense suggests that perpetrators are inherently degenerate and demonic, and most people view perpetrators of ethnic violence as less than human. The widespread acceptance of Manichean categories of good and evil has something to do with this, as it pushes humans to view violent ethnic extremists as inherently bad and to disregard any redeemable qualities they might have. Hollywood and Hollywoodized "news" programs help reinforce such views through stereotypic portrayals of cold-hearted and ruthless killers who lack any sort of human decency.

In order to go beyond overly simplistic and naïve explanations focusing on good and evil, analyses of ethnic violence must first and foremost acknowledge the humanity of the killers and objectively assess what causes them to act the way they do. And through objective analysis, it becomes clear that most perpetrators of dastardly deeds are not inherently degenerate, deranged, and demonic. Different studies of the Rwandan genocide, for example, find that prior to the genocide many civilian killers had cordial relations with their Tutsi neighbors and were not belligerent and intolerant bullies (Fujii 2009; Straus 2004).

Similarly, although it is easy to demonize the perpetrators of the Duluth lynchings after seeing their repulsive smirks and posturing next to the mangled bodies of Elias, Elmer, and Isaac, they were not deranged psychopaths incapable of love and empathy. In his exceptional analysis of the lynchings, Michael Fedo (2000) describes how most participants subsequently led "exemplary lives, becoming involved with various civic and youth programs throughout the city" (175). Even before the lynchings, most participants were considered upstanding citizens. Leonard Hedman is a particular and perplexing case. At the time of the lynching, Leonard was a twenty-three-year-old dockworker who was saving money for law school. According to police reports, Leonard attacked a police officer protecting the accused and shouted, "I got the rope! We want those niggers!" (Fedo 2000, 68). He was eventually charged with assaulting an officer and strangling Isaac McGhie. Leonard's behavior suggests a deranged and hateful individual, but Leonard's classmates remembered him as a kind, idealistic, and intelligent individual who liked to play pranks, was concerned about others, and was driven to become a lawyer. He also spoke out against lynchings earlier in his life and had actually given an impassioned speech decrying the evils of lynching at a school competition. Reciting a speech originally given by Percy E. Thomas titled "The American Infamy," Leonard declared:

> The majority of both North and South knows that lynching is an evil; but this insight must be heated to action which shall restrain the less thoughtful of the majority. We must have sentiment which guarantees a trial to the accused before a judgment bar uncorrupted by the gangrene of prejudice; we must have a sentiment that visits upon the guilty punishment as swift and unerring as the hands of God; a sentiment that restrains the shirking Sheriff from washing his hands in innocence before the mob; a sentiment that desperately determines to lift the law in its majesty far above the maddened judgment and revengeful spirits of the rabble; a sentiment that will eventually say, "killing by the mob is murder . . . and by the help of God, this American infamy must go." (Quoted in Fedo 2000, 36–37)

A powerful speech with some excellent points, and it is all the more remarkable when one considers who gave it. So what happened? Why did a seemingly upstanding young man take an active role in the grisly lynchings? Unfortunately, we will never know the exact answer to this question because Leonard refused to talk about the lynchings for the remainder of this life. Many perpetrators of ethnic violence are similar in this regard, and the accounts of those who do talk are suspect because the perpetrators usually try to justify—both to themselves and to their audiences—why they participated. These problems make it difficult to put a finger on the exact causes of ethnic violence. Still, analyses of ethnic violence are not impossible because the context and processes leading up to the violence offer important insight into the causes. If one wants to understand why Leonard and a number of his peers attacked and killed Elias, Elmer, and Isaac in Duluth, Minnesota, in 1920, one can gain considerable insight by recognizing several contextual factors. First, a discourse of white superiority dominated the United States in the 1920s and portrayed African American men as a rapacious threat to white women. Second, race relations were particularly tense in the American Midwest in 1920 after a large influx of African American migrants and a series of race riots. Third, Duluth had been facing considerable economic difficulties, and Eastern European immigrants and African Americans had been migrating to the city to work for lower wages than the local-born population. Putting all these together, we start to see what motivated Leonard and others to participate in the lynchings. The subsequent chapters highlight more general social and historical conditions that promote ethnic violence. In so doing, the analysis offers insight into what caused Leonard Hedman and other seemingly normal people to lash out and kill Others.

Definitions

Experts offer a variety of different definitions of "ethnic violence," "ethnicity," and other related concepts. Such diversity commonly contributes to conceptual confusion and misunderstandings. This section seeks to avoid these troublesome outcomes by clearly defining key concepts.

As used in this book, *ethnic violence* has three main features: It pits residents of the same country against one another, is a collective form of violence involving many people, and is motivated by ethnic difference. Because of the first definitional component, international warfare is not an example of ethnic violence. The second excludes individual hate crimes. And due to the third, violence exclusively motivated by class, party, or gender differences is not ethnic violence. In addition to these defining traits, I also limit the analysis to incidents of extreme violence causing multiple deaths and overlook episodes of ethnic violence that only involve verbal abuse, the destruction of property, and nonlethal physical assaults.

Given the centrality of ethnic difference to this form of violence, all definitions of ethnic violence must also conceptualize "*ethnicity*." This task is surprisingly difficult because "ethnicity" is an overarching concept combining multiple phenomena. Instead of trying to reduce ethnicity to one component, I conceptualize ethnicity as multifaceted: framework, structure, and consciousness all wrapped into one.

Scholars increasingly recognize ethnicity as an idea: It is a category-based cognitive framework shaping how people perceive themselves and the social world around them (Brubaker 2004; Hale 2004; Jenkins 2008). In this way, ethnicity is a matter of perception, with people seeing the world through ethnic lenses. In the pages that follow, I refer to an ethnic-based cognitive framework as an *ethnic framework*.

Yet ethnicity also has a structural side. A structure is an enduring pattern of social relations, and *ethnic structures* are social relations that are patterned by ethnicity and take a distinct, recognizable, and recurring form. Racially segregated neighborhoods and high incarceration rates among African Americans are two particular examples of ethnic structures, but ethnicity patterns social relations in many more ways, including organizational membership, occupation, discriminatory behavior, political support, the distribution of power, public rituals, and access to public goods. These structures shape the life chances of individuals and therefore make ethnicity incredibly meaningful.

Finally, an *ethnic consciousness* is an ethnic framework that is imbued with values, norms, and understandings. It is present when people not only perceive ethnicity but identify with it, value it, and are concerned about its well-being.

Sociologist Émile Durkheim (1984 [1893]) famously describes "collective consciousness," and an ethnic consciousness is a particular type of the latter. Durkheim suggests that a collective consciousness is a mental state whereby an individual focuses on the collective. Such a state is not permanent, as people continually revert back and forth between individual and collective levels of consciousness depending on the circumstances.

While ethnic frameworks, ethnic structures, and ethnic consciousness are distinct elements of ethnicity, all are interrelated. Ethnic frameworks and ethnic structures reinforce one another, with ethnic frameworks promoting ethnically patterned relations and ethnic structures shaping perceptions of ethnicity. And when both ethnic frameworks and ethnic structures are combined, they contribute to a salient and powerful ethnic consciousness: An ethnic framework influences perceptions of ethnicity, ethnic structures make ethnicity meaningful, and both are needed for people to perceive, value, identify with, and be concerned about ethnicity.

So ethnicity is a framework, structure, and consciousness, but what differentiates ethnicity from any other framework, structure, and consciousness? At the heart of ethnicity is a focus on community: An ethnic framework is based on communal categories, an ethnic structure provides the mechanical foundations for community, and an ethnic consciousness makes people value community. Ethnicity is not just any type of community, however. According to Max Weber (1968 [1921]), an ethnic community is based on perceptions of common culture and shared descent. Benedict Anderson (1983), in turn, rightly notes that most ethnic communities are broad, abstract, and overarching and include millions of strangers in an "imagined community." In this way, ethnicity is distinct from family, neighborhood, clan, and other more tangible communities that are commonly based on shared culture and descent. Importantly, "imagined" does not mean that ethnicity is fake; ethnicity is imaginary only in the sense that people perceive themselves as part of the same community even though they do not know most coethnics, commonly have major cultural differences, and rarely share blood ties.

A number of factors promote perceptions of shared culture and heritage and make something as abstract as ethnicity seem concrete and natural. Five are particularly common and influential: nation, race, language, religion, and shared history. The Quebecois ethnic community, for example, is presently based primarily on the French language, Quebecois nationalism, and a shared history of French settlement and conflict with the English (Behiels 1985). Despite the primordial feel of ethnic community, the factors that delineate ethnicity change with the social environment. The French Canadian ethnic community—a predecessor of the Quebecois ethnic community—was based on the Catholic religion, the French race, and the French language. In this way, the French language is the only defining factor that has been relatively constant over the past hundred years.

Of the main cultural and historical factors that delineate ethnic communities, three—nation, race, and religious community—are commonly used interchangeably with ethnicity, yet all are distinct concepts. As employed in this book, a *nation* denotes a political community that possesses an ideology of communal self-rule, the latter of which is commonly referred to as *nationalism*. In this way, my use of "nation" does not refer to all citizens of the same country, as many people are cocitizens but view themselves as members of different nations. Like ethnicity, different combinations of language, religion, race, and history usually delineate nations. Yet only some ethnicities have the same political components as nations, making nation a particular type of ethnicity. Nationalist violence between residents of the same country is therefore a particular type of ethnic violence.

Race, on the other hand, is not a subtype of ethnicity. Instead, I define it as a noncommunal social category based on an arbitrary combination of physical characteristics. Despite this fundamental difference, both race and ethnicity are related because many ethnicities are defined in part by race. "African American," for example, is an ethnicity based on race, nation, language, and shared history. Thus, while a Senegalese might share the same race as an African American, they do not share the same ethnicity because of different nationalities, languages, and histories. When race is a defining component of ethnicity, however, it is usually *the* most influential definitional trait, causing people to emphasize race and downplay ethnicity. In addition to the greater observability of race and the presence of racist ideologies, race's special place results from how racially informed ethnicities commonly develop: People are categorized racially, such categorization has real-world social consequences that quickly endow races with communal characteristics, and race therefore metamorphoses into an ethnicity defined by both race and communal characteristics.

Finally, a *religious community* is a set of people who practice the same religion. Similar to race, it is not an example of ethnicity but commonly defines ethnicity. Frequently, religious communities overlap with ethnicity, making a collection of people both an ethnicity and a religious community. Catholics and Protestants in Northern Ireland are notable examples. Yet religious communities and ethnicities rarely overlap perfectly. This incongruity results from the fact that religion is rarely the sole defining component of ethnicity, and the other defining factors—language, race, nation, and shared history—still apply to individuals who either are not religious or practice a different religion. Thus, only practicing Catholics and Protestants are members of religious communities, whereas nonreligious individuals from Northern Ireland with Catholic and Protestant heritage are members of Catholic and Protestant ethnicities. And unlike the Northern Ireland example, many religious communities do not overlap with ethnicities. In the contemporary United States, Catholic or Protestant ethnicities are weak or nonexistent, and the Catholic and Protestant religious communities are multi-ethnic. The reverse is also true: Many ethnicities include members who follow multiple religions. For instance, religion is not a defining component of African American ethnicity, and the African American community includes Protestants, Catholics, Muslims, Buddhists, and atheists.

Another important difference between religion and ethnicity is the type of violence that they inspire. Similar to Brubaker (2015), I define religious violence as motivated by the zealous application of religious principles and beliefs, not ethnic difference. Such violence commonly pits members of the same ethnic community against one another, such as when religious conviction pushes someone to attack an abortion clinic. Alternatively, religious violence sometimes targets entire categories of nonbelievers, such as ISIS attacks on Christians, Yedizis, and other religious minorities in Iraq and Syria. When violence targets entire religious categories in this way, one cannot assume that it is religious violence, however. Instead, it might be motivated by religious zealotry, ethnic difference, or a combination of the two. A similar distinction must be made between racial and ethnic violence, as violence that is solely motivated by racial difference is not ethnic violence. Yet nearly all episodes of racial violence have clear ethnic components, so racial violence between conationals is almost always ethnic violence.

The Argument: Modernity and Ethnic Violence

While recognizing that ethnic violence has a multitude of causes and that no two episodes have the same determinants, this book argues that modernity is the most common and influential cause of ethnic violence. The impact of modernity is largely hidden, however, because it is a structural determinant, meaning that modernity creates social conditions that increase the risk of ethnic violence. Using a forest fire as an analogy, modernity creates combustible materials that increase the chances that some proximate cause will eventually ignite a fire. As shown in Figure i.2, *Killing Others* offers evidence that modernity promotes two highly combustible conditions: an ethnic consciousness, which provides motives that push people to participate in ethnic violence, and mobilizational resources and openings, which allow people to act on motive. While multiple aspects of modernity contribute to ethnic consciousness and mobilizational opportunities, this analysis highlights modern states and education as the most influential.

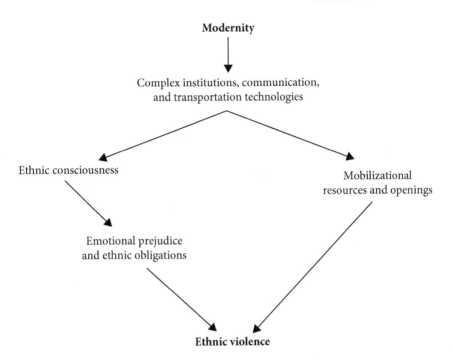

FIGURE i.2. The impact of modernity on ethnic violence

As a cognitive framework, ethnicity shapes how humans perceive, interpret, and represent the world. As a structure, ethnicity becomes relevant, meaningful, and valuable. And when combined, both frameworks and structures contribute to an ethnic consciousness whereby people perceive the world in terms of ethnicity, identify strongly with their ethnic community, and pay attention to the well-being of their ethnic community. Modernity, in turn, contributes to both the ideal and structural sides of ethnicity and therefore promotes an ethnic consciousness. Throughout the majority of human history, most people self-identified with a small set of known acquaintances, and few people developed a strong ethnic consciousness. Social transformations linked to modernity helped to create ethnic consciousnesses and spread them throughout the world. Most notably, modernity improved organizational, communication, and transportation technologies, which allowed abstract ideas of ethnicity to spread among populations living throughout large territories. These technologies also created larger and more widespread social networks and therefore contributed to ethnic structures that gave meaning to ethnic frameworks. Modernity also increased the influence of states, education, and other institutions that serve as social carriers of ethnicity, which spread ideas of ethnicity and structure relations in ways that make ethnicity highly significant.

When ethnic consciousness is powerful and widespread, it contributes to two common and influential determinants of ethnic violence: emotional prejudice and ethnic obligations. Emotional prejudice targets entire ethnic categories with hatred, anger, jealousy, resentment, fear, and other negative emotions. An ethnic consciousness is a necessary condition for emotional prejudice because it heightens the salience of ethnic difference. Moreover, emotional prejudice is most common when people value and are concerned about ethnicity.

Ethnic obligations are a second powerful and common motive for ethnic violence. Through norms and sanctions, they push people to act in ways that protect their ethnicity. An ethnic consciousness, in turn, contributes to ethnic obligations by heightening awareness of ethnic difference and causing people to value ethnicity so much that they feel obliged to protect it. And while many people willingly act on obligations because they value their ethnicity and believe they have a duty to protect it, the ethnic structures and social carriers that promote ethnic consciousness also enforce obligatory action through sanctions. Both states and education play influential roles in popularizing and enforcing the norms that underlie ethnic obligations.

In addition to influencing the motives of ethnic violence, modernity also contributes to the organization and mobilization that make possible collective violence against Others. Organization is absolutely vital for any type of collective violence, and modernity promotes a great variety of organizations. Such organizations are particularly likely to mobilize ethnic violence when they are themselves structured by ethnicity. The main social carriers of ethnicity, in turn, control organizations and resources that allow them to successfully mobilize ethnic violence. Most notably, modern states possess an impressive assortment of mobilizational resources, and ethnicized states are the most powerful mobilizers of ethnic violence. More indirectly, ethnicized states also mobilize ethnic violence by leaving political openings for ethnic violence and by encouraging civilians to attack ethnic rivals.

All in all, *Killing Others* highlights how ethnic violence is a modern menace, with modernity promoting ethnic violence through its impact on motive and on mobilization. There are two important caveats to these general findings, however. First, ethnic violence is not uniquely modern. Although modernity promotes ethnic consciousness and improves mobilizational resources, both were present to different extents in some premodern societies, especially those with states and organized religion. Modern social transformations, however, greatly strengthened ethnic consciousness, enormously expanded mobilizational resources, and spread both throughout the world, causing an abrupt spike in ethnic violence.

The second caveat is that modernity is not constant and that its changing form affects ethnic violence. This fact helps explain an important paradox: Modernity promotes ethnic violence, but the earliest modernizers have had among the lowest levels of ethnic violence over the past seventy years. *Killing Others* offers evidence that the way modernity developed in Western Europe and the former British settler colonies helped counteract modernity's earlier effects, thereby reducing the risk of ethnic violence and transforming these former champions of ethnic violence into contemporary leaders of ethnic peace. The development of robust rights-based democracy is key to containing the forces that modernity had previously unleashed, as it shapes motives and mobilizational opportunities in ways that reduce the risk of ethnic violence. Importantly, rights-based democracy changes the character and orientation of states and education and transforms them from influential determinants to important deterrents.

The Theoretical Perspective: Cognitive Modernism

To make this argument, *Killing Others* combines insights from Benedict Anderson (1983), Rogers Brubaker (2004), Stuart Kaufman (2015), Siniša Malešević (2013), Michael Mann (2005), and others to formulate a theoretical approach that I call "cognitive modernism." This approach is cognitive because it recognizes the mental side of ethnicity, with ethnic consciousness being a collectivist state of mind. At the same time, an ethnic consciousness only becomes salient when ethnic structures are present and when social carriers popularize them, and this more structural side of ethnicity works with the cognitive side to motivate and mobilize ethnic violence. And in recognizing that modernity creates structural conditions that promote ethnic consciousness and mobilize ethnic violence, this approach is modernist.

A cognitive modernist approach combines psychology and sociology, using the former to bridge the gap between biological and sociological explanations. Drawing on literature in psychology, it considers the mentalities that promote ethnic violence. These mentalities are shaped by the anatomy of the human brain and include human tendencies to divide the world into ingroups and outgroups, to form a great variety of ingroups, to be emotional toward ingroups and outgroups, and to make sacrifices for the well-being of the ingroup. While acknowledging this biological component, a cognitive modernist approach recognizes the malleability of human mentalities and places greater emphasis on the ways in which social relations shape them. Indeed, ethnic violence is much too rare to be considered an inevitability of human biology, and only certain social environments promote the mentalities that lead to ethnic violence, with modern environments being particularly nourishing.

Given the importance it places on modernity, a cognitive modernist approach has important similarities with modernization theory.[5] Most basically, both approaches focus on modern social transformations as causal determinants. While recognizing this important similarity, the approach used in this book lacks modernization theory's functionalism, progressivism, and Eurocentrism. Moreover, modernization theory claims that modernity eventually eradicates ethnic difference, with all peoples integrating into a unified nation. This book, on the other hand, views ethnic diversity and modernity as fully compatible.

A second and much more popular theoretical approach to ethnicity and ethnic violence is constructivism, which recognizes that ethnic communities are human constructs and that their strength and contours are constantly changing.[6] Constructivists suggest that humans have numerous bases of collective identity and that the social context determines which collective hat is worn at any one time. From this perspective, ethnic violence occurs when the social context heightens the salience of ethnicity, although some constructivists believe that the malleable and unstable character of ethnicity makes it difficult to accurately classify violence as ethnic or nonethnic. Like constructivism, I recognize the cognitive components of ethnicity. My approach differs from most constructivist accounts, however, because it pinpoints modernity as an influential determinant of ethnicity. Moreover, I suggest that ethnicity is commonly much stickier and more resilient than the constructivist camp recognizes. Thus whereas some constructivists claim it is impossible to actually label violence as "ethnic" because cognitive frameworks are both numerous and transformative, I recognize the need for caution in labeling violence as "ethnic" but suggest that the strength and popularity of ethnicity make ethnic violence both real and identifiable. Finally, relative to constructivists, I place greater emphasis on ethnicity's social structural side, which affects the salience of ethnicity and is the main reason why ethnicity is sometimes so sticky.

A third influential literature focuses on grievances and threats as motivators of ethnic violence.[7] This approach is varied but generally focuses on economic,

---

5. For a review of the functionalist/modernist position on ethnic violence, see chapter 4 of Malešević (2004).

6. For a review of the constructivist position, see Chandra (2012).

7. For prominent examples, see Gurr (1993), Horowitz (1985), Sambanis (2001), and Wimmer, Cederman, and Min (2009).

political, and cultural grievances and threats that are framed in terms of ethnicity. Grievances and threats commonly result from perceptions that one ethnic community has greater power, resources, or status than another. The theoretical approach of this book incorporates grievance-based theory but adjusts it in two ways: It considers how modernity contributes to grievances and threats and explicitly links both to emotional and obligatory motives.

The theoretical approach taken in this book also incorporates key elements of elite theories.[8] The elite approach notes that elites play vital roles in mobilizing ethnic violence. This book agrees but pays greater attention to why people follow elite provocateurs. People are not putty in the hands of ethnic leaders, and elites are most successful at mobilizing ethnic violence when their constituents possess ethnic consciousness, are emotionally prejudiced, and accept ethnic obligations; and ethnic violence is most likely when the leaders skillfully manipulate all three. Elites with resources are also more successful at mobilizing people. And because modernity promotes ethnic consciousness, emotional prejudice, ethnic obligations, and mobilizational resources, elites are most successful at mobilizing ethnic violence in modern environments.

Of all major theoretical perspectives on ethnicity and ethnic violence, the cognitive modernist approach is the least influenced by the instrumentalist, or rationalist, perspective.[9] The latter has gained considerable appeal in economics and political science and claims that individuals choose ethnic identities strategically in order to maximize benefits. It also suggests that ethnic violence occurs when people calculate the costs and benefits of participating in ethnic violence and choose to participate when the benefits outweigh the costs. While instrumental motives undoubtedly affect ethnic violence, this book argues that perceptions of and concerns about ethnicity are much more influential. And while communal perceptions and concerns can be analyzed in terms of costs and benefits, it is more accurate and insightful to analyze them in terms of ethnic consciousness, emotional prejudice, and obligations.

---

8. For a review of the elitist perspective, see chapter 8 of Malešević (2004).

9. For a review of the rationalist perspective, see chapter 7 of Malešević (2004).

1

THE NATURE AND NURTURE OF ETHNIC VIOLENCE

When you compare the two, it is amazing to think that chihuahuas descended from wolves only a few thousand years ago. Clearly demonstrating our creative intelligence, humans somehow transformed something big, shaggy, fierce, graceful, and athletic into a creature that can only jokingly be described by any of these adjectives. Although dangerous, wolves were easily domesticated because of their social and hierarchic natures. As a result, domesticated wolves substituted humans for their four-legged companions, and human masters asserted their authority to keep pet wolves in their place. Many early masters undoubtedly lost a finger, arm, or child to their wolves' jaws, but selective breeding helped render domesticated wolves less ferocious and more subservient. Chihuahuas, which have been bred into an innocuous pocket-sized pet, offer one extreme outcome of this process.

While the small size of chihuahuas makes them the ideal pet for Hollywood starlets wanting purse-portable pets, several popular breeds were bred to have traits that make them poor companions in most contemporary households. Border collies, for example, were bred to herd sheep and need enormous amounts of physical exercise and mental stimulation. If they fail to get both, many chew holes in walls, destroy furniture, and dig constantly. They can also be poorly suited for households with small children, as their herding instinct causes them to constantly round up their companions. The herding of children is an amusing thought, but it becomes a more serious issue when the border collie nips your daughter in the arm over and over again in an effort to get her to move.

A discussion of dogs might seem out of place in a book on ethnic violence, but the neurotic tendencies of border collies are actually an appropriate and insightful place to start, as the behavioral problems of border collies and ethnic violence are both promoted by the combination of group-wide genetic traits and changing social environments. Border collies were bred to be active and intelligent and to impulsively corral their animal companions, which created a biological need for exercise, mental stimulation, and herding. When border collies are stuck with owners who live in one-bedroom flats, have only limited time to exercise their pets, and do not have sheep to herd, their biological needs produce new behavior. A combination of genetic conditions and changing environments also lies at the heart of ethnic violence. Humans have an innate cognitive propensity to categorize people into ingroups and outgroups and to discriminate in favor of the ingroup. Throughout most of human history, this propensity pushed humans to collaborate with a small number of ingroup members and predisposed them to discriminate and act violently against unknown individuals. Modern social transformations, however, adjusted this propensity in ways that pushed many people to partake in a new type of violent behavior: ethnic violence. Any understanding of ethnic violence must therefore consider the interplay between biology and social environment.

The Biology of Ethnic Violence: Ingroups, Outgroups, and Emotions

Francis Galton was Charles Darwin's cousin. Although Galton had great respect for his cousin, he did not want to be outdone by his famous relative, so he subsequently spent his life trying to make important scientific discoveries in anthropology, meteorology, geography, statistics, and psychology. He was also among the first to use his cousin's ideas to explain human diversity, something his cousin refused to do and something that gained Galton present-day notoriety as a founding figure of eugenics. As a eugenicist, Galton denied the importance of nurture and believed that biological and social explanations were diametrically opposed to one another, and he coined the phrase "nature versus nurture."

A Galtonian explanation of ethnic violence focuses on the particular biologies of the perpetrators of violence, suggesting that hormones and the physical wirings of the brain cause some people to murder Others. A variety of evidence lends some credence to this view. One study finds that a quarter of Americans on death row experienced severe concussions in the prefrontal cortex, a region of the brain that helps control emotions, and another analysis offers evidence that convicted murderers have less activity in this region of the brain.[1] Childhood lead exposure is also linked to criminality, as lead promotes a permanent loss of gray matter in the prefrontal cortex. Various studies find that changes in lead exposure due to leaded gasoline help explain the rise and decline of violent crime throughout large parts of the world between the 1960s and 1990s (Drum 2013).

The life of Charles Whitman offers a more particular example supporting the Galtonian view. Charles was a prodigious child with an IQ of 138, placing him in the 99.9th percentile of all children. He gained renown as a twelve-year-old for his exceptional piano skills and for being the youngest person ever to become an Eagle Scout. After graduating from high school in 1959, Whitman joined the U.S. Marines and quickly rose through the ranks before his life slowly began to unravel. He became constantly angry and belligerent and proved unable to control himself. He was soon demoted for fighting and lost a Marine scholarship to the University of Texas because of poor grades and misconduct. At the age of twenty-five, he wrote the following passage in a letter:

> I don't really understand myself these days. I am supposed to be an aver-age reasonable and intelligent young man. However, lately (I can't recall when it started) I have been a victim of many unusual and irrational thoughts. These thoughts constantly recur, and it requires a tremendous mental effort to concentrate. I consulted Dr. Cochrum at the University Health Center and asked him to recommend someone that I could con-sult with about some psychiatric disorders I felt I had. I talked to a doc-tor once for about two hours and tried to convey to him my fears that I felt overcome by overwhelming violent impulses. . . . After my death I wish that an autopsy would be performed to see if there is any visible physical disorder. (Lavergne 1997, 92–93)

Shortly after writing this letter, Whitman was dead, but not before he had killed his wife and mother. And after murdering his most beloved, he climbed the bell tower at the University of Texas with a rifle and shot forty-eight oth-ers, killing sixteen in what is commonly regarded as the United States' first mass school shooting. Given the horrible atrocities that Whitman committed, doctors completed the autopsy he desired and found a tumor in his brain. And given the tumor's location and Whitman's change in comportment, many experts now believe that this tumor turned Whitman—an intelligent and well-behaved young man—into a deranged killer.

---

1. Communication with Robert Sapolsky. For more on the relationship between violence and traumatic brain injury, see Freedman and Hemenway (2000) and Sarapata et al. (1998).

Although evidence does suggest that particular biologies can predispose some people to extreme violence, a Galtonian perspective offers limited insight into the causes of ethnic violence. Most notably, we can assume that most people who participate in ethnic violence do not have tumors or brain damage. Indeed, with two thousand men participating in the Duluth lynchings, most of whom subsequently became upstanding and peaceful citizens with no signs of a frenzied and violent past, brain damage can safely be ruled out as a major cause of the lynchings of Elias, Elmer, and Isaac. And with some 200,000 Hutus actively participating in the massacre of Tutsis, a genetic-based argument is even more implausible for the Rwandan genocide.

Despite the inadequacies of the Galtonian view, nature still plays a role in ethnic violence. Instead of using biology to divide people into peaceful and violent categories, however, we need to consider how a shared biology puts all humans at risk of ethnic violence. Ironically, our sociable nature is the most important biological determinant of ethnic violence. Yet the elements of the human brain that make us sociable are multiple and competing, with some promoting peaceful relations and others predisposing us to violence. As archeologist Curtis Marean (2015) puts it, this biologically based duality makes humans both "peerless collaborators" and "ruthless competitors."

Like wolves, ants, and chimpanzees, humans are social animals. That is, we are driven to interact with other humans and experience mental trauma when deprived of human contact. Our genes therefore help to explain why solitary confinement is such a dreaded punishment among prisoners. As prison psychiatrist Sandra Schank puts it, "It's a standard psychiatric concept, if you put people in isolation, they will go insane" (Human Rights Watch 2003, 149). In addition to mental health, evidence from feral children and children who were raised in extreme isolation suggests that social isolation has a large impact on mental development: Such children are unable to develop intimate social relations, develop only the most basic communication skills, and are mentally disabled in additional ways. Along these same lines, Rene Spitz's (1945) classic study compared children raised in an orphanage with children raised in a prison nursing home. Both institutions offered adequate services, such as food and health care, but the orphans had much less social contact with their caretakers. The orphans, in turn, experienced much slower mental development and irreparable psychosomatic damage. For example, all the children in the prison nursery were walking and talking before their third birthdays, but fewer than 8 percent of the orphans were walking and talking by three. An even more extreme example comes from Emperor Frederick II of the Holy Roman Empire (1194–1250 AD), who isolated babies at birth to see what language they would eventually speak in an effort to discover the "natural" human language; he speculated it was Hebrew. According to a monk who recorded the events, the experiment failed, "for the children could not live without clappings of the hands, and gestures, and gladness of countenance, and blandishments" (Finlay 2011, 114).

Our need for social relations affects us in a variety of ways. As feral children, Spitz's study, and the victims of cruel linguistic experiments show, infants have difficulty developing into what we consider truly "human" without them. Of greater relevance to this book, we are genetically prewired to be sociable. Most notably, human emotionality and morality are rooted in the hardware of the human brain and facilitate collaboration and bonding, and our human ancestors who collaborated with one another—sharing food, shelter, and information and offering mutual security, love, and encouragement—were more likely to survive than isolated humans (Greene 2013). Even more, Charles Darwin notes that group-level evolutionary processes also promote sociability among animals, with the members of collaborative groups being more likely to survive than those in divided groups (Haidt 2012). Importantly, our ability to collaborate depends on nonviolent relations, and humans therefore evolved traits that promote peaceful interactions. Most notably, the human capacity to empathize facilitates cooperation with others even during the most difficult times and creates strong aversions to violence (Greene 2013). So powerful is this aversion that witnessing violence suffered by a protagonist on a sitcom commonly provokes empathy even though we know the violence is not real.

The flipside of being such peerless collaborators is that humans are also genetically predisposed to differentiate between people who are part of the ingroup and those who are not, and this promotes ruthless competition between groups. Anthropologist Donald Brown (1991) finds that the categorization of people into ingroups and outgroups and the favoring of ingroup members are universal tendencies across all known human cultures. Recognizing this, Rush Dozier (2002) refers to the categorization of people into ingroups and outgroups as the "binary instinct." Yet our brains are rewired through experience and learning, meaning that dividing people into ingroups and outgroups depends on the social environment. As neurologist Gary Marcus (2004) puts it, "Nature bestows upon the newborn a considerably complex brain, but one that is best seen as *prewired*—flexible and subject to change—rather than *hardwired*, fixed and immutable" (12; italics in original). In recognition of the influence of experience, "instinct" is too strong, so I use the term "binary propensity."

Evolutionary psychologists offer evidence that the binary propensity evolved because it increased the chances of human survival over our evolutionary history. While sharing and collaborating with others proved vital to human survival, our ancestors' chances of survival diminished when they offered assistance to people who failed to reciprocate, as this (from an evolutionary perspective at least) was a flagrant waste of energy and resources. Ideas of ingroup and outgroup helped to diminish nonreciprocal relationships by serving as a simple mechanism that distinguished between those who were most likely to reciprocate (i.e., people you interact with regularly) and those who were least likely to reciprocate (i.e., people you do not know). As one leading expert puts it, "By limiting aid to mutually acknowledged ingroup members, total costs and risks of nonreciprocation can be contained" (Brewer 1999, 433).

Evolutionarily, the propensity to divide people into ingroups and outgroups emerged when our ancestors lived in small groups of hunter-foragers made up of members who lived and collaborated regularly with one another. Since the rise of settled agriculture, our tendency to form ingroups and outgroups has continued, although the forms of ingroups and outgroups have changed remarkably. Humans form ingroups and outgroups easily, as seen in the example offered by Jane Elliot. She was an elementary school teacher from Iowa who decided to teach her all-white students firsthand about prejudice and discrimination after the assassination of Martin Luther King Jr. She divided her students according to eye color and discriminated against one group and then the other. She found that strong group identities formed very rapidly among the kids with similar eye color, and past friendships became unviable (Bloom 2005). The social relations that developed during the filming of the classic 1968 movie *Planet of the Apes* also highlight this tendency to form ingroups and outgroups. In the film, actors played either gorillas, chimpanzees, or orangutans, and divisions quickly developed among the actors based on their species, with actors playing gorillas eating lunch with one another at one table, actors playing chimpanzees at another, and actors playing orangutans at yet another.[2]

Along these same lines, social psychologist Henri Tajfel completed several famous experiments in which he divided groups of people at random and found that the simple act of division and categorization led to the construction of ingroups and outgroups (Tajfel 1970, 1974, 1978). His experiments also highlight human tendencies to discriminate against outgroup members and to make personal sacrifices for ingroup members. For example, he ran games that divided participants into groups at random and discovered that people actively discriminated against outgroup members and commonly chose to benefit their ingroup members instead of outgroup members even when such acts caused the actor to incur individual costs. In this way, people were willing to make individual sacrifices in order to improve the relative well-being of their groups even when these

---

2. Communication with Robert Sapolsky.

groups were created at random and had no social significance. Tajfel therefore concluded that this tendency to divide and discriminate is extremely powerful, and his work shows how obligations to ingroups are powerful even when the ingroup is seemingly meaningless.

Our binary propensity is prewired into our primitive neural system. This region regulates our basic survival responses, and these responses are made extremely quickly, as quickly as the response to flinch to avoid a moving object or to jump back when seeing a snake in the grass. The slower neocortex region of the brain, on the other hand, is able to recognize fine distinctions among categories and is the region of our brain that makes us problem solvers extraordinaire. Survival responses cannot analyze detailed information such as whether the object moving toward you is a Nerf football or a rock or whether the snake is a garter snake or a cobra. If your brain took the time to process such details, it would not be able to act quickly enough to avoid the danger, and your chance of survival would be reduced. In order to process such information quickly, the primitive brain categorizes broad entities as dangerous or benign and responds quickly to their presence. In a similar way, our primitive neural system predisposes us to categorize all people into crude dichotomies of ingroups and outgroups.

In addition to pushing humans to form ingroups and outgroups, human neurology predisposes us to ethnic violence in yet another way: through our emotions. In comparing ourselves to other animals, we humans obsess about the size of our brains and claim that our brains alone make us rational, inventive, and critical thinkers par excellence and that this separates us from the rest of the animal kingdom. Yet humans are equally unique in terms of emotions, as we experience a greater variety of emotions and more intense emotions than any other animal on the planet (Turner 2007a). Relative to other apes, the regions of our brain that play key emotional functions are roughly twice as large and have much denser neural connections with other regions of the brain (Turner 2007a, 34). Our emotions, in turn, shape our actions and interactions in a great variety of ways. According to neurologist Antonio Damasio (2005), human emotions play a vital role in the workings of a variety of neural activities from self-perception to rational calculation. To give an idea of the power of emotions, psychologist Jonathan Haidt (2012) refers to the region of our brain in charge of emotions as the elephant and the region involved with critical thinking as the rider, with the rider believing she is in charge but the elephant acting largely unconstrained. In this way, philosopher David Hume's (1975 [1738]) claim that human reason is the slave of our passions is quite accurate (415).

As some of the previous examples highlight, human emotions are clearly linked to the propensity to divide people into ingroups and outgroups. Most notably, intense emotions promote ingroup solidarity. Joy, pride, hope, and other positive emotions create attachment to ingroups and make them seem real. Negative emotions like fear, hatred, and sadness can be equally powerful in this regard. They differ from positive emotions, however, because they commonly focus on the outgroup and therefore strengthen boundaries between ingroups and outgroups and help create us-vs.-them mentalities. Renowned sociologist Georg Simmel (1955) notes this link between ingroup unity and the targeting of outgroups with negative emotions, and Karl Deutsch (1969) goes so far as to claim that nations are united by a hatred of their neighbors. The combination of our binary propensity and human emotionality, in turn, contributes to ethnic violence by creating the emotional motivation to attack Others.

Sociologists Alexandra Maryanski and Jonathan Turner (1992) extend this position, noting that intense and varied human emotions make powerful ingroups possible in the absence of prewiring that promotes rigid and universal ingroup structures. The authors recognize that apes—as well as our early human ancestors—are different from most other sociable animals because they have "a fluidity to group structures that form and disperse, only to form again in a new foraging party that may last for a few days and, at times, for months" (18). The development of strong and varied human emotions helped separate our human ancestors from other apes and promoted flexible ingroups with high levels of solidarity. Without this flexibility, abstract and illogical communities like ethnicity would not be possible, and without high levels of ingroup solidarity, ethnicity would be a much weaker motivator of violence.

Combining elements of the binary propensity, survival responses, and emotionality, the primitive neural system also plays an important role in emotional conditioning by forming and storing memories of events that caused intense emotion in the past. It therefore conditions us to react emotionally to situations that are similar to past events. To do so, it uses crude categories to classify the factors that sparked the emotions, something that links the binary propensity to emotional reactions. As such, the perception of an individual from a category that the observer has been conditioned to fear or despise can elicit negative emotions toward that individual. In one well-known study, researchers showed pictures of faces to white American participants and found that the faces of African Americans were more likely to activate the region of the brain associated with fear (Williams et al. 2006). A similar study found that these fears caused people to perceive the world in ways that reflect and heighten their emotional states. The study first showed the face of either an African American or white male on a computer and then showed a picture of either a wrench or a gun for only a fraction of a second. Participants were much more likely to erroneously respond that they saw a gun instead of a wrench when the picture of the wrench was preceded by the face of an African American (Payne 2006).

Once our primitive neural systems are conditioned to associate certain outgroups with fear, hatred, and other negative emotions, a variety of cognitive processes make these conditioned responses resistant to change even in the face of inconsistent information (Harrington 2004, 68). Outgroup prejudices are also extremely powerful in another way: They affect how our brains actually perceive outgroups. One study finds that individuals who observe despised outgroups are less likely to stimulate the region of the brain that is usually used when observing other humans, suggesting that stereotyped outgroups are in effect objectified and dehumanized by our brains (Fiske 2009). Supporting this conclusion, another study finds that people are less likely to attribute complex secondary emotions like love and hope to negatively stereotyped outgroups (Leyens et al. 2003). In this way, prejudicial conditioning of the primitive neural system facilitates violence against outgroups by obstructing empathy, thereby helping to overcome the side of our neural prewiring that deters violence.

Emotional responses are linked to the binary propensity in additional ways. When humans perceive the world in terms of ingroups and outgroups, we respond emotionally to perceived threats to our ingroup even when these threats do not threaten us individually. Sociologist Émile Durkheim (1965 [1912]) famously describes how humans have two different types of "social sentiments," one of which binds us to other people and one of which binds us to the entire ingroup. He emphasizes that the latter can be enormously powerful, as the social group has a sacred element that individuals lack. Similarly, a large interdisciplinary literature finds that people inherently look out for the relative well-being of their communities by comparing them to other communities and experience intense emotions, including joy, anger, fear, and jealousy, based on the relative status of their communities (Cottrell and Neuberg 2005; Fiske 2011; Fiske, Cudy, and Glick 2002; Horowitz 1985; Petersen 2002).

It is not simply the prewirings of our brains that contribute to us-them dichotomies, discrimination, and emotional prejudice. Studies find that the hormone oxytocin, which is linked to empathy, trust, and cooperation, also plays a role. Large amounts of oxytocin are released during childbirth, which—in addition to provoking contractions—facilitate mother-child bonding. Similarly, studies find that the level of oxytocin in the bloodstream increases in children when they interact with their mothers. While these characteristics have led some to call oxytocin the "love" or "social capital" hormone, studies also find that its effects—empathy, trust, and cooperation—are limited to ingroup members. Even more, laboratory experiments that administer oxytocin nasally to participants find that oxytocin promotes discrimination against outgroup members. For example, one study presented participants with hypothetical moral dilemmas in which one individual among many had to be sacrificed to save the group, and participants were asked to select the unfortunate member. Those participants who were administered a placebo tended to choose the individual at random, whereas participants who were administered oxytocin were much more likely to choose an individual from an outgroup (De Dreu et al. 2010, De Dreu et al. 2011).

So competing biological mechanisms help explain why humans are both peaceful and violent, with brains that are prewired to promote both interpersonal cooperation and intercommunal conflict. When, however, does one tendency dominate the other? That is, when does our collaborative streak overcome our ruthless side and vice versa? By itself, biology does not offer a clear answer to this question. Instead, one must look at the circumstances in which people find themselves, as some situations and experiences activate our ruthless traits and suppress our more peaceful characters while others privilege collaboration over violence. As a segue into this discussion, it is helpful to consider one final biological trait that is strongly related to violence but that is commonly ignored by studies of ethnic violence: sex.

Men and Violence

In the United States, 90 percent of people charged with homicide are males, and evidence from other countries suggests that murder is a masculine activity throughout the world (United States Department of Justice 2011). Similar data on ethnic violence are unavailable, but there is no reason to believe that women are more involved in ethnic violence. This is not because women lack the binary propensity and do not discriminate against Others. Something else accounts for this discrepancy, and evolutionary biology suggests that the answer is in our genes.

One notable biological difference between the sexes is physical size and strength. Although many women are bigger and stronger than many of their male counterparts, the average male is bigger and stronger than the average female, and these physical differences might contribute to masculine violence. The average American male, for example, has a five-inch and thirty-pound advantage over the average American female, and the world record for the bench press is 117.5 kilograms for women but 345 kilograms for men (World Powerlifting Federation 2015). Biological differences resulting from pregnancy and child care might also limit female participation in violence. Pregnancy, which places women in a particularly vulnerable state for long periods, makes women vulnerable during violent confrontations. And because infants depend on their mothers for breast milk during their first year of life, female participation in violence is also limited after childbirth. This being said, if relatively small size, pregnancy, and breastfeeding restrain violent behavior, their combined impact is likely declining in many contemporary social environments. Birth control, declining fertility, changing gender roles, child care, and the availability of baby formula free women from these potential biological constraints that prevent them from participating in violence. Similarly, guns, tanks, and drones render even the weakest person potentially deadly. A tragic example that demonstrates this last point occurred in Hayden, Idaho, in 2014, when a two-year-old boy shot and killed his mother with a handgun.

Hormones are another biological trait that might contribute to differences in violence between men and women. Most notably, testosterone levels are higher in men and are linked to aggressive behavior. Studies of mice find that castration greatly reduces aggressive behavior but that testosterone replacement subsequently increases aggression among the castrated rodents. The findings of testosterone studies on humans are less clear and more complex (Mims 2007). One complicating factor is that testosterone is a common outcome of aggression, which suggests that the direction of causation might be reversed. Moreover, the impact of testosterone appears to depend on the social context. As one expert notes, "testosterone is generated to prepare the body to respond to competition and/or challenges to one's status. Any stimulus or event which signals either of these things can trigger an increase in testosterone levels" (Mims 2007). Thus, testosterone might not promote aggression in many contexts but is linked to aggression in competitive and threatening environments. For example, one study finds that males with high levels of testosterone are more likely to react aggressively to threats to their manliness than males with low levels of testosterone (Willer et al. 2013).

These examples suggest that biology helps to explain why men are significantly more likely to participate in ethnic violence than are women. Yet one must question biological explanations because of limited evidence and because biology does not offer insight into variation in masculine violence over space and time. Indeed, men are more violent in some places than others, masculinities are presently transforming throughout large parts of the world, and biology cannot explain either (Anderson 2009; Gutmann 2003; Kimmel 2005; Segal 1990). Instead of biology, many sociologists offer evidence that the social environment promotes gendered behavior and that some masculinities contribute to the gendering of violence more than others (Banerjee 2012; Bowker 1998; Hatty 2000; Kaufman 1987; O'Toole and Schiffman 2007). Still, sociological explanations have difficulty explaining why violence is a male affair in virtually all cultures in the world and why Amazonian warriors are a myth rather than a reality.

So who is right? Does nature or nurture promote male violence? The answer to this question is almost certainly some combination of the two. As the previous discussion suggests, the social environment mediates the impact of physical size, pregnancy, breastfeeding, and testosterone. Some cultures and contexts limit but fail to eliminate the biological determinants of male violence (think contemporary Sweden). In Afghanistan and elsewhere, however, the social environment magnifies the influence of biology and produces hyper-masculinities that encourage male violence. In a similar way, the biological predispositions to divide people into ingroups and outgroups and to favor the ingroup also interact with the social environment to promote ethnic violence in some places but not others.

The Social Determinants of Ethnic Violence

As described previously, many believe a brain tumor caused Charles Whitman to orchestrate America's first mass school shooting. The main problem with this explanation is that most humans with similar brain damage are not prone to violence. Research into this variation finds that the type of brain damage suffered by Whitman does not promote violence on its own. Instead, brain damage is most likely to promote violent behavior when combined with a violent past. In Whitman's case, his father was violent and severely abused all members of the family; Charles joined the Marines the day after his father nearly beat him to death.

The impact of the binary propensity on ethnic violence has important parallels with the Whitman example. The binary propensity is based on biology and makes possible ethnic violence; ethnic violence would likely be nonexistent without a psychological tendency to categorize people into ingroups and outgroups, place great value on ingroups, and be emotional toward the ingroup. Yet reducing ethnic violence to human biology offers little insight into the causes of ethnic violence because few people participate in ethnic violence even though nearly all humans possess these biological traits. Indeed, as described previously, other biological traits promote peaceful social interaction, and biology cannot explain why violent predispositions prevail in some instances but not in others. Ultimately, the social environment determines why some people participate in ethnic violence at certain times.

At the most elementary level, ethnic violence requires the perception of ethnic-based ingroups and outgroups, but ethnicity is an abstract and seemingly unnatural way to categorize humans and must be learned. Our binary propensity therefore can only contribute to ethnic violence in environments that push people to possess ethnic frameworks. In addition, emotional prejudice and obligations are linked to both the binary propensity and ethnic violence, but the form and intensity of emotions and obligations depend on the social environment. Finally, ethnic violence is a form of collective action, which requires social environments that facilitate collective mobilization and create openings for violent behavior. Another look at the lynchings of Elias, Elmer, and Isaac in Duluth, Minnesota, highlights how the social environment influences ethnic violence in these ways.

Ethnic Difference and Ethnic Violence

So why did residents of Duluth murder Elias, Elmer, and Isaac? Although an answer to this question has many components, one is fundamental: Many white residents of Duluth perceived ethnic difference and placed great value on ethnicity. That is, the participants in the lynchings possessed an ethnic consciousness.

Ethnicity is commonly viewed as a concrete thing: It is a coherent and well-defined group linked by shared culture. More recent work in psychology and sociology, however, claims that ethnicity is, first and foremost, a categorical framework shaping how people perceive themselves and the social world around them (Anderson 1983; Brubaker 2004; Jenkins 2008). And when viewed as a cognitive framework, it is easy to see the relationship between ethnicity and the binary propensity, as people use ethnicity to categorize others into new and abstract ingroups and multiple and equally abstract outgroups.

While all humans have an innate tendency to perceive ingroups and outgroups, ethnicity is an abstract communal category, and people have to learn ethnic frameworks. Indeed, "community" logically refers to a group of known individuals, but ethnic communities are not based on acquaintance: People do not know the overwhelming majority of the members of their ethnic communities, and known acquaintances are frequently members of different ethnic communities. Instead of acquaintance, ethnicity is based on abstract criteria like language group, fabled historical origins, religion, physical appearance, and wardrobe. Yet people do not always wear ethnic lenses. As self-categorization theory in psychology and the situational school of anthropology both note, the salience of ethnic frameworks depends on the social context, with some contexts—especially those with ethnic structures—pushing people to see the world through ethnic frameworks and to place great value on ethnicity (Turner et al. 1994; Waters 1990; Wimmer 2013a). In this way, ethnic frameworks are most influential when they are combined with ethnic structures, and the combination of ethnic frameworks and ethnic structures promotes an ethnic consciousness whereby people perceive, value, identify with, and look out for the well-being of ethnicity.

The social context of Duluth in the 1920s heightened ethnic consciousness and caused people to interpret an alleged rape in terms of ethnicity. One legacy of slavery was a racist ideology that declared that African Americans were inferior to white Americans. Moreover, the United States developed a form of nationalism that proclaimed white Protestants the only true members of the American nation (Gerstle 2001; Horsman 1981). This ethnic nationalism was taught in schools in the early twentieth century and was both widespread and powerful. The Ku Klux Klan preached this nationalism and used it to attract six million members in the mid-1920s, a figure representing more than a quarter of all adult white Protestant American males (McVeigh 2009). At this time, the KKK was strongest in the Midwest.

Two additional factors further strengthened ethnic consciousness among Duluth residents. First, the lynchings occurred at the peak of the Great Migration, during which millions of African Americans moved from the South to the North. Most residents of Duluth therefore found themselves face to face with African Americans for the first time. Second, several dozen race riots occurred in the United States in the summer and early fall of 1919, a period commonly referred to as "Red Summer." Many of the riots were particularly violent because African American veterans had gained confidence during the First World War and unlike in the past they fought back. W. E. B. Du Bois (2014) encouraged and celebrated such resistance in his powerful editorial "Returning Soldiers," which ends with a call for resistance: "We *return*. We *return from fighting*. We *return fighting*" (161; italics in original). Importantly, the race riots received extensive press coverage, and the residents of Duluth read these accounts.

Emotional Prejudice and Ethnic Violence

An ethnic consciousness was a fundamental determinant of the Duluth lynchings, but it was hardly the only thing contributing to the killings. In addition, residents targeted African Americans with negative emotions that impeded empathy and motivated the killings. That is, many white residents of Duluth were emotionally prejudiced and despised and feared African Americans simply because they were African Americans. Emotional prejudice, in turn, is one of the most common and influential motives of ethnic violence.

Besides increasing the salience of ethnicity and highlighting ethnic difference, racist ideologies also made Elias, Elmer, and Isaac clear targets of intense emotional prejudice. Although Frederick Douglass had died a quarter-century before the Duluth lynchings, he understood as well as anyone the emotional prejudice that contributed to the violence. Douglass was one of America's greatest thinkers, but he never knew his age because he was born into slavery and separated from his mother as an infant. Despite his enslavement, Douglass somehow learned to read and write and became a leading lecturer and writer of the abolition movement after he escaped to the northern United States as a young adult. Mary Todd Lincoln was supposedly so moved by the speech Douglass gave at her husband's funeral that she gave him President Lincoln's walking stick as a memento. Douglass's written work is equally moving. In one of his best-known essays, Douglass coined the phrase "color line" as well as a lesser-known phrase—"diseased imagination"—to describe xenophobic emotional prejudice, and he suggested that it causes people to hate people they have never met and know nothing about. He writes:

> Few evils are less accessible to the force of reason, or more tenacious of life and power, than a long-standing prejudice. It is a moral disorder, which creates the conditions necessary to its own existence, and fortifies itself by refusing all contradiction. It paints a hateful picture according to its own *diseased imagination*, and distorts the features of the fancied original to suit the portrait. As those who believe in the visibility of ghosts can easily see them, so it is always easy to see repulsive qualities in those we despise and hate. (Douglass 1881, 567; italics added)

Hatred, anger, fear, resentment, jealousy, and other emotions are vital elements of diseased imaginations; people imagine whole communities as dangerous, blame them for hardship, despise them for their imagined inadequacies, and resent their affluence. It is therefore hardly surprising that emotions are a focus of several contemporary analyses of ethnic violence (Horowitz 1985; Kaufman 2001; Petersen 2002). As noted in the first section of this chapter, emotions play an important role in turning us-them dichotomies into aggression, and this role is genetically prewired. These emotions do not simply arise instantaneously from the brain, however. Instead, the social environment must trigger them (Kemper 1978). As sociologist Jack Barbalet (2002) puts it, "The Emotion is *in* the social relationship" (4; italics in original).

Social environments that promote perceptions of hardship, danger, and competition are most likely to spark negative emotions (Duckitt 2003). And the greater the perceived hardship, danger, and competition, the greater the negative emotions. Most importantly, these social contexts commonly threaten power, resources, status, values, beliefs, and identities, and these threats unleash powerful negative emotions (Duckitt 2003; Mackie, Devos, and Smith 2000). Both psychological and sociological studies, in turn, find that perceived hardship, danger, competition, and threats increase ethnic consciousness and orient negative emotions toward ethnic Others (Brustein 2003; Duckitt 2003; Hale 2004; Hogg and Mullin 1999; Straus 2004; Turner 2007b). In Duluth, racism and recent race riots contributed to antipathy and fear. Moreover, economic hardship and the Great Migration caused many white residents to scapegoat African Americans for "stealing" the jobs of "real" Americans.

While individual perceptions of hardship, danger, and competition promote negative emotions that underlie emotional prejudice, the belief that one's ethnic community is threatened by hardship, danger, and competition are even more powerful determinants. Threats to community are influential determinants of emotional prejudice because they elicit powerful emotions. As psychologist Susan Fiske (2002) notes, "The state of people's own wallets does not motivate their degree of prejudice. Instead, the most reliable indicator is perceived threat to one's in-group" (127). One reason why collective threats and hardships evoke powerful emotions is their righteous character; a concern for the greater good is more virtuous and justifiable than self-interest. This righteousness can intensify emotions through a self-legitimizing process whereby people recognize that they have good reason to be emotional and believe they are doing society a service by punishing offenders, which promotes an escalation into what sociologist Jack Katz (1988) refers to as a "righteous rage." We see this in the Duluth lynchings, with white residents infuriated by the perceived moral, physical, and sexual threat posed to their community by African Americans. In addition to affecting emotions, a concern for community also promotes ethnic violence because it affects more people and increases the number of potential participants. Indeed, emotions caused by communal concern can motivate many people to participate in ethnic violence, whereas individual concerns have a more limited potential to motivate collective violence against Others.

Some people experience greater emotions over the well-being of their ethnicity than do others, and different factors help to explain such variation. The presence of ethnic frameworks is important: Emotional reactions to perceptions of communal well-being can only occur if people perceive the world through ethnic lenses. An ethnic consciousness predisposes people to emotional prejudice in additional ways. For one, a heightened attachment to a social collective creates potent emotional reactions whenever the collective is harmed or threatened (Duckitt 2003). Moreover, an ethnic consciousness shapes perceptions of threats to ethnicity. A variety of studies, for example, find that people are more likely to perceive threats and react emotionally to them when they identify strongly with and value their ethnicity (Musgrove and McGarty 2008; Operario and Fiske 2001; Rydell et al. 2008; van Zomeren, Spears, and Leach 2008).

Anger, hatred, resentment, fear, and jealousy are distinct emotions that commonly motivate ethnic violence, but they can be difficult to separate because one blends into another, reinforces the others, and can be a pathway leading to the others (Berkowitz 1993). Indeed, when people are asked how they feel during unpleasant situations, they commonly report a cocktail of negative emotions. Fear, anger, and resentment, for example, heighten antipathy toward other groups and contribute to hatred. Similarly, hatred pushes people to view despised individuals as rivals and scapegoats, which promotes anger and resentment. It is therefore fruitful to consider the combined impact of all different emotions instead of tediously trying to disaggregate them.

Obligations and Ethnic Violence

Emotions were in all likelihood the single most important motive pushing thousands of Duluth residents to kill Elias, Elmer, and Isaac, but other motives also shaped the actions of the participants. Obligation was a second influential motive. Many residents of Duluth believed they had a duty to teach the three African Americans a lesson for what they saw as an egregious affront to their community. Such retributive violence was seen as a way of reasserting the dominance of white Protestants and showing everyone what happens when Others mess with them. This obligatory motive was self-applied by many, as people felt a sense of duty to protect their ethnic community. Some participants, however, needed a push from their peers. This pressure came in a variety of ways, including denigrating looks, cajoling, and questioning the honor and manliness of individuals. When combined with a personal sense of obligation, external pressure undoubtedly coaxed many to participate.

The Duluth lynchings show how obligations were both self-motivating and enforced by peers. For many episodes of ethnic violence, however, externally imposed obligations take a much different form: They are enforced through institutional channels. While religious institutions, communal organizations, and civic associations commonly enforce obligations in this way, the state is easily the most influential obligatory institution. State obligations affect the actions of state agents, who are sometimes given orders to participate in ethnic violence. States can also use their authority to pressure civilians to participate in ethnic violence. Such state-imposed obligations are most common in cases of extreme ethnic violence, such as ethnic civil war and genocide. Importantly, institutional obligations are not detached from informal obligations to peers, family, and others. Participants in collective violence, for example, are more likely to risk their lives for ethnic obligations when such obligations coincide with obligations to family and fellow combatants (Collins 2008; Kalyvas 2006; Mann 2005; McCauley 1995; Malešević 2013). And regardless of whether states, family, or strangers apply the pressure, people are more likely to follow ethnic obligations when they believe it is their duty to do so.

Obligatory motives can show an honorable side of ethnic violence: Many people participate in ethnic violence in an effort to protect the well-being of their community *despite* the considerable risks that come with participating in it. Given the right circumstances, a person who puts the collective before the individual and is willing to use violence for the well-being of the community is a hero, and this gives such violence a moral character and makes it an example of what Alan Page Fiske and Tage Shakti Rai (2015) call "virtuous violence." This laudable character helps to explain why many perpetrators of ethnic violence—as was the case with the Duluth lynchings—are upstanding individuals who are active in community affairs, concerned about their community's well-being, and well-respected by their peers. Along these same lines, Daniel Chirot and Clark McCauley (2006) note that "the obverse of genocide is identification with a loved group—friends, family, village, clan, tribe, class, nation, or religion on whose behalf the massacres are carried out" (75–76). We therefore need to be wary of demonizing people who participate in ethnic violence, as they commonly support and participate in ethnic violence not because they are self-absorbed psychopaths but because they are concerned about the well-being of their community. Émile Durkheim (1979 [1897]) notes that extreme concern for community can lead to altruistic suicide whereby people willingly give up their lives for the sake of the community, and an all-consuming concern for community can also promote altruistic violence against Others. The ignoble outcomes of ethnic violence can therefore be driven by a noble neurosis.

Although ethnic obligations and emotional prejudice are distinct motives, they commonly go hand-in-hand with and reinforce one another, making it difficult to disentangle the two. Obligations depend on pre-existing ethnic consciousness, as people do not act on ethnic obligations if they do not perceive ethnic difference, identify strongly with their ethnicity, possess norms and values related to the well-being of the ethnic community, and pressure one another to act on obligations. Obligations become much more powerful when they are backed by emotions such as anger, hatred, fear, and jealousy. We see this with the Duluth lynchings, where the negative emotions that targeted Elias, Elmer, and Isaac made the obligations seem all the more important. At the same time, obligations channel emotions into action by legitimizing and encouraging violence. When combined, emotions and obligations are a potent force motivating ethnic violence. During the Duluth lynchings, both obligations and emotions combined to promote a righteous rage, and the latter was in all likelihood the most powerful motivating force.

Mobilizational Resources, Political Opportunities, and Ethnic Violence

Duluth residents were emotionally prejudiced and felt an obligation to participate in the lynchings, and this helps explain the motivation behind the murders of Elias, Elmer, and Isaac. Yet a large literature on social movements finds that motive is an imperfect predictor of collective action because it is difficult to mobilize people even when many of them share powerful motives (McAdam 1982; Skocpol 1979; Tilly 1978). Most notably, all forms of contentious collective action require mobilizational resources and openings, and even the strongest motives have difficulty mobilizing ethnic violence without both.

Relative to other types of ethnic violence, the lynchings in Duluth required only limited mobilizational resources because the event was very short. Still, spreading the word about the alleged rape and the mobilization of two thousand men did require mobilizational resources. The sociological literature highlights a variety of resources facilitating such collective mobilization (Jenkins 1983; McCarthy and Zald 1977). Collective forms of violence, for example, require some means of coordination whereby activists encourage and organize violence against outgroup members. Communication resources that allow leaders to spread plans to a large group of people are therefore vital. Organizational resources, such as associations and clubs, also facilitate broad-based mobilization by offering pre-existing organizational structures that can be used for recruitment and mobilization. Material resources are also important. For example, money allows leaders to purchase goods needed for the movement. Human resources are needed to help organize and coordinate the movement and have considerable bearing on mobilizational success. While all these resources are influential, cultural and symbolic resources are particularly good at mobilizing violent ethnic movements (Brass 1997; Kaufman 2001). Most notably, movement mobilizers are able to draw on cultural and symbolic resources to frame issues in ways that inspire or oblige participation (Benford and Snow 2000). In effect, this framing helps to activate ethnic consciousness, which facilitates mobilization.

Although mobilizational resources make possible ethnic violence, one's ability to use such resources depends on the presence of a political opening, and states are the most influential determinants of such openings. With the help of police officers, the military, and judges, the state is supposed to maintain a rule of law and curtail unlawful violence. Many therefore link the rise of powerful states to a decline in violence (Hobbes 1957 [1651]; Fearon and Laitin 2003). Still, many states do not possess the capacities needed to curtail violence, and three factors determine which states can contain ethnic violence: bureaucratic organization, which facilitates coordinated state action; infrastructural power, which allows the state to be physically present throughout its territory; and state inclusiveness, which enables the state to gather information and engage social actors (Goodwin 2005; Lange 2009).

Notably, the political institutions in Duluth were bureaucratic, had impressive infrastructural power, and were relatively inclusive. The case therefore highlights how political actors only close openings for ethnic violence when they are both capable and willing, and the will was lacking in Duluth. The lack of desire to stop ethnic violence is most common in ethnicized states, that is, when members of one ethnicity dominate the state and use it to look out for the well-being of their ethnic community. In fact, ethnicized states commonly employ their own enormous resources to actually mobilize ethnic violence. Politics in Duluth in the 1920s were highly ethnicized, with a government that was made up of whites for the benefit of whites. Although the local government did not use its mobilizational resources to participate in the lynchings, the ethnicized character of politics created a political opening that made the lynchings possible. To their credit, several police officers fought hard and risked their lives to protect the African American prisoners, but many officers sympathized with the mob and either laid down their arms or fought half-heartedly. A few shots would have stopped the mob in their tracks and prevented the lynchings. The police, however, had orders not to shoot; the commissioner of public safety declared that the blood of one white man was not worth the lives of a few African Americans (Fedo 2000, 90). There was also little concern among the murderous mob about the legal repercussions of their actions. What court would convict whites who were just being "good" citizens? Although the outraged governor of Minnesota initially ensured that people were charged for the murders, strong public support for the mob eventually resulted in all charges being dropped. Therefore no one was ever convicted for the despicable murders of these three young African American men, although Leonard Hedman's participation did prevent him from going to law school; he subsequently ran a resort.

Modernity and Ethnic Violence

As noted at the beginning of this chapter, urban lives commonly promote new forms of canine neurosis, as this "modern" environment places border collies in closer contact with young children and does not allow them the exercise and stimulation they require. In a similar way, ethnic violence has its roots in cognitive propensities to categorize people into ingroups and outgroups, react emotionally to ingroups and outgroups, and feel obligations toward ingroups, but it is most commonly unleashed by "modern" social environments. Modernity either began or amplified a number of major social transformations, and many of these shaped ethnic consciousness, emotional prejudice, ethnic obligations, mobilizational resources, and political openings. As a result of modern social transformations, more and more people developed powerful ethnic consciousnesses, which played a vital role in redefining ethnically based us-them dichotomies and therefore created the most basic requirement for ethnic violence. Even more, ethnic consciousness contributed to emotional prejudice whenever ethnicity was threatened and promoted ethnic obligations to look out for the well-being of the ethnic ingroup. Finally, these new environments offered mobilizational resources and openings that allowed many to organize collective violence against ethnic rivals. Analyses of ethnic violence must therefore pay close attention to modernity.

2

MODERNITY AND ETHNIC VIOLENCE

My wife and I once had a small disagreement during a taxi ride through a rural region of India. The disagreement began after she casually remarked that the region was not very "modern." With a heavy dose of academic condescension, I replied that she should avoid using "modern" because our driver likely found her statement insulting. Indeed, whereas "modern" can have either positive or negative connotations, being labeled its opposite is a universal insult. The previous two chapters use "modern" and "modernity" frequently, showing that I am unable to heed my own haughty advice. My excuse for such hypocrisy is the lack of alternative concepts that adequately capture what "modern" and "modernity" represent. And for the sake of presentation, it is more efficient to simply use these problematic terms instead of listing time and again the numerous processes and characteristics that the terms represent. Yet to limit as much as possible the value-laden character of the terms "modern" and "modernity," it is necessary to explore their genealogies and clearly conceptualize them. This chapter begins with these tasks before reviewing opposing arguments about the impact of modernity on ethnic violence.

The Origins and Forms of Modernity

The renowned Roman statesman and scholar Cassiodorus is commonly credited with coining the term "modern" (*modernus*) in the fifth century AD, and he used it to refer to the Roman Empire's Christian era, as opposed to the pagan era that had preceded it.[1] The term was rarely used over the next millennium, but a heated seventeenth-century debate in the French Academy between the so-called Moderns and Ancients over whether contemporary or classical culture was superior helped to popularize the term among French intellectuals. Shortly thereafter, the French Enlightenment usurped the term and used it to refer to reason, individualism, and science. As philosopher Jürgen Habermas (1981) writes, Enlightenment thinkers believed that modernity would "further understandings of the world and of the self, would promote moral progress, the justice of institutions, and even the happiness of human beings" (9). Ultimately, Enlightenment thinkers saw modernity as both a means and an end, with modern rationalism and knowledge promoting some sort of this-worldly modern paradise. It was at this time that "modern" gained an exuberantly positive connotation linked to progress.

Although the French writer and romanticist Chateaubriand first used the term "modernity" (*modernité*), the French poet Charles Baudelaire (1821–1867) popularized it. Baudelaire helped to create an association between "modernity" and the avant-garde, especially in art, and he used "modernity" to refer to the ephemeral character of life and existence in urban metropolises, claiming that "modern" art must highlight and represent this character. In Baudelaire's most famous work, *Les Fleurs du Mal*, he does just this, presenting death, decay, suffering, and sex as beautiful and sublime components of modern life in mid-nineteenth-century Paris. Several of his poems glorify workers, beggars, prostitutes, gamblers, the elderly, and immigrants as the antiheroic underbelly of modern Paris.

Shortly after Baudelaire popularized the term "modernity," a number of the first sociologists borrowed it, though they had a very different take on what modernity is. Instead of celebrating the deviant side of modernity and trying to depict it artistically, they considered how modernity transformed social relations and tried using scientific methods to understand the causes and consequences of modernity. In fact, sociology's disciplinary origins are firmly rooted in the concept, as the first sociologists strove to better understand the major social transformations associated with modernity. Even today, acclaimed sociologist Anthony Giddens refers to sociology as "the study of modernity" (Giddens and Pierson 1998, 94). The work of Ferdinand Tönnies, Émile Durkheim, and Max Weber all highlight early sociological attempts to make sense of modernity.

Tönnies (1855–1936) was the first German sociologist, and he influenced the nascent discipline by writing more than nine hundred sociological works,

---

1. For a more in-depth genealogical analysis of "modern" and "modernity," see Jauss (1982).

including his most influential work, *Gemeinschaft und Gesellschaft* (2001 [1887]). In it, he argues that modern and premodern societies are fundamentally different. *Gemeinschaft*, commonly translated as "community," refers to social relations based on acquaintance, shared experiences, and mutual understanding, with familial relations being notable examples. Individuals participating in these social relations view themselves as part of the collective and actively seek to pursue the goals of the group, often at considerable personal expense. *Gesellschaft*, on the other hand, is translated as "civil society" and refers to social relations that allow people to pursue their individual interests. Whereas norms dealing with conformism, obligation, and exclusion help regulate social relations characterized by *Gemeinschaft*, law, the police, and the state regulate *Gesellschaft*-based social relations. Ultimately, Tönnies saw modern social relations as increasingly dominated by *Gesellschaft* instead of *Gemeinschaft*. In this way, modernity promotes individualism and allows people to better pursue their wills by freeing them from traditional social shackles that promote disciplined conformism.

The work of Durkheim (1858–1917), a French academic who founded sociology as an academic discipline, also analyzes the social effects of modernity. His work parallels that of Tönnies, but instead of *Gemeinschaft* and *Gesellschaft* Durkheim (1984 [1893]) focuses on mechanical and organic solidarity. Durkheim conceived of societies as a special type of living organism and was most interested in the factors holding these social organisms together. He believed that mechanical solidarity promoted cohesion in premodern societies and was based on personal ties and conformism. Everyone knew everyone else and was supposed to act exactly the same, and there were strict norms regulating social relations. He referred to this as mechanical solidarity because everyone was like a machine, seemingly acting in the same preprogrammed ways. With modernity, mechanical solidarity was no longer possible because people did not know everyone and because the strict rules of conformism and obligation broke down in the face of large and diverse populations. Mechanical solidarity was replaced by organic solidarity, a term Durkheim used because he saw modern society as based on a division of labor whereby diverse formal institutions served certain functions and worked together to allow the whole of society to survive. Just as organs serve a specific function and work together to allow an individual organism to survive, the same thing occurs in modern societies, with the state making decisions for the social body, the economy providing material goods, and education imparting norms and knowledge. This division of labor forced people to hold specialized positions in the social body and caused all people to depend on unknown others for their livelihoods. Durkheim believed that it was through this extreme interdependence that modern forms of solidarity arose.

The work of Weber (1864–1920) also deals with modernity. One of the most influential sociologists of all time, Weber had an encyclopedic knowledge of human history and wrote about everything from religion to the family to the economy to politics. His greatest concern, however, was exploring the factors that allowed Western Europe to emerge as the global economic and political power-house, a topic that forced him to consider the causes of modernity. Although Weber believed that an eclectic combination of factors promoted modernity, he paid close attention to a favorite topic of the Enlightenment: rationalization (Kalberg 1980). He believed that European social relations had become increasingly rational over the previous few centuries, that is, people used science and abstract reasoning to guide their actions instead of depending on mystic beliefs and habit. Such rationalization, in turn, had major effects on social relations and promoted new organizations and institutions. Bureaucracy, the rule of law, and capitalism offer three notable examples of rational social organization.

As founding figures of sociology, Tönnies, Durkheim, and Weber all influenced subsequent generations of social scientists, and different aspects of their works were combined into a single theory of social development: modernization theory. This theory gained great popularity in the United States and elsewhere after the Second World War and remained a dominant paradigm of development in many capitalist countries until the 1970s. It claimed that development involves a transformation from traditional and simplistic to modern and complex, and it saw modernity as both inevitable and highly desirable, as the social institutions of modern societies are supposedly a sign of progress. The work of Walt Rostow exemplifies this theory. Rostow was an influential advisor to both John F. Kennedy and Lyndon B. Johnson and the author of several books. In *The Stages of Economic Growth* (1960), Rostow offers a social evolutionary view of modernization, claiming that all countries go through the same five-step process of economic modernization: traditional society, the development of preconditions for economic takeoff, economic takeoff, drive to maturity, and mass consumption, with the final stage being characterized by personal freedom and wealth.

In the early twenty-first century, it is hard to find a social scientist who supports classic modernization theory, and there are several factors that help explain the theory's unpopularity. For one, modernization theory offers an overly universal view of social change, with traditional societies inevitably becoming modern and following the same developmental trajectories as previous societies. History has shown that universal and unidirectional social change is hardly inevitable and that a number of varieties of modernity exist, and many social scientists offer evidence that the social environment and historical period have enormous implications on the way modern social processes unravel (Cardoso and Faletto 1979; Wallerstein 1976). In addition, modernization theory suggests that modernization is unique and disregards the enormous social changes that have occurred since the invention of settled agriculture. Yet the changes occurring over the past few centuries are not the only ones that matter, and we must therefore remove all blinders that hide the enormous social changes that occurred over the past ten thousand years. Finally, modernization theory describes modernization as good and defines modernization based on the particular social changes that occurred in Western Europe and North America. In this way, the characteristics of Western Europe and North America are depicted as universally desirable while characteristics of other regions are not, which justifies and perpetuates extreme international inequalities. In addition to promoting Eurocentrism, this bias pushes people to overlook the negative consequences of modernity.

There is much to these criticisms, and they explain the mass extinction of modernization theorists over the past forty years. Despite the baggage that comes with it, however, "modernity" is still a valuable sociological concept. Although we must realize that modernity is not inevitable, that there are multiple routes to and several varieties of modernity, that we should not ignore premodern social change, and that we must avoid equating modernity with unfettered progress, analyses of modernity help to highlight major social transformations that have occurred throughout the world over the past few centuries and that have had great repercussions for humanity. These include the proliferation of capitalism, industrialization, powerful states, nationalism, mass education, urbanism, the sciences, and democracy. Such transformations integrated people into larger and larger social institutions and promoted social differentiation characterized by a growing division of labor and specialization. And "modernity" helps capture these interrelated processes better than any other term. I therefore use "modernity" to refer to a set of interrelated social processes, including the development of powerful states, the geographic expansion of social networks, growing urbanization, economic differentiation and industrialization, scientific development, the institutionalization of religions with numerous practitioners, the development of a complex division of labor, and mass educational expansion. Throughout this book, whenever I use the terms "modernity" and "modern," I am referring to this set of interrelated processes.

To better grasp a complex concept like modernity, it is helpful to contrast it with premodernity, and hunter-forager lifestyles offer a stark and insightful comparison. For some 97 percent of human history, our human ancestors lived as hunter-foragers and used rudimentary technologies to extract life's necessities from their environments. Because the environments varied greatly and because people found different solutions to the same problems, these hunter-foraging societies differed from one another in important ways. While recognizing such variation, these societies commonly shared a number of general traits.

One key similarity concerns how hunter-foragers met their nutritional needs. As the term implies, hunter-foragers hunted wild animals and collected wild seeds, fruits, vegetables, and roots. There was a division of labor, with some individuals specializing in hunting, others in foraging, and still others in making the tools needed to hunt animals and gather food. Yet this division of labor was limited, and most people had considerable knowledge of the whole repertoire of activities that were necessary to extract resources from the environment and protect themselves from the elements. Another common characteristic of hunter-forager societies was their small size, which ranged from a few dozen to a few hundred. Large numbers were usually impossible to sustain because of the limited amount of food that could be acquired from the environment through hunting and foraging. Both small numbers and a limited division of labor, in turn, promoted what anthropologists refer to as acephalous communities, or communities lacking formal governments and hierarchies. The limited division of labor also had implications for education, which was informal and involved the transfer of knowledge and beliefs from one generation to the next through daily social interactions. Literacy was unknown in hunter-forager societies, which limited the ability to store and transmit information. Finally, the extreme dependence of hunter-foragers on their environment had implications for religion: hunter-foragers commonly practiced polytheistic religions that worshiped the environment, the great provider of all things. Similar to education and government, there were no formal religious institutions, which was a result of illiteracy and the limited division of labor.

Fast-forward to modern human societies, and we see very different characteristics. Most people living in modern societies do not produce their own food; they purchase it. This situation is the result of settled agriculture and new technological developments—ranging from tractors to fertilizer to genetic modification—that make possible mass agricultural production. With only a small fraction of the population producing food, the vast majority of people must find some way to acquire foodstuff, and an exchange economy is the main institution for this. With the advent of new technologies that allow people to produce a variety of goods and services, the capitalist exchange economy has exploded. This economic system requires an extremely complex division of labor and considerable specialization, with individuals having occupations that help provide one particular good or service. Modern societies are also characterized by mass education, with nearly all individuals spending most of their childhoods and adolescence in formal institutions that are explicitly designed to transfer knowledge, skills, outlooks, and norms from teacher to student. One important outcome of mass education is universal literacy, and the latter has shaped all social institutions. Systems of writing and literacy, for example, make possible the institutionalization of religions whereby sacred texts promote standard religious beliefs and practices among large numbers of people. Because the economic and technological transformations occurring with modernization place humans in seeming control of the environment, these religions no longer focus on the environment as provider and commonly view humans as the rightful masters of the earth. As the Bible states in Genesis, "Be fruitful and multiply, and fill the earth and subdue it; and have dominion over the fish of the sea and over the birds of the air and over every living thing that moves upon the earth." Modern societies are also enormous in scale, with millions of people living in close proximity to one another in growing urban metropolises. Large populations create problems that necessitate a formal government that implements decisions affecting all members of the political community, and bureaucratic organizations make possible large and effective states that implement a variety of policies ranging from economic management to social welfare provisioning to the maintenance of peace and stability.

As this brief comparison shows, the differences between hunter-forager societies and modern societies are enormous and fundamental; these are remarkably different social worlds. When one compares modern societies to premodern societies with settled agriculture, however, there are many more similarities. A look at Europe during the Middle Ages helps highlight how modernity built on pre-existing social processes but ultimately transformed such processes in very important ways that separate modernity from premodernity.

Relative to earlier times, the population size of medieval Europe was quite large, more people were literate, states were present, the division of labor was expanding, mass institutionalized religions were present, urbanization was increasing, and an exchange economy was growing (Bartlett 1993). Many of the attributes we associate with modernity were therefore already present, but one must not make too much of these similarities. Indeed, a comparison of medieval and contemporary Europe highlights important differences in degree and character (Crone 2003). In the Middle Ages, formal education and literacy were limited to a minuscule group of elites, with the overwhelming majority of the population remaining uneducated and illiterate. Educational institutions, in turn, focused primarily on religious instruction, and science was largely absent and undeveloped. The division of labor was also much more limited in the Middle Ages. Historian Georges Duby (1980) describes a tripartite division of labor whereby a few prayed, a few fought, and the rest worked. The overwhelming majority of the workers were peasant farmers who produced most of their daily needs. The exchange economy had a limited presence outside of urban areas, and the cities were tiny in comparison to the urban metropolises that emerged over the next few centuries: Only 5 percent of Europe's population lived in urban areas by 1500, as opposed to nearly 25 percent in 1890 and 75 percent today (de Vries 1984, 39, 46). Moreover, the states in the Middle Ages were very different from the states that exist today. They had limited territorial presence, were extremely dependent on local elites to implement decisions, and were organized based on personal relations and ownership rather than bureaucratic rules. Their activities were also much more limited. Most notably, while contemporary states provide diverse public goods and services, these were almost completely neglected during the Middle Ages.

This comparison clearly highlights that modernity continued processes that had begun with the advent of settled agriculture thousands of years ago, and there was not a sudden, radical shift transforming premodern societies into modern ones. Nonetheless, there was a period of more punctuated transformation in Europe between roughly 1650 and 1900, a period that German historian Reinhart Koselleck (2002) refers to as the "saddle period" separating premodernity and modernity. According to Koselleck, these social transformations were so great that the subjective realities of people changed, which is evident in the changing meanings of many common concepts during the saddle period. Before the saddle period, basic concepts like "history," "revolution," "progress," "politics," "society," "law," and "development" had very different meanings, but during the transition new meanings crystalized into a new conceptual schema that allowed people to make sense of the social structural changes caused by modernity.

As historian Christopher Bayly (2004) notes in his monumental study *The Birth of the Modern World*, Europe was not isolated from the rest of the world at the time modernity arose, and other regions of the world influenced its form as they modernized on their own. Despite this, Western Europe emerged as the epicenter of modernity, and Europe influenced how other places modernized over the next 250 years. This influence began with the modernization of the United States in the early nineteenth century and the modernization of the remaining British settler colonies shortly thereafter. We also see modernity's influence in the Latin American settler colonies and Eastern Europe beginning in the first half of the nineteenth century. Outside of Europe and the regions of European settlement, Japan was among the first to modernize, beginning an extremely aggressive campaign to modernize in the mid-nineteenth century after the Meiji Restoration. For the majority of Africa and Asia, the social processes constituting modernity only became a major transformative force in the late nineteenth and early twentieth centuries.

Modernity did not magically proliferate into all corners of the world. In large parts of the world, modernizing processes had indigenous roots. In addition, advances in transportation and communication technologies were already at work promoting globalization, and a variety of global processes pushed and pulled modernity throughout the world. In the British and Latin American settler colonies, the transfer of peoples who had already experienced the beginnings of modernity was an important force behind modernity's proliferation. Besides bringing the rudimentary components of modernity with them, settlers also looked toward Europe as an admirable example and actively mimicked the modernizing processes that were taking place there. Later, European and North American capitalists, missionaries, and colonists pushed modernity into diverse corners of the world. In turn, many political leaders outside Europe and North America recognized the danger that the modern regions of the world posed to their very existence and purposefully copied many elements of modernity in an effort to fend off Western conquest. Worried by American belligerence and European imperialism, for example, Japan sent officials to Germany to study its state in an effort to build a powerful state back in Japan, and it also sent economic actors abroad to copy the industrial techniques of the United States. By the twentieth century, powerful global institutions and actors such as the United Nations, World Bank, and nongovernmental organizations entered the fray and used both carrots and sticks to encourage peoples throughout the world to mimic modernity.

It is important to note that there was not only one way to modernize; there were a variety of modernities, and all countries modernized in their own unique ways (Schmidt 2006). Just as McDonald's offers chicken masala burgers in India, poutine in Quebec, lobster roles in New England, and beer in Belgium, local conditions interact with global forces to create different forms of modernity. Most notably, the social contexts in which modernity arose varied, different forces promoted modernity in different regions, and modernizing processes began in different time periods and occurred in different orders. All these factors caused the processes constituting modernity to develop in different ways.

Modernity and Violence: Rival Perspectives

If you ask a sample of people how modernity affects ethnic violence, you will likely get mixed responses. Some will point to a number of twentieth- and twenty-first-century atrocities as evidence that things have gotten more violent with modernity. Others, however, will equate premodernity with barbarianism and claim that modernity promotes peace. Scholars of violence are split along the same lines, with the classic modernist position believing that modernity promotes peace and the revised modernist position suggesting that modernity increases violence.

The Classic Modernist View of Violence

Joseph Conrad's novella *Heart of Darkness* offers a clear example of the classic position equating modernity with peace. The story takes place at the turn of the twentieth century, and the plot involves an Englishman named Marlow leading an expedition deep into the Congolese rainforest to find Kurtz, a star trader who had gone mad. The novella depicts a thin line between civilization and primitivism, with all modern technologies breaking down and littering the landscape as Marlow works his way up the Congo River in search of Kurtz. More importantly, civilization has shaped the character of people, but modern mentalities are as fragile as modern technologies. Kurtz, who had been living among Africans acquiring ivory, is overcome by the primitivism of his surroundings and loses his civilized character to become a ruthless barbarian, which is shown by the decapitated heads impaled on the stakes surrounding his residence. Thus, during a final instance of lucidity before his death, Kurtz recognizes that primitivism has shorn away modernity's influence to uncover his own heart of darkness and is disturbed by what he has become, gasping in his final breaths, "The horror! The horror!"

Despite the bleak story line, a more optimistic message is hidden in the novella. Conrad was a lifelong British imperialist, and he saw the Empire as helping to bring "light" to some of the "darker" regions of the world. This view is evident at the very beginning of the novella, when Marlow begins to tell Kurtz's story to his fellow sailors as they set sail from London on the Thames years after Kurtz's death. Marlow breaks the silence surrounding the sailors, exclaiming in reference to England, "'And this also . . . has been one of the dark places of the earth' (Conrad 1999 [1899], 49). He continues: 'I was thinking of very old times, when the Romans first came here, nineteen hundred years ago—the other day. . . . Light came out of this river since—you say Knights? Yes; but it is like a running blaze on a plain, like a flash of lightning in the clouds. We live in the flicker—may it last as long as the old earth keeps rolling! But darkness was here yesterday'" (50). Like Rome's civilizing influence in England, Conrad suggests that the enlightenment of the Belgian Congo also seems a possibility, although Kurtz's story shows that such efforts are difficult, dangerous, and uncertain.

Conrad was not unique among his contemporaries in linking ruthless violence to primitivism and peaceful social order to modernity. In fact, he was a product of his time, as the classic modernist position dominated the social sciences and public opinion in Europe and North America throughout his life. One basic underlying claim of nearly all early sociologists was that modern environments offer a superior means of containing violence. Durkheim, for one, emphasizes how modernity promotes interdependence and the development of broad norms, both of which help limit confrontation and conflict between strangers. He also notes that premodern societies commonly employ extreme corporal punishment and execution for relatively minor infractions but that less violent methods replace brutal punishments in modern times. Others, like Weber, note that modernity is linked to powerful states, which regulate social relations and implement a rule of law and thereby help contain violence.

Steven Pinker's (2011) *The Better Angels of Our Nature* offers one well-known contemporary example of the classic modernist perspective. Pinker considers nearly all types of violence and assembles a great variety of evidence suggesting that modernity promotes more peaceful relations. One important element of his argument draws on the work of Thomas Hobbes and Max Weber in describing how modern states regulate social relations in ways that limit the ability of people to kill one another. Paralleling Durkheim's work, Pinker also points to a humanitarian revolution that began with the Enlightenment and helped delegitimize forms of violence that had previously been common, such as slavery, torture, execution, and superstitious murders. Similarly, Pinker also draws on the work of sociologist Norbert Elias, who famously described how cultural changes have increasingly restrained violent behavior in Europe over the past several centuries.

Pulitzer-prize-winning evolutionary biologist Jared Diamond (2012) also supports the classic modernist position in *The World Until Yesterday*. The book compares modern lifestyles to the lifestyles of hunter-foragers and horticulturalists who use limited technologies. Diamond describes premodern societies as participating in seemingly endless cycles of warfare that produce many more victims of violence than even the most violent modern societies. He therefore concludes that violence decreased dramatically with modernity. Although focusing only on Western Europe, historian Robert Muchembled (2012) arrives at a similar conclusion. He describes how brutality and violence have declined over the past seven centuries, and his explanation focuses on a "civilizing process" whereby mechanisms of social control removed masculine violence from the public sphere.

The Revised Modernist View of Violence

A note left by a prisoner who was forced to remove bodies from the gas chambers of Auschwitz makes a powerful and eloquent claim against the classic modernist position: "For although even animals have been restrained by civilization—their hooves have been dulled and their cruelty greatly curbed—man has not, but has become a beast. The more highly developed a culture, the more cruel its murderers, the more civilized a society, the greater its barbarians; as development increases, its deeds become more terrible" (Stone 1999, 367). After witnessing how modern governments employed chemical and organizational technologies to annihilate millions of people, it is easy to see how this individual came to such a conclusion. He is not alone in this regard: The revised modernist position—as exemplified by the works of Hannah Arendt (1966), Hans Joas (2003), Michael Mann (2005), James Scott (1998), and Andreas Wimmer (2013b)—suggests that modernity is an influential cause of violence.

Although Arendt (1966) arrives at a very different conclusion than Durkheim (1984 [1893]), her position borrows key elements of Durkheimian social theory. In particular, she draws on Durkheim's concept of anomie, a condition in which social norms are confused, unclear, or absent due to society's transition from mechanical to organic solidarity. Durkheim linked anomie to suicide, crime, violence, and other negative outcomes, but he believed that this state was only temporary and would soon lead to a new and superior society. Arendt largely accepts Durkheim's claims of anomie but rejects his rosy conclusions. Her pessimism is due in no small part to the fact that she was a German Jew who lived through the Second World War. Looking at the causes of the Nazi atrocities, Arendt suggests that modernity produced a mass society in which people were free to act as they wished because traditional values and institutions had been destroyed. Such destruction contributed to the rise of totalitarian movements, and the combination of anomie and totalitarianism was, according to Arendt, a deadly cocktail that unleashed some of the worst atrocities the world has ever seen.

The views of sociologists Michael Mann (2005) and Andreas Wimmer (2013b) differ from that of Arendt, but they nonetheless arrive at similar conclusions. They focus on nationalism and the state as fundamental elements of modernity and offer evidence that both are linked to severe violence. In particular, the nation-state principle—which suggests that all communities should control their own state and rule themselves—commonly motivates people to eliminate nonnationals. Mann, for instance, sees this as a driving force behind a variety of twentieth-century genocides, and the gas chambers of Auschwitz were therefore part of this deadly process. Similarly, Wimmer notes that state discrimination against minorities commonly motivates nationalist reactions that spark violence.

Anthropologist James C. Scott (1998) makes more general claims in his book *Seeing Like a State* and does not focus on nationalism and nation-states. He notes that high modern ideologies commonly push states to disregard the well-being of their citizens and to implement modernizing policies that actually brutalize their populations. Stalin's collectivization efforts in the Soviet Union offer one example.

Importantly, most scholars taking a revised modernist position differ from Scott and focus explicitly on the impact of modernity on ethnic violence.

Alternatively, classic modernists analyze nearly all types of violence. Given this difference, advocates of each position commonly talk past one another, as places with low levels of overall violence sometimes experience severe ethnic violence. The classic and revised modernist positions thus need not be in opposition to one another, and it is possible that both are correct. Generally speaking, however, classic and revised modernists offer rival views, as classic modernists usually assume that all types of violence follow similar trajectories and revised modernists commonly expand their claims beyond ethnic violence. For this book, I only consider their claims about ethnic violence.

Quantitative Evidence of Historic Trends in Ethnic Violence

So who is right? Does modernity contain or exacerbate ethnic violence? Although evidence is limited, different datasets on ethnic violence offer insight into long-term trends in ethnic violence, and these trends can be used to test the competing claims. One dataset compiled by Andreas Wimmer and Brian Min (2006) notes the characteristics of all wars with at least one thousand battle deaths that occurred between 1816 and 2001. This dataset recognizes different categories of war, including two types of ethnic warfare: wars of nationalist secession, whereby a community mobilizes to fight for separation and communal self-rule; and ethnic wars, whereby different communities mobilize to fight for greater control of the existing state. Figure 2.1 combines both nationalist and ethnic civil wars into a single "ethnic" category and includes two additional categories: international wars and civil wars that were nonethnic in character. The figure shows that ethnic wars made up approximately 20 percent of all wars between 1816 and 1930, suggesting that it was an important form of war, albeit far from the most common form. After the 1930s, however, ethnic civil wars increased dramatically and became the most common form of warfare, with more than 60 percent of all wars being ethnic civil wars in the 1990s. Coinciding with the revised modernist perspective, we therefore see sharp increases in ethnic violence relative to other types of violence at the very time when modernity was proliferating throughout the world.

Figure 2.2 uses the same data but looks at the sheer number of ethnic wars per decade. At the same time that ethnic warfare became the most common form of warfare, its numbers increased dramatically, showing that ethnic civil wars have become more and more common. Although there were only a handful of ethnic wars per decade until the 1940s, this number exploded in the 1950s, and thirty-four ethnic wars occurred during the 1990s alone.

Other datasets on ethnic violence have less historical depth but paint a similar picture over a shorter period of time. Figure 2.3 presents data on ethnic violence from four different datasets: Ethnic Power Relations (EPR) (Wimmer,

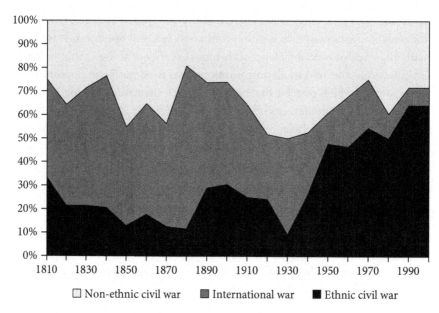

FIGURE 2.1. Types of warfare by decade, 1816–1999. Source: Wimmer and Min (2006).

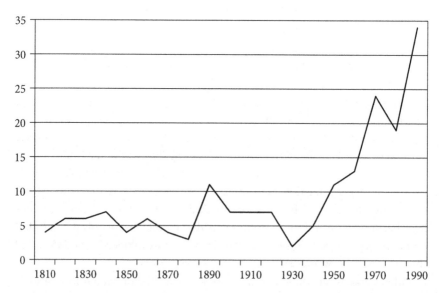

FIGURE 2.2. Number of ethnic wars per decade, 1816–1999. Source: Wimmer and Min (2006).

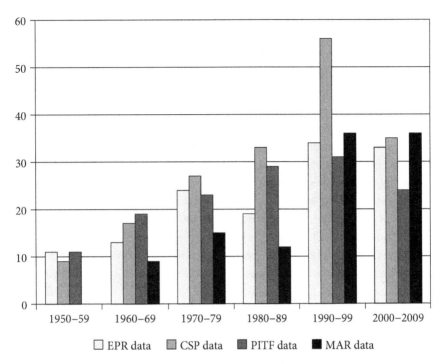

FIGURE 2.3.   Episodes of ethnic violence by decade, 1950–2009. Sources: Wimmer, Cederman, and Min (2009); Marshall (2014); Political Instability Task Force (2013); Bennett and Davenport (2003).

Cederman, and Min 2009), the Center for Systemic Peace (CSP) (Marshall 2014), the Political Instability Task Force (PITF) (2013), and Minorities at Risk (MAR) (Bennett and Davenport 2003).[2] Both the EPR and the PITF datasets measure ethnic civil wars that pit a state against an organized ethnic opponent. Because both use slightly different definitions of civil war, they categorize cases of ethnic civil war differently. Alternatively, the MAR dataset scores the presence of severe cases of civilian-on-civilian violence taking the form of either ethnic riots or warfare, meaning that it disregards ethnic civil wars that lack civilian-on-civilian violence. The cases of ethnic violence in the MAR dataset are therefore quite different from those noted by either EPR or PITF. Finally, the CSP data is in between the two, as it analyzes ethnic warfare that either pits the state against ethnic adversaries, involves severe civilian-on-civilian violence, or both. In Figure 2.3, all four

---

2. Because MAR stopped collecting data in 2006, the total number of episodes of severe ethnic violence shown in the figure excludes episodes between 2007 and 2009.

datasets show a rising trend in ethnic violence, although two show declines over the past decade, with the CSP data showing a significant decline. Thus, although data from EPR, CSP, PITF, and MAR do not extend back far enough to show the long-term rise in ethnic violence since the beginning of the nineteenth century, they corroborate data from Wimmer and Min (2006) showing a growth in ethnic violence with the spread of modernity.

Instead of violent episodes, another way to measure ethnic violence is by calculating the number of deaths it has caused. This measure is much more speculative because calculations of deaths are crude estimations, but the measure is a better indicator of the scale of violence. Of all datasets, only CSP (Marshall 2014) estimates the number of deaths caused by severe episodes of ethnic violence, and Figure 2.4 presents the number of deaths per 100,000 people for ten-year periods since 1950. The overall trajectory is similar to that in Figure 2.3, although it rises earlier and declines after 2000. The earlier rise is influenced by the ethnic civil war in Bangladesh/Pakistan, which was the most deadly episode of ethnic violence during this sixty-year period and is estimated to have killed one million people. The decline during the first decade of the twenty-first century was influenced by a fall in the number of violent episodes from fifty-six in the 1990s to thirty-five in the 2000s. Notably, only the CSP data show a significant decline in episodes of ethnic violence after the 1990s, suggesting that the other datasets would not reveal the same reduction if they included data on deaths.

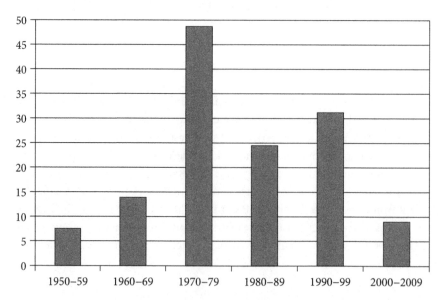

FIGURE 2.4.   Deaths per 100,000 people caused by ethnic violence, 1950–2009. Source: Marshall (2014).

Qualitative Evidence of Historic Trends in Ethnic Violence

All in all, these data support the revised modernist position linking modernity and ethnic violence. To convincingly show that ethnic violence has increased with modernity, however, one must explore trends in ethnic violence long before the saddle period, and some have collected such data. Pinker (2011) and Diamond (2012), for example, use anthropological and archeological studies to estimate the violent death rates in early premodern societies. Unfortunately, these data have very important limitations.[3] Moreover, they measure all types of violence, not just ethnic violence. And because other types of violence do not necessarily follow the same trajectory as ethnic violence, these data cannot be used to measure long-term trends in ethnic violence. Indeed, by a number of measures, Latin America is the most violent region in the world today, but it has low levels of ethnic violence.

More qualitative data can provide insight into long-term trends in ethnic violence, but the qualitative evidence is vast, varied, and incomplete. As a result, a number of different interpretations are possible, with some supporting the modernist position and others supporting the claims of revised modernists. My own interpretation is that both modernist and revised modernist positions make important points but that—when focusing on ethnic violence—the evidence conforms most closely to revised modernist claims. A review of the evidence suggests that violence between ingroups and outgroups has been present throughout human history, but *ethnic* violence became much more prevalent in modern times.

The historical record offers strong evidence that people have been killing each other throughout human history, which refutes past claims of the "peaceful savage" (Keeley 1996; Pinker 2011). Still, it appears that the type of violence has transformed over time as a result of changing social environments, meaning that some types of violence were more common in the past while others are more

---

3. For a variety of reasons, many doubt the accuracy and validity of the data on premodern violence used by Pinker and Diamond. First, anthropologist Brian Ferguson (2012a) scrutinizes the archeological data used by Pinker and Diamond and finds that they grossly exaggerate deaths via warfare. Second, there is little data on violence in premodern societies, and we cannot be sure that the available data highlight a general picture: Anthropologists are more likely to gather data on violence among more violent peoples, and archeologists might find a disproportionate share of skeletal remains in mass graves, the latter of which are linked to warfare. Another critique concerns the impact of external actors on violence. Excluding the archeological data on premodern societies who lived prior to the advent of settled agriculture, the hunter-forager societies with information on violence did not exist in a state of pristine isolation. Instead, they were in contact with other more modern peoples, and the latter might have caused higher rates of violence among the world's last hunter-foragers.

prevalent in the present. Anthropologist Raymond Kelly (2000), for example, argues that homicides were common among hunter-foragers but that warfare only emerged after the advent of settled agriculture. A more recent and extensive analysis by anthropologists Douglas Fry and Patrik Söderberg (2013) supports these claims, finding that organized violence between groups was extremely rare among hunter-foragers but that homicide was common. Anthropologist Keith Otterbein (2004) arrives at a slightly different conclusion. He agrees that settled agriculture made military organization and thereby warfare possible but argues that those hunter-foragers who hunted large game frequently participated in warfare, as hunting dangerous animals depends on two technologies—lethal weaponry and organization—that make warfare possible.

Paralleling these findings, the available historical evidence suggests that certain "modern" social contexts dramatically increase the risk of ethnic violence. Most premodern violence between unknowns pits foreigner against foreigner, whereas modern ethnic violence involves conflict between conationals that is motivated by ethnic difference. Ethnic violence is therefore only possible when states are present and rule over a large number of peoples, something that has only recently become the norm. Beyond semantics, ethnic violence depends on widespread ethnic consciousness, and the latter requires advanced communication technologies, mass education, and powerful states. In premodern times, large states, communication technologies, and education were much more limited, which impeded the social requisites of ethnic violence. As noted in the first section of this chapter, however, many modern social transformations began prior to the saddle period, which would have increased the risk of ethnic violence in some premodern social environments. These modernizing transformations continued and intensified as societies passed through the saddle period into the modern era, and the risk of ethnic violence grew accordingly.

Some historians and social scientists disagree with my revised modernist interpretations of history.[4] Scholars taking this position usually present a two-pronged critique of the revised modernist position. First, they claim that collective categories of people have existed for thousands of years and that ethnicity is not new. Second, they point to premodern violence between people from different communities as proof that ethnic violence was widespread.

Both critiques are difficult to assess because the evidence needed to adjudicate between the competing claims is varied and sparse. Much of the evidence used to make the first critique is from ancient written sources using collective categories

---

4. For an alternative view of ethnicity as very long-standing, see Gat (2013).

like "Akkadian" or "Sumerian" to refer to groups of people. In fact, every ancient civilization with systems of writing had collective social categories, suggesting the existence of ethnicity. Yet ancient communal categories and ethnicities should not be confounded. Moreover, ancient manuscripts were written by elites for elites, meaning they are in no way representative of the vast majority of past populations. A brief look at premodern Europe highlights these countercritiques.

Early modern Europe is a particularly appropriate case for looking into the premodern history of ethnic violence because a relatively large number of historical relics offering insight into the mentalities of the time have survived. And because medieval Europe preceded modernity, one can explore changes in mentalities as modernity developed. One way to look into the presence of ethnic categories is to explore the literary record to see what types of categories were used to make sense of communities. Within Europe, linguists and conceptual historians note the rise of new concepts that refer to and make sense of abstract communities of strangers beginning in the seventeenth and eighteenth centuries. These concepts include "people," "nation," "race," and—much later—"ethnicity" (Banton 1997; Braude 1997; Greenfeld 1992; Kohn 1956; Voegelin 1940; Zernatto 1944). Prior to that, communal terms were more localized and specific. In medieval Europe, the Latin term "gens"—commonly translated as "people"—usually referred to individuals of similar origins but focused on small groups linked either by blood or a small locality such as a town or city (Hudson 1996). The *Dictionary of Old Danish (1300–1700)*, for instance, defines "people" as a family concept: "my people and my father's house with fathers, family, and mothers, my first kin, my great-grandfather, my family founder" (Korsgaard 2014, 12). It was only in the eighteenth and nineteenth centuries that a broader and more abstract idea of Danish "people" emerged.

The Danish intellectuals who promoted these new ideas of community were influenced by England, which developed large and abstract ideas of community relatively early (Korsgaard 2014; Greenfeld 1992). Thus, in the mid-seventeenth century, British philosopher Thomas Hobbes (1949 [1642]) carefully distinguished between a "people" and a "multitude," defining the former as a collection of individuals "that is *one*, having *one will*, and to whom *one action* may be attributed; none of these can properly be said of a multitude" (135; italics in original). This conceptualization clearly anthropomorphizes the community, something that is even more evident in the famous image in Hobbes' *Leviathan* (1957 [1651]), which depicts the English commonwealth as a monarchy made up of a number of peoples, thereby creating a unified social organism out of the English people (see Figure 2.5).

At the time Hobbes was writing, the term "people" was reserved primarily for the English nobility, with the peasants considered as merely part of the

FIGURE 2.5.   The frontispiece of Hobbes' *Leviathan* (1651).

"multitude." Hobbes and others who helped to popularize communal concepts were also writing for elite audiences. As sociologist Michael Mann (1986, 439) notes, the English nation was based on class and power up until the eighteenth and nineteenth centuries, a situation that was also the case elsewhere in Europe. Even more, these ideas of a national community were largely limited to elites and the growing class of professionals and the intelligentsia, with the masses being unacquainted with abstract ethnic frameworks and possessing much more localized communal identities (Anderson 1983; Greenfeld 1992; Hroch 1985; Kedourie 1960).

The second major critique against revised modernist interpretations of the historical evidence is that people from different communities were killing one another long before modernity. Much of this violence, however, was between foreigners, meaning it was something different from ethnic violence. Moreover, violence between conationals is commonly motivated by something other than ethnic difference. In considering past examples of violence between conationals from different communities, most were not examples of ethnic violence because something other than ethnic difference motivated the violence. The most common of these premodern motives were fear, interests, and religious zealotry.

In several premodern environments, fear of unknown individuals commonly motivated violence. Such fear was greatest when resources were scarce, making fight a better option than flight. Another important cause of fear of unknowns was the absence of external authorities, which—especially in resource-scarce environments—made encounters with strangers a risky affair (Kelly 2000). Such fear of outsiders pushed people to either fight or flee whenever they encountered strangers, and it caused people to view strangers as dangerous and degenerate. The Central !Kung of the Kalahari, for example, referred to themselves as "ju/wasi," which translates into the people who are honest, good, and not harmful. Alternatively, they referred to everyone else—including people speaking the same language—as "ju/dole," or people who are strange, bad, and harmful (Diamond 2012, 50–51). And like other hunter-foragers, the supposedly peaceful !Kung frequently attacked and killed unknowns who were trespassing in their territory. The Sentinelese also highlight this tendency. They are the sole humans inhabiting a small island in the Bay of Bengal off the coast of Burma and are one of the last remaining groups of hunter-foragers left in the world. Little is known of them—not even the size of their population—because they commonly attack outsiders they encounter.

Although fear commonly contributes to modern ethnic violence, modern motives are different in important ways. First, modern ethnic violence usually results from a toxic combination of xenophobic emotions, including hatred, anger, resentment, and jealousy, in addition to fear. And when fear motivates modern ethnic violence, it is commonly fear for the well-being of an abstract ethnic community, not fear for individual or familial well-being. Another difference concerns who is the target of fear. The !Kung and Sentinelese targeted all strangers, whereas modern ethnic violence is based on abstract categories, with people fearing only certain ethnicities. In this way, premodern fear does not depend on ethnic difference, and the latter is a defining component of ethnic violence. Moreover, people in modern societies know and interact with people they fear, meaning that contemporary emotional prejudice commonly targets acquaintances. Even more strikingly, strangers make up the overwhelming majority of modern ingroups, so most of the strangers we meet are part of our ingroup, whereas premodern peoples usually categorize all strangers into the outgroup.

From a historical perspective, one cannot make too much of a fuss about statelessness as a cause of premodern violence because many stateless societies found ways to regulate violence between communities and because states became a major source of violence once they emerged some six thousand years ago (Malešević 2013; Otterbein 2004). Thus there is very little archeological evidence of collective violence and warfare in the southern Levant for several thousand years after the advent of settled agriculture, but many signs of violent strife and warfare are present after the rise of the Egyptian state, which forcibly incorporated the region into the growing Egyptian empire (Ferguson 2012b). Such imperialistic conquest and violence was quite common after the rise of ancient states, as the armies of proto-states conquered neighboring peoples. According to historians of genocide, these conquests offer among the first evidence of purposive attempts to annihilate communities of strangers.

While ancient conquests suggest that there is nothing inherently modern about large-scale violence between ingroups and outgroups, this too does not fit the definition of ethnic violence because it involves invaders attacking foreigners, whereas ethnic violence involves people killing conationals. Premodern violence via conquest and modern ethnic violence also differ greatly in terms of motive. Premodern conquest is generally driven by a desire for land, power, and wealth, meaning that greed and need are the dominant motives. Alternatively, modern ethnic violence is more commonly motivated by emotional prejudice and ethnic obligations, and both depend on ethnic difference. Along this line of argument, historian Walter Rodney (1972) notes that ethnic violence had no premodern equivalent in Africa. Discussing the ethnic violence in Nigeria that killed as many as two million civilians between 1967 and 1970, he writes, "[N]owhere in the history of pre-colonial independent Nigeria can anyone point to the massacre of Ibos by Hausas or any incident which suggests that people up to the 19th century were fighting each other because of ethnic origin. Of course there were wars, but they had a rational basis in trade rivalry, religious contentions, and the clashes of political expansion" (229).

Rodney includes religion along with material interests and power in his list of the causes of premodern violence in Africa. Although religion can be an important basis of ethnicity, it commonly promotes a different type of collective violence: Norms and values from religious doctrines motivate violence, with religious zealots targeting sinners and nonbelievers. In early modern Europe, one sees religious zealotry with the violent Christian Crusades against the Muslim "heathens," pogroms targeting Jews in Germany and Eastern Europe, the prosecution of Jews and Muslims during the Spanish Inquisition, and the violent expulsion of Protestant Huguenots in France. Mythic accounts of religious-based violence are also present in the Bible. According to Numbers 31:7–19:

> [The Israelites] did battle against [idol-worshiping] Midian, as the Lord had commanded Moses, and killed every male. . . . Israelites took the women of Midian and their little ones captive; and they took all their cattle, their flocks, and all their goods as booty. All their towns where they had settled, and all their encampments, they burned, but they took all the spoil and all the booty, both people and animals. . . .

Moses became angry with the officers of the army, the commanders of thousands and the commanders of hundreds, who had come from service in the war. Moses said to them, 'Have you allowed all the women to live? These women here, on Balaam's advice, made the Israelites act treacherously against the Lord in the affair of Peor, so that the plague came among the congregation of the Lord. Now therefore, kill every male among the little ones, and kill every woman who has known a man by sleeping with him. But all the young girls who have not known a man by sleeping with him, keep alive for yourselves.'

In a way similar to this myth, religious zealotry played a role in the much more recent and very real atrocities committed by ISIS in Iraq and Syria.

As described in the introduction, zealous religious violence commonly overlaps with ethnic violence, but it is distinct from ethnic violence. Whereas ethnic violence is motivated by ethnic difference, zealotry is based on religious ideology and occurs when fanatical followers attack others for failing to follow the creed. Moreover, the obligations involved in zealous violence are to deities, whereas the obligations that underlie ethnic violence are to ethnicity. Finally, zealous violence targets all sinners and nonbelievers, not particular ethnicities, and victims of religious zealotry are often members of the same community as the religious zealots; they might even be family members.

Yet religions that are capable of inspiring zealous violence are also capable of promoting distinct religious communities, and the latter can metamorphose into an ethnic community. Religious violence therefore commonly has an ethnic component, and several examples of religious violence—including ISIS—are driven by both religious and ethnic difference. The transformation of religious violence into ethnic violence is most likely when religions are organized and based on written documents because these religions possess communication and organization technologies that help instill religious-based consciousness among larger numbers of people. Similarly, some states had also begun to develop ideas of nation-based ethnicity prior to the modern era. Although these premodern states were more likely to participate in international warfare and conquest, ideas of ethnic difference undoubtedly emerged among conationals and contributed to ethnic violence. Relatively speaking, however, religious-based and nation-based ethnic violence were rare in premodern times for two reasons: Few places had the social requirements for ethnicity until relatively recently, and, when present, an ethnic consciousness was usually concentrated among a thin strata of elites.

Both the quantitative and qualitative analyses support the revised modernist position linking modernity to ethnic violence. The quantitative data show that ethnic violence became increasingly common as modernity proliferated throughout the world. Moreover, the qualitative evidence suggests that premodern violence between ingroups and outgroups rarely conformed to definitions of ethnic violence and that the basic form and motives of violence between ingroups and outgroups transformed with the advent of modernity. While offering initial evidence that modernity is an influential structural determinant of ethnic violence, we cannot have too much confidence in these findings because the analysis does not highlight mechanisms linking modernity to ethnic violence. The next five chapters offer insight into these mechanisms and thereby increase our confidence that ethnic violence is—by and large—a modern menace.

3

TEACHING PEACE OR VIOLENCE?

Because of human diversity, poor data, and the extremely complicated nature of our social world, the social sciences are inexact sciences, and one must view all social scientific claims with a heavy dose of skepticism. To increase our confidence in the validity of social scientific findings, a major goal of nearly all social scientists is to collect more and better data about the social world. Many social scientists also tweak their research designs in the hope of performing "tough" tests that offer particularly powerful insight into the validity of theories. For example, social scientists might develop an experimental design that allows the researcher to control for alternative theories. Social scientists might also test a theory on a case that seems unlikely to support the theory, believing that such a case would provide particularly powerful evidence should the case ultimately support the theory.

This chapter employs a tough test to explore the impact of modernity on ethnic violence. It focuses on a central component of modernity that does not appear to promote ethnic violence. In fact, my claims that this component commonly contributes to ethnic violence likely strikes most readers as utter nonsense, as popular beliefs and a large literature suggest that it promotes peace and tolerance, not hatred and violence. This component is education.

Questioning Tolerance Education

Few things are as revered as education. Whether liberal or conservative, American or Angolan, rich or poor, educated or uneducated, seemingly everyone recognizes education as a source of diverse and important benefits. Human development, for example, is commonly conceptualized as improving the well-being of populations, and education is widely used as a core measure of well-being. Of greater relevance to this book, many believe that education promotes peace and tolerance, with innumerable claims that education is a cure for the likes of gang violence, racial bigotry, and even terrorism. Such views are hardly new; thousands of years ago Aristotle and Plato described education as a vital determinant of peaceful human relations (Elias 2013). More recently, the United Nations Educational, Scientific, and Cultural Organization (UNESCO) (1995) described education as "the most effective means of preventing intolerance."

A number of analyses of political and racial tolerance in the United States support the claims of Plato, Aristotle, and UNESCO. These works use individual-level survey data and find that education is positively related to different measures of tolerance (Bobo and Licari 1989; Quillian 1996; Tuch 1987). That is, the higher a respondent's education level, the greater the chance he or she will respond in ways demonstrating tolerance. The authors of this body of work suggest that the relationship between education and tolerance is causal and point to two mechanisms. First, education enhances the ability of individuals to think critically and connect ideas, and these cognitive skills allow individuals to empathize with and extend norms to people from different backgrounds. As a consequence, people are more likely to respect differences instead of discriminating. The second mechanism deals with how schools socialize students. It proposes that schools socialize individuals to hold and uphold values of equality and human rights and that these values promote more tolerant and peaceful interactions with people from different backgrounds.

There is little doubt that education has the potential to promote tolerance in both ways, but universal claims that education promotes peaceful social relations must be questioned on a variety of grounds. For one, the results of past analyses are frequently much more mixed than most recognize. Some analyses fail to find a significant relationship between education and tolerance, and others even find a negative relationship. One of the earliest studies of this kind in the United States found that education is positively related to anti-Semitism, with 34 percent of respondents with a college education expressing dislike for Jews as opposed to only 18 percent of people with a high school education and 14 percent of people with a grammar school education (Campbell 1952). Several analyses also find that the relationship between education and tolerance varies greatly depending on the exact issue and the wording of the questions. One study, for example, finds that the educated are less likely to hold traditional stereotypes, to favor discriminatory policies, and to reject casual contacts with minority group members, but they are more likely to hold certain derogatory stereotypes, favor some forms of informal discrimination, and oppose intimate contact with minorities (Stember 1961).

Another potential problem with past findings is case selection. Previous studies focus primarily on the United States and generalize based on the unique American experience. One study of anti-Semitic attitudes in Austria, France, Germany, and the United States, for example, finds large variation in the relationship between education and tolerance in the different countries (Weil 1985). Similarly, studies that explore changes in tolerant attitudes over time in the United States find that tolerant attitudes have transformed and become more prevalent, showing that any relationship between education and tolerance is not static and must be considered historically.

Self-reporting surveys, which commonly provide erroneous results to survey questions that have socially appropriate responses, might also bias the findings. For example, people frequently give inflated responses to questions about church attendance, the amount of money donated to charity, and—for men at least—the frequency of intercourse. In the case of education and tolerance, the educated might be socialized to believe that tolerance is valued and therefore be more likely to respond in ways that portray themselves in a favorable light. So when an interviewer asks a respondent if African Americans should have the same rights as whites, an educated white respondent might be more likely to respond in a tolerant way even if he or she is not actually more tolerant. An influential study by sociologist Mary Jackman (1978) supports this view. She finds that educated individuals are more likely to show higher levels of tolerance toward racial integration in abstract survey questions but are no more likely to provide racially tolerant responses to questions that require the respondent to apply ideas of racial tolerance to real-world circumstances. "Increasing years of education," she concludes, "lead to a greater familiarity with the appropriate democratic position on racial integration but not to a stronger commitment to racial integration" (322). Similarly, another study finds that the educated are less likely to claim they hold anti-Semitic stereotypes but more likely to support social club discrimination against Jews (Selznick and Steinberg 1969).

Beyond potential empirical problems with past analyses, logistical considerations force one to reconsider the impact of education on tolerance. Most of the literature suggests that formal schooling can promote tolerance, but this outcome requires an appropriate curriculum focused on diversity and mutual understanding as well as a large, motivated, and capable staff. In the real world, such a curriculum must be meticulously constructed and commonly faces stiff opposition from powerful and entrenched interests, and few schools are lucky enough to have a large number of talented and inspired teachers. The most important

requirements of tolerance education are therefore either absent or in short supply in many places.

Education, Hate Groups, and Ethnic Violence

Although commonsensical, the tolerance hypothesis is not based on solid empirical evidence, which raises the possibility that education might only contribute to peace and tolerance in some cases. Instead of attitudinal surveys, another
way to test the tolerance hypothesis is to analyze the educational backgrounds of
intolerant, hateful, and violent people and the relationship between education
and ethnic violence, a task that this section begins.

Education and the Nazis

Hate groups epitomize Frederick Douglass's idea of diseased imagination, and
many hate groups are actively involved in ethnic violence. One of the most notorious hate groups of all time was the National Socialist German Workers' Party,
better known as the Nazi Party. It was founded in 1919 and ruled Germany under
Hitler from 1933 until his military defeat in 1945. This ultranationalist party
used brute coercion to pursue its objectives, and its most notorious goal was
the protection of Aryan racial purity by excluding and eliminating non-Aryans.
Although the Nazis preached the inferiority of a variety of groups, they focused
on Jews, and anti-Semitism was a core element of their exclusionary nationalism.
In pursuit of national purity, the Nazi Party orchestrated the killings of Others on
a scale the world had never seen.

In an effort to better understand the causes of Nazi atrocities, several historians and sociologists have investigated the bases of Nazi support. These works
look at the backgrounds of people who voted for the Nazis, party members, and
party officials. Data on educational attainment are usually lacking, and the literature focuses on the class and occupation of Nazi supporters, members, and officials. Yet because all education beyond the primary level prepared students for
the professions, class is an excellent predictor of education for prewar Germany.

In stark opposition to Seymour Martin Lipset's (1963) well-known claims
that the Nazis came to power through the support of the lower middle classes,
there is presently a general consensus that the middle and upper classes were their
strongest supporters. As a leading expert on the topic notes, "It was the support from established social circles, from the elite, which was significantly
over-represented in both the membership and—especially—the leadership
of the Nazi Movement" (Muhlberger 2003, 80). Another leading historian of

the Nazi Party muses, "What seems most remarkable in this context was the vulnerability of the educated bourgeoisie to National Socialist propaganda" (Mommsen 1996, 344).

Voting patterns offer important insight into who supported the Nazis. In an early analysis, sociologist Richard Hamilton (1982) finds that electoral support was weakest in lower-class districts, strong in middle-class districts, and very strong in upper-class districts. Using much more extensive data, political scientist Jürgen Falter (1990) highlights the same pattern: The middle and upper classes were much more likely to vote for Nazis, and Nazi supporters switched allegiance from parties traditionally serving the educated elites.

And while the upper and middle classes voted for the Nazis in large numbers, their support is even more evident when looking at party membership. According to historian Michael Kater (1983), members of the lower class were underrepresented among Nazi Party members despite the active efforts of Nazi elites to gain worker support. Middle-class members were moderately overrepresented, but the upper class—and thereby the most educated members of German society—was heavily overrepresented. In 1923, for example, upper-class membership was 325 percent greater than expected given its share of the population, whereas lower-class Germans were underrepresented among Nazi Party members by 35 percent (242–43). After Hitler's ascension to power, many more people joined the Nazis, but the base of support remained unchanged: Members of the upper class were overrepresented among new Nazi Party members in 1933 by 335 percent, whereas the lower class was underrepresented by 45 percent. Considering specific occupations, Kater finds that teachers, students, lawyers, engineers, academics, and doctors were at greatest risk of joining the Nazi Party both before and after the Nazis gained control of the German state (242–43).

The pattern of upper-class support for the Nazis is even stronger among Nazi officials. For example, gauleiters were the regional heads of the Nazi Party, and upper-class Germans were overrepresented among them by a factor of fifteen both before and after the Nazis' rise to power (Kater 1983, 256–57). Even members of the *SS-Totenkopfverbände* (*SS-TV*), the organization running the concentration camps, were well-educated. Although the upper class made up less than 3 percent of the population, one-third of the *SS-TV* had upper-class backgrounds (Ziegler 1989, 132). University students, doctors, and academics were particularly overrepresented.

Unlike analyses of voter support and party membership, data on the educational background is available for some Nazi personnel, and these Nazis were very educated relative to the general population. One-quarter of SS members, for example, had a university education at a time when only 2 to 4 percent of the German population was able to attend university (Zeigler 1989, 115). Even

among the *Einsatzgruppen*, the notorious paramilitary branch that actually implemented the "final solution," one-third of all members held university degrees
(Weiss 2003, 54). Taking a large sample of Nazi war criminals, sociologist Michael
Mann (2000) highlights a similar pattern: 40 percent of war criminals were university graduates.

Education and the KKK

Faced with declining membership in 2013, the Ku Klux Klan (KKK) sought
broader support by downplaying its racism and emphasizing its patriotism. With
considerable irony, the arrest of two New York Klansmen a few months later actually demonstrated greater tolerance and patriotism, as the two were caught trying
to sell an x-ray gun to Jews—a group that was previously a favorite target of the
Klan—in order to kill Muslims—a group that is now framed as enemy number one
in America's war on terror. Even if the Klan can avoid additional bad publicity from
incidents such as this, their efforts to downplay racism seem doomed to failure because nothing—with the possible exception of the Nazis—epitomizes racism more
than the KKK. Like the Nazis, the Klan therefore offers a window into whether
members of hate groups are relatively educated or uneducated. Unfortunately, the
KKK is a secret society and does not publish information on the characteristics
of its members, making such an analysis difficult. It is not impossible, however.
A growing body of work on the Second Klan, which began in 1915 and reached its
zenith in the mid-1920s, offers insight into the education of Klan members.

With between five and six million members, the Second Klan was much larger
and more active than the Klan movements that preceded and followed it. It was
active in nearly all states, but its largest following was in the Midwest. Although
women were unable to join the KKK, they were also strong supporters and had
their own independent organization, the Women of the Ku Klux Klan (WKKK).
The KKK and WKKK of the 1920s were right-wing nationalistic organizations
that attracted Protestant members through many platforms. At the heart of their
message were claims that the great American nation (i.e., white Protestants)
needed protection from diverse and deadly threats. While these supposed men-
aces included communists, criminal elements, gambling, and even alcohol, the
KKK is most notorious for its verbal, symbolic, and physical assaults on African
Americans, Catholics, foreigners, and Jews.

The normal assumption is that members of the KKK and the WKKK were
uneducated, socially isolated, and economically vulnerable. A famous assessment
of the Klan movement in the 1920s characterizes it as led by ignorant lower-class
masses who mobilized out of fear and competition with minority groups (Lipset
and Raab 1970). Over the past two decades, some lists of KKK membership

have emerged, and they provide evidence pointing to a very different conclusion. Working with membership lists of KKK chapters in California, Colorado, Georgia, Illinois, Indiana, and Oregon, diverse historians have come to a general conclusion that membership differed from place to place but represented all segments of society (Cocoltchos 1992; Goldberg 1992; Horowitz 1992; Jackson 1967; MacLean 1994; Moore 1997; Toy 1992). Different qualitative analyses of the KKK in Oklahoma, Pennsylvania, and Texas and of the WKKK in Indiana even suggest that the regional elite were common members (Blee 1991; Brown 1984; Burbank 1971; Jenkins 1997; Lay 1992).

Besides simply showing that Klan members came from a variety of class backgrounds, studies of the Klan in Denver, Indianapolis, and Anaheim provide comparative data on Klan members and the general population. As shown in Figure 3.1, Klan members in Denver and Indianapolis came from all classes. When compared to the general population, however, they are underrepresented among blue-collar workers and overrepresented among white-collar workers. In Anaheim, 43 percent of Klan members had middle-class occupations compared to only 32 percent of the general population (Cocoltchos 1992). Moreover, Klan members in Anaheim were twice as likely to be registered to vote and three times as likely to be a member of a civic association than members of the general population (Cocoltchos 1992). Others also find that Klan members were very active in politics and strongly represented in the Masons, Kiwanis, and other

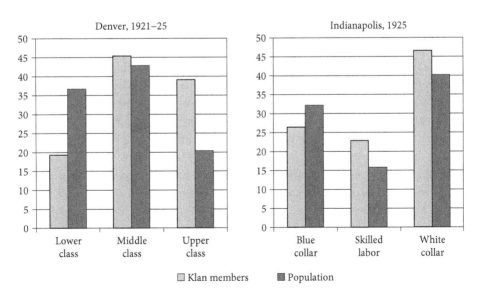

FIGURE 3.1 Klan membership by class. Sources: Goldberg (1992, 52); Moore (1997, 63, 66).

civic associations (Blee 1991, 121; Goldberg 1992, 51; Lay 1992, 73; MacLean 1994, 54; McVeigh 2009; Toy 1992, 167). Given their overrepresentation among white-collar jobs and their participation in civic associations, Klan members appear to have been both relatively educated and active in community affairs, not the ignorant and isolated masses that many so commonly assume.

Another way to gain insight into the educational background of Klan members is to compare regional rates of KKK membership with average education level by region. Such an analysis provides insight into whether KKK membership is more common among regions with relatively educated or uneducated populations. Although data on regional rates of KKK membership are very difficult to find, Indiana has data for both the KKK and the WKKK by county. Census data from 1920, in turn, offer insight into average school enrollment by county. By itself, school enrollment is a good predictor of Klan membership in Indiana, explaining 14 percent of KKK membership and 23 percent of WKKK membership. Even when controlling for immigrants, blacks, Catholics, economic conditions, and population growth, education remains a powerful predictor of Klan activities. In fact, its explanatory power increases when controlling for other factors associated with Klan membership.[1]

Notably, the Indiana Klan—like elsewhere—paid great attention to education and demanded educational reforms aimed at expanding and improving the educational system; the Indiana Klan even tried unsuccessfully to buy Valparaiso University. The great value Klan members placed on education is clearly evident in a speech given at a national Klan convention in 1923 by Hiram Evans, an imperial wizard between 1922 and 1939 and a man who created "black squads" to attack and torture minorities when he was a Klan leader in Dallas: "One of the principal duties of the Klan today is to build up a great free educational system. Fifty percent of our taxes should go towards education instead of only five percent. Go home and talk education among the Klansmen and soon your representatives in congress will see the light and will be voting to make America the best educated country on earth so that through education our children's children can care for themselves and be a value to their state" (McVeigh 2009, 112).

With the recent release of the 1940 census, it is now possible to gain direct insight into the educational background of some members of the Second Klan. A list of Klan members from Denver, Colorado, during the mid-1920s provides

---

1. Unpublished analysis by the author. The data on KKK membership by county are from Moore (1997). The county-level data on school enrollment rate for fourteen- to twenty-year-olds, foreign-born population, African American population, Catholic population, and per capita industrial and agrarian production (log), and percent change in population are from the United States Census Bureau (1920). Data on WKKK membership are from Blee (1991).

the addresses of most Klan members, allowing researchers to gather information on the educational attainment of Klan members. To do just this, I have taken a sample of Klan members and used the census to gather information on their educational attainment.[2] On average, the Klan members had 10.4 years of education compared to only 8.9 among all males aged forty-five and older living in Denver in 1940. Figure 3.2 compares Klan members to non–Klan members by level of

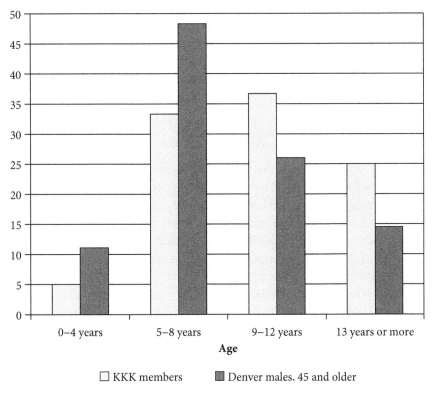

☐ KKK members ■ Denver males, 45 and older

FIGURE 3.2 Education of KKK members and the general public in Denver by age, 1920s.

2. Unpublished analysis by the author. I gathered data on KKK members at the Colorado Historical Society. Because of the large number of memberships, I took two samples of KKK members (KKK registration numbers 569 to 2,112 and 14,979 to 15,410). The membership list gave the residential address of most members but did not list their education levels. To find their education levels, I looked up the addresses of KKK members using the 1940 census, which was the first US census to gather information on education. Using this technique, I was only able to gather information from the census for KKK members who—in 1940—lived at the same address they listed as their home address in the KKK registry. Data on the average education of males living in Denver aged forty-five and older comes from the 1940 census.

educational attainment. The figure clearly shows that KKK members were much more likely to have at least nine years of education: More than 60 percent of Klan members completed at least nine years of education versus only 40 perent for all males living in Denver aged forty-five and older. This difference is particularly stark at the higher levels of education, as Klan members were almost twice as likely to have attended college for at least one year.

One example of an educated individual who was in my sample is Benjamin Stapleton, who was the 1,128th registered member of the Denver Klan and had completed sixteen years of education. Stapleton was a five-term mayor of Denver, and his name litters the Denver landscape, with a street, a district, a park, and Denver's first international airport (closed in 1995) all bearing his name. With obvious irony, Stapleton Central Park is located on Martin Luther King Jr. Boulevard.

Education and Terrorist Violence

According to Nobel laureate Elie Wiesel, "Education is the way to eliminate terrorism" (Jai 2001). Yet Wiesel was highly educated and was a former member of Irgun, a group Enders Walter and Todd Sandler (2006) claim helped to revolutionize modern terrorist techniques in its effort to establish an independent Jewish state in Palestine. Similarly, Hannah Arendt, Albert Einstein, and many other Jewish intellectuals decried Irgun as "a terrorist, right-wing, chauvinist organization" (Abramowitz et al. 1948).

Wiesel is not unique in this regard, as many members of terrorist organizations are highly educated. The 9/11 bombers, for example, were not ignorant fools. As one journalist notes, they "were adults with education and skill ... [who had] spent years studying and training in the United States" (Wilgoren 2001). Mohammed Atta was the leader of the bombers and offers a striking example: He was the son of a prominent Egyptian lawyer and brother of two university professors, excelled in school, and pursued postgraduate studies in urban planning in Germany. The perpetrators of the 2007 Glasgow Airport bombing were even more educated: Seven of the eight people arrested were either doctors or medical residents.

While these examples are anecdotal, empirical analyses suggest that they conform to general patterns. Political scientist Robert Pape (2005) analyzes data on sixty-seven suicide attackers in Lebanon, the Palestinian territories, and Israel and finds that 54 percent had some postsecondary education, compared with only 7 percent of all Lebanese Shia and 18 percent of all Palestinian males. In a more thorough analysis of violence committed by Hamas and Palestinian Islamic Jihad against

Israelis, economist Claude Berrebi (2007) analyzes data on 335 militants who were either arrested or killed between 1987 and 2002. He finds that 96 percent had at least a high school education and that 65 percent had postsecondary education. Alternatively, while controlling for age, sex, and religion, the comparable figures for the Palestinian population were only 51 percent and 15 percent, respectively, which means that the militants of these organizations were twice as likely to have completed high school and four times as likely to have postsecondary education.

Members of non-Muslim organizations using terrorist methods also have relatively high levels of education. In an early study of the causes of terrorism completed in the 1970s, for example, Charles Russell and Bowman Miller (1978) generate a large database on terrorist attacks and their perpetrators. Most of these 350 terrorists were from Western Europe and Latin America, although some were also from Asia and the Middle East. Based on their analysis, Bowman and Miller conclude that "the vast majority of those individuals involved in terrorist activities as cadres or leaders are quite well educated. In fact, approximately two-thirds of those identified as terrorists are persons with some university training, university graduates, or postgraduate students" (89).

Education and Ethnic Violence

Terrorist violence commonly involves attacks on individuals from different ethnic communities. Terrorism can thus be a particular type of ethnic violence. Broader analyses of ethnic violence, in turn, offer mounting evidence that education commonly contributes to violence against Others.

One way to explore the impact of education on ethnic violence is to test whether regions with higher levels of education and more rapid educational expansion are more or less likely to experience ethnic violence. In *Educations in Ethnic Violence* (Lange 2012), I look into this and find that countries with higher levels of education and more rapidly expanding educational enrollment are at considerably *greater* risk of intense ethnic violence. Importantly, although the relationship is strong for all countries in the world with available data, only a subset of cases drives the relationship. In wealthy countries with effective states and robust democracies, education is unrelated to ethnic violence. In nonwealthy countries with relatively ineffective states and limited democracies, on the other hand, education is strongly and positively related to ethnic violence. In this way, education appears to increase the risk of interethnic violence, although this impact depends on other factors.

My analysis uses aggregate data exploring whether a country's level of education is related to its level of ethnic violence, but other studies explore the relationship at the individual level. One study uses survey data on young women in contemporary Kenya and compares girls who won scholarships to attend school with girls who were not awarded scholarships and subsequently did not attend school (Friedman et al. 2011). The girls who won scholarships were 30 percent more likely to claim that their ethnic identity was important. They were also more frustrated by their lack of opportunities and much more likely to support political violence. A different study uses survey data from nine African countries to explore how competition affects ethnic identification (Bannon, Miguel, and Posner 2004). It finds that competition intensifies ethnic identification but that this effect is especially strong among people with relatively high levels of education. And more than simply showing that education contributes to characteristics that are linked to ethnic violence, analyses find that education is one of strongest predictors of participation in the Rwandan genocide (Brehm 2013; Verwimp 2005).

Linking Education to Violence

A common joke among professors is that exams should be abolished to save lives, as there is a strong relationship between the dates of exams and the deaths of grandparents (almost always grandmothers in my experience). The joke is funny—at least among heartless academics—because it highlights the problem of inferring causality when the data used to establish a relationship is faulty (i.e., some students lie to get out of exams). Inferring causation from relationships can also lead to erroneous conclusions when relationships are spurious. For example, the presence of storks is positively related to birth rates, but this obviously does not mean that storks deliver babies. Instead, storks are usually present in rural areas, and rural areas—for a variety of reasons not involving storks—experience higher birth rates than urban areas. In order to avoid errors caused by bad data and spuriousness, researchers must seek mechanisms that potentially underlie relationships. For instance, one mechanism that helps explain higher birth rates in rural areas is a cost-benefit mechanism: Children in rural areas are less expensive to raise and offer greater economic returns and support, so rural couples commonly choose to have more offspring.

Thus far, this chapter has only highlighted a relationship between education and ethnic violence, so we cannot be certain that education actually contributes to violence in any way. Instead, the findings might be based on inaccurate data, or the relationship between education and ethnic violence might be spurious. To look into whether education actually contributes to violence and intolerance in some way, we must therefore consider mechanisms that potentially underlie the relationship. Chapter 1 describes four general mechanisms that might explain the relationship between education and ethnic violence: Education might strengthen ethnic consciousness, intensify emotional prejudice, create ethnic obligations, and provide mobilizational resources. Another look at the Nazis highlights all four at work.[3]

Education and Ethnic Violence in Nazi Germany

According to historian George Mosse (1964), education was the main institution spreading the racist nationalist ideology that the Nazis usurped and intensified, and this ideology shaped the contours and strength of a German national consciousness. In so doing, education contributed to emotional prejudice and ethnic obligations, both of which motivated anti-Semitic violence. Moreover, education provided a variety of mobilizational resources that put these motives into action.

After the unification of Germany in 1871, German schools taught extremely nationalistic curricula in a concerted effort to create a homogenous national community among a population that had previously been divided among a number of separate polities (Weymar 1961). The hyper-nationalism taught in schools went hand-in-hand with claims of Aryan racial superiority. Textbooks and lectures at secondary schools and universities preached and legitimized the doctrine of Aryan racial superiority to such an extent that it gained cliché status by the time the Nazis came to power. One historian therefore concludes, "We would not be so surprised that a highly educated nation spawned the Nazis if we looked at the reading lists and textbooks in the schools that preceded them" (Weiss 2003, 32). This racism was linked to the German Romantic Movement, which glorified the German "*volk*" and claimed that all true Germans possessed a transcendental essence that "was fused to man's innermost nature, and represented the source of his creativity, his depth of feeling, his individuality, and his unity with other members of the Volk" (Mosse 1964, 4). Under Hitler, this racist nationalism of education increased. As Hitler (1971 [1925]) described in *Mein Kampf*, the ultimate goal of education "must be to burn the racial sense and racial feeling into the instinct and the intellect, the heart and brain of youth entrusted

---

3. This analysis of education and support for the Nazis draws on and reformulates my work from *Educations in Ethnic Violence* (Lange 2012).

to it. No boy or girl must leave school without having been led to an ultimate realization of the necessity and essence of blood purity" (427).

Education also contributed to an ethnic consciousness more indirectly by increasing individual access to artistic and literary works that represented and glorified the nation. Due to state patronage and a strong national consciousness among the German intelligentsia, the arts objectified the German nation and thereby created a powerful emotional attachment to the nation (Mosse 1975). One only needs to consider Richard Wagner's operas—which are full of nationalistic myths and symbols—for an example (Mosse 1975; Viereck 2004). Similarly, the educated devoured nationalist literatures depicting the nation as real and important.

In addition to imparting a strong national consciousness, German education also increased emotional prejudice by intensifying hatred, anger, and fear targeted against Jews. German schools did not create anti-Semitism, but German education helped popularize and legitimize it (Blackburn 1985; Mosse 1964). The hyper-nationalistic ideology taught in German schools divided and ranked the world's races. Inevitably, Aryans were placed on top of the racial hierarchy, and Jews were relegated to the bottom. Historian George Mosse (1964) finds that the *volkisch* nationalism taught in schools pigeonholed Jews as the antithesis of the German *volk*. "Not only was the essential nature of the Jews incompatible with the inner character of the German Volk," he writes, "but their national religion made them an irreconcilable foreign element on German soil" (38). Figure 3.3 depicts this discriminatory education in practice, with the curriculum effectively racializing and dehumanizing Jews. And hand-in-hand with this formal curriculum, schools heightened anti-Semitism through other forms of discrimination. Fraternities and educational associations, for example, commonly excluded and demeaned Jews, and many teachers actively harassed and humiliated their Jewish students. To help Jewish students avoid such unwanted attention, a Jewish journal regularly published a list of schools that were not openly anti-Semitic (Mosse 1964, 268).

Education also contributed to anti-Semitism more indirectly by increasing individual access to the arts and literature, both of which commonly contained overtly anti-Semitic messages. In addition to racist depictions of Jews in paintings, plays, and operas, many books were blatantly anti-Semitic and played a particularly influential role in strengthening anti-Semitism. These works include the writings of Theodor Fritsch, whose *Handbook of Anti-Semitism* appeared in thirty-seven editions between 1896 and 1914; Heinrich von Treitschke, who coined the expression "the Jews are our misfortune"; H. S. Chamberlain, who described the history of mankind as the struggle between Aryans and Jews; and Julius Langbehn and Paul de Lagarde, both of whom berated the Jews as a

„Die Judennaſe iſt an ihrer Spitze gebogen. Sie ſieht aus wie ein Sechſer..."

FIGURE 3.3 Teaching anti-Semitism in German schools. Source: *Der Giftpilz* (The Poison Mushroom) by Ernst Meimer (Nuremberg: Der Strumer, 1938).

national menace. One leading expert pays particular attention to the final three authors and notes that they wrote for a very educated audience:

> Chamberlain, Lagarde, and Langbehn, unlike many anti-Semites in the West, did not write for the ignorant, the uneducated, or the powerless. Their admirers came from the highest ranks of German society, including the Kaiser, his military officers, and the aristocracy. Countless schoolteachers and academics were avid readers, as were members of

> German student organizations, middle-class youth movements, the Pan
> German League, the Agrarian Bund, the German Conservative party,
> and leaders of a variety of anti-Semitic movements. (Weiss 2003, 35)

While education contributed to anti-Semitism both directly and indirectly, education also had the potential to intensify anger, hatred, and fear of Jews in two additional ways. First, education heightened expectations and assertiveness, both of which promoted anger and frustration in the context of an abysmal economy that stifled the aspirations of millions of educated Germans and a post-Versailles geopolitical order that effectively made Germany a second-class power. Second, education strengthened a national consciousness and thereby increased the attention Germans paid to threats to the national community, something that heightened fear in such difficult times. Rampant anti-Semitism, in turn, helped to target Jews with these emotions.

Education was quite possibly the pre-eminent means of receiving respect, privilege, and a high-paying job in pre-Nazi Germany. An ideology known as *bildung* held a hegemonic position in the German education system and proclaimed education the most important source of cultivation and social worth (Hahn 1998; Ringer 1967). As a consequence, the educated were self-confident and possessed high expectations, both of which increased the chances of being angered by hardship and acting aggressively against perceived threats. In the 1920s and 1930s, in turn, Germany was racked with economic, political, and geopolitical crises that frustrated many, including the educated. Along these lines, sociologists Thomas Scheff and Suzanne Retzinger (1991) link these hardships to shame, anger, and scapegoating.

The anger caused by this hardship targeted a variety of actors, including the government. Jews were another common target, and they were scapegoated mercilessly. Anti-Semitism helps explain why Germans blamed Jews for their hardships because this ethnic ideology pushed Germans to recognize Jews as a distinct category of people and to despise them. In addition, Jews were doing relatively well in several professions, including law, medicine, and academia. Because only the educated had access to these jobs and because the experiences and observations of the educated allowed them to see the prominent positions of Jews in the professions, they were the most likely to scapegoat Jews for "stealing" jobs from "real" Germans. Importantly, one must not mistake scapegoating as simply the result of individual hardship. Rather, communal hardship is an equally influential cause of scapegoating, and the educated were more likely to scapegoat Jews for communal hardship because of education's impact on their national consciousness, anti-Semitic views, and experiences. This helps explain why many educated middle-class and upper-class Germans scapegoated Jews for Germany's hardship even when they did not experience hardships personally.

The anger that pushed Germans to scapegoat Jews and support the Nazis cannot easily be separated from fear, as both emotions had similar determinants and reinforced one another. Most notably, the hardships that educated Germans saw and experienced not only angered them but sparked fear of German national decline. Anti-Semitism, in turn, was not only virulent in its strength but virulent in its characterization of Jews: It portrayed them as a malignant disease sapping the great German nation of its strength and glory, and it encouraged the elimination of the Jewish menace. Similarly, the combination of ethnic consciousness with fear of German national decline and disgrace caused individuals to pay close attention to the statuses of Jews and "real" Germans, and the relatively high status of the former heightened fear and anger and thereby motivated efforts to eliminate Jews.

Hatred, anger, and fear all contributed to genocidal violence against Jews, but emotional prejudice was not the only motive. Another influential motive was obligation. The horrific ethnic violence in Nazi Germany was state-led and highly institutionalized, meaning that most perpetrators of the ethnic violence were state agents who were simply following orders. Recognizing the bureaucratic apparatus that implemented the "final solution," Hannah Arendt (2006) famously claims that SS Lieutenant Colonel Adolf Eichmann and other perpetrators of the genocide lacked emotional motivation and simply acted out of "sheer thoughtlessness" and obligation as cogs in an impersonal statist machine.

The hyper-nationalism preached in German schools, in turn, pressured students to serve Germany without reservation and predisposed many educated Germans to act on nationalist obligations. Ever since German unification, German education hammered home the message that all Germans have a duty to serve the Fatherland and must do everything in their power to increase its glory. One analysis of the German educational system by two American academics in the 1920s, for example, found that it obsessed on creating obligations to serve the nation (Alexander and Parker 1929). "The essential aim of the school as it is now conceived," they write, "is to fire youth with enthusiasm for service to the race, and to make each generation conscious that its fate is indissolubly linked with the fate of its people" (291). Giving ominous warnings about the potential consequences of such education, they conclude, "Grave danger may lie in this conception of education for it might lead to national arrogance or to imperialistic greed for power" (291).

One clearly sees this sense of duty in the patriotic societies that emerged during the 1890s and flourished during the Weimar period, and these societies highlight a link between education and a strong sense of ethnic obligation. German patriot societies were focused on making Germany a great nation through a variety of means, including geopolitical expansion and belligerence. They were worried about Germany's geopolitical decline after the First World War, and many of their members saw Hitler as a means of reasserting Germany's rightful place as a world power. Believing that Jews threatened the German nation, nearly all patriotic societies preached anti-Semitism.

Historian Roger Chickering (1984) investigates the educational background of the local officials of patriotic societies and finds that they were extremely well-educated: 70 percent had at least some university education, and 30 percent possessed doctorates. In a more detailed analysis of one patriotic society, he discovers that the long-term members were even more educated than the local leaders. Chickering also compares the educational background of patriotic society members with that of their main rival, the German Peace Society, a renowned association promoting international peace, democracy, and multiculturalism and claiming several Nobel laureates among its membership. The Peace Society's local officials were well-educated relative to the German population, but the leaders of the patriotic societies were nearly twice as likely to have high levels of education.

Importantly, obligations commonly worked hand-in-hand with emotional prejudice to promote ethnic violence against Jews. Arendt's famous claims about the banality of violence have been thoroughly critiqued, with in-depth studies showing that Eichmann was not simply following orders. Instead, he was a "fanatical racist" and "ruthless anti-Semite," and this emotional prejudice caused him to willingly follow orders (Cesarani 2004; Stangneth 2014). In this way, anti-Semitism helped many Germans to fulfill some despicable obligations. And even if some people who followed orders were not anti-Semitic, the state leaders who concocted the horrific policies were driven in large part by emotional prejudice against Jews.

Finally, mobilizational resources also help to explain why the educated were at greater risk of supporting the Nazis. For example, the Nazis used cultural resources to frame their movement, and the educated were more responsive to these frames because their education increased familiarity with the myths and symbols used by the Nazis. Education also offered more tangible mobilizational resources that aided the Nazi movement. One notable example is university associations. University students jumped on the Nazi bandwagon early, and one-quarter of all university students were members of the Nazi Student Association in 1930 (Proctor 1988). With such large numbers, Nazi students dominated student councils and university politics even before Hitler came to power in 1933, and they played an influential role in the Nazi party before Hitler's ascendency to the chancellorship (Steinberg 1977).

In addition to simply exploiting the mobilizational resources of schools and universities, the Nazis co-opted upper- and middle-class associations and thereby engaged the educated in the Nazi movement relatively easily and rapidly. More than any other party, the Nazis actively organized, infiltrated, and co-opted civil societal associations. Such efforts proved successful because many associations shared the Nazi platform of divisive nationalism, hatred of the Weimar regime, and anti-Semitism. And when co-opted, associations facilitated Nazi recruitment and mobilization efforts and thereby helped to propel Hitler into power on the backs of educated and socially active Germans (Berman 1997; Koshar 1990).

Doctors and Ethnic Violence in Nazi Germany

A review of the literature offers evidence that education promoted a strong national consciousness, targeted Jews with xenophobic emotions, and popularized national obligations. In addition, the educated controlled mobilizational resources and used them to participate in the Nazi movement. All four, in turn, help to explain the relationship between education and support for the Nazi Party. After such a broad analysis of education's impact on Nazi support, however, it is helpful to look at a more specific example. Doctors provide one very intriguing case.

Because doctors are almost universally regarded as humanitarian caretakers, it may come as a surprise that few other occupational groups rivaled doctors in their active support of the Nazis: 45 percent of doctors joined the Nazi Party, 31 percent joined the Nazi Physicians' League, 26 percent joined the SA, and 7 percent joined the SS (Kater 2002, 80). Although the last statistic might not seem very large, the SS was relatively small, and nearly half of all SS members with a university education studied medicine (Ziegler 1989). Through their active participation in Nazi policies, at least four hundred doctors committed crimes against humanity (Kater 1989). According to Hugh Gallagher (1990), doctors were so active in the Nazi Party that "the Nazi administration was as close as the world has come to being a medical state: a government run in accordance with 'doctor's orders'" (91).

Education placed doctors at a greater risk of supporting the Nazis by instilling a powerful national consciousness and promoting anti-Semitism. Doctors, in turn, spent as much of their lives in school as any elite occupational group and were hardly immune to this influence. Even more, eugenics was a subdiscipline of medicine and "had become a scientific orthodoxy in the German medical community" before the Nazis rose to power (Proctor 1988, 38). By giving pseudo-scientific proof of Aryan superiority and Jewish inferiority, eugenics effectively legitimized anti-Semitism.

Medical historians also place considerable weight on fear and anger as determinants of strong Nazi support among doctors. Although the existential threat caused by Germany's difficult geopolitical position contributed to these emotions and was potentially the most important cause of emotional prejudice, previous analyses emphasize economic hardship and competition with Jews (Kater 1984; Proctor 1988). Doctors had high expectations for economic mobility and prestige. This common feeling of privilege and merit was the result of the elitist origins of German universities, the elite background of most doctors, and the past mobility and status of doctors. During the Weimar period, however, many doctors were unable to attain these expectations because they were either unemployed or underemployed. Given their hardships, combined with great expectations for social mobility, many doctors were angry and turned to the Nazis as a means of expressing their discontent (Kater 1989; Lange 2012; Proctor 1988; Weiss 1996).

Many also blamed Jews for unfairly stealing jobs and made emotional appeals to remove them from the medical establishment. In addition to their anti-Semitic educations, several "Aryan" doctors pinpointed Jews as a menace because Jews were greatly overrepresented within the profession: Although Jews made up only 1 percent of the total German population, they constituted 16 percent of German doctors in 1900, and this percentage rose to 40 percent in some larger cities (Kater 1987, 35). "In their efforts to oust Jewish colleagues from the profession," historian Michael Kater (1984) writes, "Gentile medical students and doctors stopped short of nothing" (151). Importantly, both unemployed and employed doctors held anti-Semitic views and supported the Nazis, suggesting that the desire to eliminate their Jewish colleagues was caused by anger, fear, and hatred in addition to self-interest.

Ethnic obligations also pushed many doctors to support the Nazis. Specifically, German medical schools cultivated a nationalistic form of humanitarianism that encouraged concern for the well-being of the entire German nation, and this pushed medical students to accept drastic measures in an effort to "heal" the nation. Noting the link between medicine, social well-being, and extremism, historian Eric Weitz (2003) writes that "science and medicine had begun to provide the ideas and techniques by which the population could be manipulated, purged of its ailing elements and refined to the lofty stage of pristine purity. Biology had developed techniques of immunization against harmful bacteria; it was now possible to imagine biological-political techniques for dealing with the harmful scourges of human society" (50). Although it promotes despicable actions and outcomes, there is something virtuous about looking out for the well-being of an imagined social body. Along these lines, Jewish philosopher and sociologist Raymond Aron, who was a professor in Germany between 1930 and 1933, recalled that his most "upstanding" students were Nazis.[4]

---

4. Correspondence with John A. Hall.

Finally, doctors participated in associations that were either co-opted by or formed under the supervision of the Nazi Party, and this is another reason for their overrepresentation among Nazi supporters. Doctors were very active in civic and professional associations such as the patriotic societies, and the Nazi Party infiltrated these associations to mobilize them. Moreover, the Nazis helped doctors to create a medical association with direct ties to the Nazis, the National Socialist German Physician's League (NSAB). The latter soon eclipsed all other medical associations to become the dominant medical association. According to one medical historian, the NSAB's success resulted from the skillful infiltration and absorption of "traditional physicians' organizations into the party's own physicians' league" (Weyers 1998, 47). Another historian claimed that "[t]he NSAB acted as a catalyst for the social and organizational bonding between the Nazi Party and the upper bourgeoisie" (Kater 1986, 171).

Education can undoubtedly promote peace and tolerance, but this chapter shows that hateful and violent people are commonly highly educated. Moreover, it offers evidence that education commonly contributes to intolerance and violence in four ways: by strengthening ethnic consciousness, promoting emotional prejudice, pushing ethnic obligation, and increasing mobilizational resources. In subsequent chapters, this book continues to explore the impact of education on ethnic violence but expands its scope to consider the influence of additional elements of modernity, especially states. Additionally, it focuses on ethnic consciousness, emotional prejudice, ethnic obligations, and mobilizational opportunities, beginning with the first.

4

THE ORIGINS OF ETHNIC CONSCIOUSNESS

The tops of many mountain ranges have fossilized remains of creatures that lived on the ocean floor millions of years ago. Early attempts to explain this anomaly turned to the Bible and saw these fossils as proof of a flood so great that aquatic creatures lived atop submerged peaks. Besides religious conviction, this explanation had considerable appeal because it coincided with the common perception of mountains as eternal and unchanging. So if mountains were always there, then sea life must have worked its way up the mountains somehow, and a flood offers one logical explanation. Today, the diluvian hypothesis seems utterly absurd; it is common knowledge that mountains are not unchanging but slowly rose from the seabed over millions of years to become towering masses of rock, and the aquatic fossils are from the period before colliding tectonic plates pushed ancient seabeds into the sky.

As well as any other, this geological example highlights how even the most magnificent and enormous transformations can be hidden from human observation either because they occurred in the distant past or because they changed at an extremely slow pace. The present chapter describes another example of an enormous and radical transformation that is hidden in history: the rise of powerful ethnic consciousnesses shared by large numbers of strangers. Today ethnicity seems utterly natural, and this creates the impression that we have always been members of ethnic communities. In fact, because ethnic communities are perceived as universal, philosopher and social anthropologist Ernest Gellner (1983) notes that people who cannot be categorized into an ethnicity—more specifically, a nation—are perceived as deviant and provoke feelings of revulsion. Similar to the discovery of aquatic fossils high in the mountains, however, archeological, anthropological, and historical evidence force one to recognize that our impression of the naturalness of large human communities is false. Indeed, "nation," "race," "ethnicity," and other categories that refer to large communities of strangers are all modern conceptual constructs that only entered the popular lexicon with their contemporary meanings during the past two centuries (Banton 1997; Braude 1997; Greenfeld 1992; Kohn 1956; Voegelin 1940; Zernatto 1944). Before then, few people possessed an ethnic consciousness.

This chapter describes the processes shaping the contours, salience, and proliferation of ethnic consciousness over the past two centuries. While of general interest, such an analysis is a necessary component of this book's analysis because ethnic violence requires the division of peoples into ethnic-based ingroups and outgroups. Moreover, an ethnic consciousness contributes to ethnic violence through its effects on emotional prejudice and ethnic obligations.

From Communities of Acquaintances to Communities of Strangers

Chapter 1 described how humans are genetically predisposed to form ingroups and outgroups and how human emotionality promotes ingroup solidarity, both of which suggest that communal consciousness is prewired into our brains. The influence of our biology does not stop here, however, as our creative intelligence interacts with our emotionality and has important implications on ingroups and outgroups. Most notably, our adaptability and problem-solving skills have allowed us to dramatically transform the social environments we inhabit, and our social environments are starkly different from those our ancestors lived in when our cognitive propensity to categorize people into ingroups and outgroups developed hundreds of thousands of years ago. We have, in turn, used our creative intelligence to form new types of communal consciousness to make sense of our changing world, something that was possible because human biology does not delineate ingroup structures (Maryanski and Turner 1992).

The human propensity to categorize people into ingroups and outgroups developed when our progenitors lived as hunter-foragers in small bands of individuals. In this situation, communal categorization was quite simple: One's community consisted of a band or collection of related bands, so everyone knew all members of their ingroup. Here the ingroup was for all intents and purposes a large extended family with whom one interacted on a regular basis. Alternatively, everyone who was not a member of the band was in the outgroup. In reality, the ingroup transformed according to the social situation, with some situations causing a more circumscribed delineation of ingroups than others. Thus one might view the collection of related bands as the ingroup when faced with an external adversary but restrict the ingroup to one's immediate band when competing with members of related bands. Along these lines, a famous Bedouin saying claims, "I against my brothers, I and my brothers against my cousins, I and my brothers and my cousins against the world." Importantly, although known acquaintances could either be in the ingroup or the outgroup depending on the situation, unknown individuals were almost inevitably part of the outgroup.

Humans lived as hunter-foragers throughout the overwhelming majority of our existence, but the hunter-forager lifestyle teeters on the verge of extinction today, with only a few tiny communities maintaining this lifestyle in the most isolated of environments. This greatest of transformations began roughly ten thousand years ago and was triggered by the emergence of settled agriculture, which gradually spread throughout the world and allowed people to reap more food per unit of land through new, more labor-intensive activities. As a result of both proliferation and independent development, most humans lived via settled agriculture by the beginning of the Christian era. During the period of European imperialism, in turn, most of the world's remaining hunter-foragers were conquered and their livelihoods destroyed. There was nothing new about the introduction of settled agriculture via conquest, however. Such conflict and conquest by invaders with superior technologies and numbers had been common since the early days of settled agriculture. This is a large part of the story of how settled agriculture conquered the world.

The rise of settled agriculture had major effects on human communities. Although there was enormous variation, most early agriculturalists seem to have lived in small farming communities (Piggott 1965). Individuals living within these communities likely interacted regularly with their relatives and neighbors and maintained a familial or regional communal identity that extended beyond their household to the clan or village. Still, settled agriculture dramatically transformed the unit of production from that of the community among hunter-foragers to that of the household among settled agriculturalists. Similarly, instead of more communal families, households now became the basic family unit. Things were similar among people who practiced animal husbandry, as they commonly lived among their immediate clan but maintained relations with a larger set of clans sharing a common lineage (Crone 2003).

Later, with the rise of states and the first so-called "civilizational" societies some five thousand years ago, things changed even further. New technologies made possible greater population densities and the emergence of a more complex division of labor in which a growing number of people made their living outside of agriculture. Soon urban areas began to form. As these urban areas grew, people could no longer know everyone they interacted with and lived among. According to anthropologist Robin Dunbar (1992), the neocortex region of the human brain places a cognitive limit on the number of people with whom an individual can have stable social relations, and he estimates that this limit is around 150, give or take a few dozen. Knowing everyone, in turn, helps overcome potential problems with reciprocity by increasing both trust in one another and social pressure to respect the interests of others. Considering the latter, knowing everyone in your community makes peer pressure a powerful force, as what others think of you has considerable implications on your livelihood. If someone starts a rumor that you cannot be trusted, this information will quickly spread to everyone in the community and will likely affect the willingness of others to share their resources with you. Gossiping—while looked down on by many—therefore plays an important role in maintaining trust and reciprocity among the community.

Dunbar arrives at 150 based on an equation dividing the size of our neocortex by the size of our entire brains. Although seemingly crude, this equation does an excellent job of predicting the size of communities of all primates, ranging from chimpanzees to macaques to humans. The size of hunter-forager communities also supports his claims. Of the twenty-one hunter-gatherer communities for which researchers have carefully documented group size, he finds that all had populations around 150, with the average for all groups being 148. He also notes that Hutterites, a religious group similar to the Amish, divide their communities after their populations reach 150 because they believe it is too difficult to control communal members after the size of the community surpasses this number. Similarly, Dunbar notes that standard military units are capped at approximately 150, which makes greater cohesion and discipline possible.

Growing urbanism caused human contacts to expand far beyond 150 people, meaning that people were no longer able to know and have regular social relations with everyone they lived among. In this way, the old dividing line between ingroup and outgroup simply broke down in the face of overwhelming numbers, as new living conditions outgrew the limits of the human brain. Despite this limitation, human brains are well-equipped to deal with new environments, so humans did not simply stop perceiving ingroups and outgroups and become either individualists or universalists. As Tajfel's (1970, 1978) experiments show, the binary propensity is both powerful and adaptive, and humans therefore developed new categories of ingroups and outgroups to reflect our new environments.

Team sports offer a telling example of how the propensity to categorize people into ingroups and outgroups can be transposed to a new social situation completely different from that in which it originally developed. Forgetting about actual athletes, the brains of fans quickly identify team members and other fans as members of their ingroup (i.e., Yankee Nation and Cowboy Country) and perceive the athletic competition as a battle between ingroup members and outgroup members. This helps to explain why observing team sports causes biological reactions similar to those caused by participating in warfare and why riled-up sports fans commonly turn violent. One study showed Boston Red Sox and New York Yankee fans films of both Red Sox and Yankee players being beaned by pitches and took images of the subjects' neural activities during the showings (Cikara, Botvinick, and Fiske 2011). The study found that the regions of the brain involved in pain and empathy were active when members of their favored team were beaned but that the regions of the brain involved in pleasure were active when the members of the rival team were beaned. The fact that sports creates strong ingroup attachment also explains why governments from around the world pour money into the Olympics in the hope of strengthening national unity and pride. Along these same lines, John Carlin's book *Playing the Enemy* (later adapted into the film *Invictus*) offers a telling account of how Nelson Mandela made a concerted effort to use rugby as a means of increasing badly needed national unity in postapartheid South Africa.

With growing population density and the rise of communities that were bigger than Dunbar's number, humans did not start playing team sports and acquire team-based ingroup identities. On this topic, the historical record is limited. There is some evidence that abstract communities similar to ethnicity began to form in some places, such as ancient Greece, Rome, and Israel (Kohn 1956). These were exceptions, however, and smaller social aggregates like clan, village, and neighborhood usually remained the most important defining elements of community. Additional changes were needed for the rise of a salient communal consciousness for much larger communities made up of unknown comembers. A larger and more encompassing communal consciousness required, above all else, a revolutionary way of thinking; one needed to start thinking of community as something other than the people you know, interact with, and collaborate with. Some sort of abstraction like team sports was necessary.

Different factors contributed to the rise of these new and abstract conceptualizations of community, but citizenship emerged as one important basis on which new ideas of community were built. Citizenship-based communal consciousness likely emerged in small city polities like those in ancient Greece. Plato's writings highlight his own effort to construct a new community of citizens among strangers in Greek city-states. In *The Republic*, he insists on the primacy of the national community (i.e., the city-state) and describes ways in which one can diminish the hold of households and more local communities, which still dominated the Greek city-states during his lifetime. For this, he discussed the desirability of having a form of communal marriage and child rearing, which would help to break familial bonds in the hope of strengthening the new national community. In fact, with his emphasis on communal marriage and child rearing, it seems that Plato wanted to make the new community more like one big family. Following the basic message of Plato's writings, Kleisthenes, a famous Athenian reformer, broke up family-style political units in 508 BC and created larger groupings that combined people from different regions and backgrounds (Manville 1990).

In Athens and other Greek city-states, the political leaders began granting citizenship to city inhabitants, and this helped form the basis of new communal frameworks and consciousnesses. Citizenship proved very important in ancient Greece because slavery was common—between 70 and 90 percent of the inhabitants of ancient Athens and Sparta were slaves—and citizens could not be enslaved. It was not simply in ancient Greece that one sees the rise of citizenship in city-states. In medieval and Renaissance Europe, for example, citizenship was also granted to inhabitants of various cities throughout large parts of Western Europe. As in ancient Greece, citizenship could also be an important sign of freedom and status, and it demarcated true members of the community from nonmembers. Only true members were able to participate in city politics and receive certain rights to public goods. The rights of citizenship also came with obligations, however, including taxation, public works, and military conscription.

While city-state-based communal consciousness offers a window into the origins of communities of strangers, city-states were still relatively small, meaning that the new frameworks and concepts used to make sense of larger communities were not enormously abstract. Athenians might not have known all their co-citizens, but they could walk around their city in a day and observe their new community firsthand. Moreover, the size of the cities—Athens was the biggest Greek city and had about twenty thousand people at its height—meant that only a few degrees of separation existed between most inhabitants, so people randomly meeting on the street likely shared acquaintances.

One must therefore turn to larger political units to understand the great degree of abstraction that was needed to create gigantic communities with members who lived in distant regions and with whom comembers would never interact. According to Benedict Anderson (1983), these are truly *imagined communities*. Such communities of strangers first emerged in medium-sized empires that subsequently became nation-states. It proved difficult to construct abstract communities of strangers in large polities, and many modernizing processes contributed to their rise. In particular, modernity strengthened and proliferated institutions that served as influential social carriers of ethnicity. According to Max Weber, a social carrier patterns social relations by shaping the cognitive frameworks, values, norms, beliefs, and interests of multiple actors (Kalberg 1994, 58–62).

States, education, and religions spread the norms, values, beliefs, frameworks, and identities that underlie an ethnic consciousness and are therefore ethnicity's most influential social carriers.

States and Communal Identities

According to the famous Roman statesman Cicero, "Parents are dear; dear are children, relatives, friends; but one's native land embraces all our loves; and who that is true would hesitate to give his life for her, if by his death he could render her a service?" (Singer 2011, 51). The quote shows how Cicero sought to cultivate a sense of patriotism and ethnic obligation and links this to an important need of states: soldiers willing to risk their lives for the state. For statesmen, this is obviously a very important need, as armies are needed to protect states (as well as the leaders who run them).

Two additional factors push state officials to try to instill their subjects with an ethnic consciousness. First, states require resources, and taxing subjects is an important source of state revenue. And when subjects believe they are giving resources for the benefit of the greater community, they are more willing to pay taxes. Second, states sometimes try to create unified national communities in an effort to limit antistate rebellions, as the rise of larger and more intrusive states commonly sparks local opposition. By reshaping and expanding ideas of community, state intrusions become more legitimate, thereby reducing such opposition.

Although many early states attempted to cultivate an ethnic consciousness so subjects would identify with and value the nation, this was a long and difficult project. Similar to the Greek city-states, these European states granted citizenship to the population in exchange for services, taxes, and subservience. As renowned sociologist Charles Tilly (1985) famously notes, the granting of certain citizenship rights made it easier for the rulers to extract these obligations from the populace and helped to change the form of state "protection" from Mafia-style racketeering to a more benign protection whereby the state actually looked out for the well-being of its citizens. What differed from the Greek city-states and made these efforts extraordinary is that most of Western Europe was not made up of city-states. Instead, most of the population resided in medium-sized and large empires in which a central power retained control over the peripheral regions of their territories through local intermediaries who gathered taxes, regulated social relations, and gave military support to the center when called upon for assistance. This type of state is commonly referred to as a composite state (or composite monarchy), whereby a single ruler controls diverse territories but governs the territories through local authorities (Elliott 1992). The local authorities and the people they govern, in turn, are granted different degrees of political and cultural autonomy from the central monarch. More generally, such control via intermediaries possessing considerable political autonomy is commonly referred to as indirect rule. The Holy Roman Empire (and subsequently the Austrian and Austro-Hungarian Empires), the Swedish Empire, the Ottoman Empire, and the Russian Empire were also composite states, although larger in terms of territory and population. While the Holy Roman, Swedish, Russian, and Ottoman Empires ultimately broke apart, France, the United Kingdom, and Spain maintained most of their territories by building (with different degrees of success) nation-states. Such transformations involved major state reforms that promoted direct rule as well as concerted efforts to forge a common national consciousness among the populations (Tilly 1992).

Direct rule had long been employed in European city-states, but organizational, communication, and transportation technologies limited the use of this model among larger populations living in much vaster territories. Indeed, technological limits made it difficult to communicate and monitor individuals in faraway places, and this promoted more decentralized forms of rule through local intermediaries (Innis 2007). Such indirect forms of rule, in turn, proved sufficiently effective throughout most of history. Over time, however, bureaucratic innovations and improvements in communication and transportation made possible more direct forms of rule in composite states, especially by the eighteenth and nineteenth centuries (Ertman 1997; Weber 1968 [1921]). France, Spain, and the United Kingdom were in particularly good positions to implement direct rule because they already had relatively large and effective states that could implement the reforms. Moreover, the extreme warfare that occurred in Europe between the seventeenth and twentieth centuries created an incentive for their leaders to create more directly ruled states. As Charles Tilly (1992) famously notes, warfare created a strong need for more and more resources, most notably money and soldiers. Indirect rule did not offer an effective means of extracting either, which led to a need to rule more directly. We see this with the growing power of France after the centralizing policies of Louis XIV. The French Revolution and the subsequent Napoleonic Reforms, in turn, built on this pre-existing state to create the first extremely direct form of rule within a composite state, and the revolutionary state allowed Napoleon to conquer much of Europe (at least temporarily). Through conquest, in turn, Napoleon built more direct forms of rule throughout large parts of western and central Europe.

The move toward direct rule underlay the growing strength of European states but also posed a risk, as local populations—usually encouraged by disgruntled former intermediaries who were disempowered by the new form of rule—commonly opposed direct state intervention. Such resistance was initially put down ruthlessly. Eventually, however, several state officials turned to nationalism as a more peaceful way to overcome this opposition. Indeed, the combination of citizenship, direct rule, and nascent democracy promoted one of the most powerful ideas the world has ever known: the nation-state, whereby a state rules in the interests of a unified political community and makes communal self-rule possible. This idea of communal self-rule was not completely new, as communities—ranging from hunter-foragers to city-states—had always ruled (or at least sought to rule) themselves. Yet the nation-state model differed from previous forms of self-rule in several important ways.

First, sociologist Siniša Malešević (2013) notes that nation-states were unique in the organizational power that underlay them. With direct rule and bureaucratic organization, new modern states emerged. These states were enormously powerful and used their diverse capabilities to regulate social relations in ways that helped build new and abstract ideas of the national community. Second, the nation-state model contained an idea of communal unity that was lacking in most previous political communities. As Malešević (2013, 109) notes, there was no *liberté* or *egalité* without *fraternité* within the nation-state. Third, in seeming contradiction to the second point, the nation-state model sought self-rule within a much larger and enormously more diverse population, and this required the removal of many aspects of self-rule at the local level. Given the large number of local communities within the borders of these former composite states, the nation-state model required major transformations that weakened local communities and created a more unified national community. State officials had a difficult time nationalizing their subjects, however. Just how does one go about either destroying or radically transforming a local communal consciousness and replacing it with a national consciousness that is largely meaningless and seemingly irrational? Indeed, a community of strangers is an oxymoron, and such an idea seemed idiotic to people with strong local identities, especially the rural peasantry.

Exclusion was one brutal strategy that states employed in pursuit of national unification. The Spanish Inquisition, for example, sought to protect the orthodoxy of Catholicism, and the Spanish government expelled all Jews and Muslims who were unwilling to convert (while subsequently torturing many of those who converted). Similarly, tens of thousands of French Protestants (known as Huguenots) were brutally attacked and murdered during the sixteenth and seventeenth centuries, actions that caused surviving Huguenots to flee to Protestant countries. In this way, leaders in both Spain and France excluded those they felt could not possibly be part of the national community.

Most works on state-led nation building in Western Europe overlook violent exclusion and focus on more peaceful processes. A seminal text showing the more peaceful dynamics of nation building is Eugen Weber's *Peasants into Frenchmen* (1976). The book describes how the post-Napoleonic French state played an active role in the Herculean task of transforming a diverse and dispersed population into the prototypical national community. Indeed, the French state proved so successful that people today forget that France was a diverse country with hundreds of different languages and dialects only a century and a half ago. Overall, Weber's analysis supports Malešević's (2013) more general claims that a modern state with enormous organizational capacity was needed to popularize a national consciousness.

According to Weber, French officials employed a multipronged policy over several generations to instill a national consciousness. One way was through military conscription, which forced men to leave their local communities and work with other men from all over the republic while being indoctrinated into the nation through teachings and training. Indeed, sociologists commonly recognize that the military is a "total institution," meaning that it has its own set of norms, values, and outlooks and therefore serves as a powerful means of resocialization (Goffman 1961). Under Napoleon, France became the first country to make the military a total institution and to implement universal military conscription, and the military remolded soldiers into Frenchmen until 2001, when universal conscription ended.

Weber notes additional ways in which the French state helped to forge a national consciousness. Massive public investment in internal transportation and the state-led expansion of a national market helped facilitate long-distance interaction and communication, which expanded social relations in a way that gave a certain reality to the French nation. State-led public rituals and the propagation of ethnic myths and symbols also helped build and create emotional attachment to national communities.[1] Jean-Jacques Rousseau recognized the nation-building power of public rituals and symbols long ago and recommended that the Polish government begin a tradition of holding a patriotic celebration around a monument representing the glories of the Polish peoples in an effort to spark greater patriotism (Mosse 1975, 73). Moreover, the state's provision of a growing list of public goods to citizens provided benefits that came with citizenship, effectively holding out a carrot and encouraging people to think of themselves and others in

---

1. Eugen Weber largely overlooked the importance of ritual, myths, and symbols. For insightful analyses on this topic, see Berezin (1997) and Mosse (1975).

terms of nation. Of all the state policies that helped to forge a French nation, educational expansion is the factor on which Weber places greatest emphasis. Indeed, such is the influence of education on nation building that one must consider it separately.

Education and Ethnic Consciousness

According to Albert Guérard (1959), "France, like all nations, is an increasing consciousness. She exists in the minds of men, because men have faith in her existence" (ix). Schools played a pivotal role in laying the seeds of and nourishing the French national consciousness. They did so in a variety of ways.

First, the French educational system taught exclusively in French, which created a common national language. Linguistic unity, in turn, gave the nation a certain concreteness that made it seem real and thereby more acceptable to the population. The impact of education on linguistic unity proved so successful that most people do not realize that France had considerable linguistic diversity only 150 years ago. The impact of education on linguistic unity had an important gendered component: Other languages and dialects proved difficult to stamp out when only boys went to school, and French only became the dominant mother tongue throughout France after the onset of mass female education, suggesting there is a reason why we call it the "mother tongue."

French teachers also bombarded students with ideas of nation and patriotism, and this is a second way through which education promoted a French national consciousness. Eugen Weber (1976) notes, for example, that all French students were forced to complete assignments asking them to describe the "fatherland," an abstract and incomprehensible question for many unindoctrinated French youth. With help, students were able to make sense of the new national community and provided responses like "The fatherland is not your village, your province, it is all of France. The fatherland is like a great family. Your fatherland is you. It is your family, it is your people" (Weber 1976, 333). One clearly sees how students struggled to transpose a familial and local consciousness onto the nation, something that was aided by curricula teaching that the nation was a type of family, hence the terms "fatherland," "motherland," and "homeland." This merging of nation and family was not limited to France, and it highlights the kin-based elements of nation and ethnicity more broadly. According to political scientist Walker Connor (1994), "The new universality with which certain images and phrases appear—blood, family, brothers, sisters, mother, forefathers, ancestors, home—and the proven success of such invocations in eliciting massive popular responses tell us much about the nature of national identity" (205). Similarly, Mabel Berezin (1999) notes that family metaphors are a powerful tool for building common national consciousness because they resonate emotionally with people, as most people have strong emotional attachments to their family.

Schools also helped to build a French national consciousness by teaching French national history, which described the origins and exploits of the French nation and helped to make it real in the minds of students. Like national histories elsewhere, the nationalizing French curricula focused on the supposed origins of the French people (the Gauls), the factors (such as language and religion) that made someone French, and the historical trials and tribulations of the glorious French nation. The nation-building goal of history classes is evident in the results of an 1897 survey of French students who were completing high school; 80 percent of respondents claimed that that the primary purpose of history was to promote patriotism (Weber 1976, 333).

Schools also acquainted students with symbols that made a national community of strangers more concrete. Examples include the French flag and national anthem, Marianne,[2] and Joan of Arc. Of all symbols, however, maps of France were among the most powerful because they helped ground the emerging national consciousness in a physical reality. French schools universally displayed maps of France that gave a concrete idea of what this abstract entity referred to as "France" actually was. Importantly, the maps allowed students to see with their own eyes that their local communities were a tiny part of this larger whole, thereby helping them to better imagine this novel national idea. Similar to Hobbes' visual depiction of the leviathan, they were able to see themselves as one of the people that join together to form the national body.

Notably, Eugen Weber is not alone in pinpointing education as a critical determinant of nation building. Other scholars include Benedict Anderson, Keith Darden, Karl Deutsch, Ernest Gellner, Eric Hobsbawm, and Miroslav Hroch. Darden's (forthcoming) work is unique because he focuses exclusively on the role of education, whereas the rest consider processes of modernization more broadly and analyze mass education as one influential element of modernity. Although it is difficult to differentiate the impact of education from that of urbanization, state building, capitalism, and other aspects of modernity, education appears particularly well-suited for building an abstract ethnic consciousness for different reasons.

First, schools are resocializing agents par excellence, and they train students to participate in a complex institution. Educational resocialization involves

---

2. Marianne is a popular depiction of a proud woman who symbolizes liberty, equality, and fraternity.

learning a vast quantity of new norms and perspectives, especially a total respect for school authorities. Teachers are both gatekeepers of knowledge and
well-trained disciplinarians. In this way, students are broken down and rebuilt to
facilitate the learning process. As Harry Gracey (1975) famously notes, kindergarten is like military boot camp. Kindergarteners, he writes, "have learned to go
through routines and to follow orders with unquestioning obedience, even when
these make no sense to them. They have been disciplined to do as they are told by
an authoritative person without significant protest." Importantly, this authority
can easily be used to shape student identities when teachers tell students that they
are members of a particular community.

A second reason for the influence of education involves the skills and knowledge that education imparts. Literacy, for example, allows people to access
literature—such as newspapers and novels—that describes larger communities as real, concrete entities. According to Benedict Anderson (1983), literature
depicts and glorifies ethnic communities and influences many to imagine that
they are part of large communities of unknown members. As a consequence,
Anderson links the rise of nationalism to the invention of the printing press and
the subsequent proliferation of print media. N. F. S. Grundtvig (1783–1872),
whose lifelong efforts to craft a Danish national community earned him recognition as the father of the Danish nation, paid considerable attention to the role literary imagery played in building an ethnic consciousness long before Anderson
was even born. In particular, he described how emotive and inspirational narratives give life to nations, referring to these new communities as "poetic realities"
(Korsgaard 2015, 200).

Eugen Weber (1976) also recognizes the importance of literature, focusing on
Augustine Fouillée's children's book *La Tour de la France par Deux Enfants*. The
book was written in 1877, sold seven million copies by 1915, was used in schools
until 1950, and remains in print to this day. It recounts the tale of two children
who lost their father during the Franco-Prussian War of 1870, struggled to return
to France after Germany conquered Alsace-Lorraine, and subsequently toured
France in search of relatives and friends. The book is extremely patriotic and
helps to integrate the French population into a singular entity through the travels
and adventures of the children. The final chapter, entitled "I Love France," wraps
up the children's adventures by hammering home the central message:

> At the same time of year six years ago, Andre and Julian fell asleep
> under a mountain evergreen the day before crossing the Vosges Moun-
> tains; and when the sun rose that morning, the two children—all alone
> and without support—kneeled on French soil once again and cried:
> "Beloved France, we are your children and want to become worthy of
> you!" They kept their word. The years passed, but their hearts have not

changed; they grew up encouraging one another to do good deeds at all times; they will always stay loyal to the two things they learned to love at such a young age: Duty and Homeland.

Besides literacy, abstract thinking is another skill taught at school that facilitates the construction of a large and intangible ethnicity. According to political scientist Keith Darden (forthcoming), education teaches abstract ways of analyzing the world. In particular, he notes an early study by Soviet anthropologist Alexander Luria that found that the ability to think abstractly does not come naturally and is promoted by formal education. Luria tested the abstract reasoning of different peoples throughout the Soviet Union in the 1920s and found that rural peasants and indigenous peoples without any education had extreme difficulty understanding and applying abstract concepts. According to Luria, this was not because the peasants were inherently less intelligent; it was caused by two factors: Their livelihoods did not depend on abstract concepts, and abstract thinking must be learned. Ethnicity, in turn, is not based on acquaintance or other meaningful criteria and is an abstract concept. In this way, education helps people grasp abstract communities, something that is vital in order for them to start seeing and valuing ethnicity. Put differently, it helps create the *imagination* that is needed to *imagine nation*.

The abstract thinking that allows people to make sense of intangible communities depends greatly on the concepts people employ to interpret the world. We see this in the French example, with students being force-fed new concepts like "fatherland" that ultimately helped them understand what it meant to be French. As Johan Heilbron, Lars Magnusson, and Bjorn Wittrock (1998) note, a number of social concepts like "nation" and "society" were either created or had their meanings radically altered during the late eighteenth and early nineteenth centuries. The rise and spread of these concepts was linked to the founding of the social sciences, which emerged in the nineteenth century to try to make sense of the enormous transformations associated with modernity. These social concepts were subsequently taught in schools and provided students with a conceptual toolbox that helped them to think about communities of strangers and to make sense of their changing social worlds.

These examples highlight how education can promote an ethnic consciousness in a peaceful manner, but there is also a conflictual and destructive side to this process. Most notably, students who fail to conform to the ethnic ideal become Others and are penalized, excluded, ridiculed, and harassed. The education of indigenous peoples in Canada and the United States showcases the darker side of educating ethnicity.

Beginning in the 1870s, American and Canadian governments took hundreds of thousands of indigenous children from their families and forced them to live

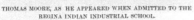

THOMAS MOORE, AS HE APPEARED WHEN ADMITTED TO THE
REGINA INDIAN INDUSTRIAL SCHOOL.

THOMAS MOORE, AFTER TUITION AT THE REGINA INDIAN
INDUSTRIAL SCHOOL.

FIGURE 4.1.   Thomas Moore before and after residential school. Source: Department of Indian Affairs (1897), Saskatchewan Archives Board R-A8223-1.

in residential schools. These schools sought to separate indigenous children from their families and communities as much as possible in order to take the "Indian out of the Indian" and assimilate them into the dominant settler cultures. This goal is evident in the before-and-after photos of one young student—shown in Figure 4.1—published by the Canadian Department of Indian Affairs in 1896 to highlight the "fine" work the residential schools were doing. Although the photo suggests that the indigenous students assimilated into the settler cultures and were "whitened," the students were not incorporated into mainstream American and Canadian societies. Instead, popular ideas of racial inferiority and the race-based character of the Canadian and American nations caused their continued exclusion. As a result, the children were told that they were no longer Dakota or Cree, but this void was not replaced by anything new, which placed them in cultural limbo.

As part of this program of cultural genocide, students of residential schools were abused in a variety of ways. Because the ultimate goal of these schools was assimilation, teachers and administrators meted out extreme punishments—including sticking needles through tongues and solitary confinement—whenever students spoke their native languages or acted like "Indians." The schools also attracted predators, and evidence suggests that most children attending the schools experienced physical and sexual abuse. American and Canadian governments preyed on the children in their own shameful ways; reminiscent of the

Nazis, the Canadian government actually performed medical experiments on residential schoolchildren in the 1940s and 1950s.

Through such horrific residential school experiences, indigenous cultures were destroyed but not replaced, and children were humiliated and abused by the authorities who served as their surrogate parents. Both of these outcomes commonly destroyed any sense of self-worth and left deep psychological scars. Highlighting the ill effects of this abuse, several studies find that residential school survivors are much more likely to be depressed, abusive, chemically dependent, and suicidal; the most common mental illness among residential school survivors is posttraumatic stress disorder (Corrado and Cohen 2003; Elias et al. 2012; Bombay, Matheson, and Anisman 2011). Sadly, this residential school "syndrome" is also present in many children and grandchildren of residential school survivors, which shows that the harmful effects have been passed down to subsequent generations who witnessed and experienced residential schools through the behavior of their parents and grandparents.

Religion and Communal Identities

In addition to states and education, religion—in particular mass organized religion—also contributes to the construction of ethnic consciousness. In fact, organized religion played an important role in forging many the first large communities of strangers among early civilizations (Hall 1986; Mann 1986). Several aspects of religions promote collective consciousness. First, religions socialize followers to think of themselves as part of the same religious community, and they pressure people to act in certain ways that demonstrate communal membership—ranging from circumcision to prohibitions on certain types of food to wardrobe. Similarly, religion helps to create a moral community that lives according to specific religious rules. Finally, religions commonly use rituals and symbols to build ideas of community and to objectify it. A notable example of a ritual that builds and strengthens a communal framework is communion among Christians: All participants symbolically eat the body of Christ and drink his blood, which unifies participants by putting a little bit of Christ in all participants.

In places with a centralized and organized religion and a growing cadre of literate elites, the impact of religion on a communal consciousness began well before modernity's saddle period. Sociologist Anthony Smith (2003), for example, argues that thousands of years ago many Jews believed they were part of a large religious community. In medieval Europe, national consciousness was largely absent, but a religious consciousness was present and helped forge Europeans from diverse regions into a united force that went off to try to reconquer the Holy Lands during the Crusades. According to historian Robert Bartlett (1993, 254), beginning in the mid-eleventh century we see the growth of "Christendom," a concept that increasingly gained a territorial component and helped to integrate Europeans into one community until the Reformation and the rise of nationalism.

Large religious communities are not necessarily the same thing as ethnic communities, however. Ethnicity designates a community based on subjective ideas of heritage and descent, whereas shared religious beliefs are the principal bases of religious community. In this way, people can change religious communities by adopting new religious beliefs and practices, but ethnicity is much more difficult to change because people perceive it as ascribed. An Israeli Jew who converts to Islam, for example, will remain a Jew in terms of ethnicity.

While recognizing that religious communities and ethnicities are distinct, the two commonly overlap. Most notably, many ethnicities are partially defined by religion, and religious communities sometimes transform into ethnic communities. The change from religious community to ethnicity is most common when some combination of language, heritage, race, and nation overlap with religion, thereby endowing religious communities with additional defining traits beyond shared religious beliefs. This transformation also depends on organizations, institutions, and other social actors that are able to spread a religious-based collective consciousness throughout populations. States and education have played particularly important roles in this regard by shaping the contours and salience of ethnicity and spreading an ethnic consciousness among large numbers of people.

States frequently enforce official religions and use them as a means of building and delineating national communities, something that is evident with diverse Buddhist, Christian, Jewish, and Muslim states around the world today (Loizides 2009). Within Europe, the Treaty of Westphalia in 1648 recognized that the religion of the ruler was the religion of the territory, thereby strengthening the groundwork for religious-based national communities. Important places of worship often starkly highlight this link between religion, state, and nation. The walls of London's St. Paul's Cathedral, for example, are decorated with plaques and statues of national war heroes, and the crypt includes giant and ornate tombs of such figures as the Duke of Wellington, who defeated Napoleon at Waterloo, and Horatio Nelson, who defeated Napoleon's navy in the Battle of Trafalgar. In this way, one goes to St. Paul's to effectively worship both God and nation. Further up the Thames at Westminster Abbey, in turn, past kings and queens are buried and new kings and queens are crowned. We therefore see how states commonly usurp control of religions to exploit their nation-building capabilities.

Scholars explain this link between religion and nation in different ways. Sociologist Anthony Smith (1993) claims that religions are premodern cultural markers that state officials and other nationalists employ to show the deep historical roots of the nation and strengthen national consciousness. Alternatively, historian Miroslav Hroch (1985) notes that shared religion promotes "inward ties" that make abstract ideas of nation more tangible and therefore facilitate state-led nation building. Historian George Mosse (1975) combines elements of both Smith and Hroch by focusing on rituals and symbols. Noting Huizinga's (1924) analysis of how fifteenth-century Christianity made abstract ideas and beliefs more concrete and believable through the use of myths and symbols, Mosse describes how states copied these techniques to make nations equally alive and tangible, causing people to effectively worship nations as sacred objects.

Education has also helped to ethnicize religious communities. Most notably, religious organizations commonly operate schools. While the first religious schools focused on training religious leaders, by the 1600s Protestants began opening many schools, teaching a variety of academic disciplines in addition to religion, and they sought to spread education to the masses. They opened these more popular schools to allow followers to read the scripture and as a tactic to attract new followers. Other religions subsequently copied Protestants and opened their own multidisciplinary schools. As described in the next chapter, these schools have helped to popularize and strengthen ethnic consciousness in a variety of places.

The Micro-Dynamics and Context of Ethnic Frameworks

States, education, and religion therefore play extremely important roles in molding and popularizing ethnic consciousness. Once created, however, other activities play equally important—if not more important—roles in sustaining an ethnic consciousness. Focusing on nations, social psychologist Michael Billig (1995) notes that seemingly banal elements of everyday life help nourish ethnicity and endow it with meaning and potential emotion.[3] Billig notes that mundane aspects of ethnicity are constantly repeated to such an extent that we hardly recognize them, fail to question them, and are shaped enormously by them. Examples include flags, national sports competitions, statues, postcards of national landmarks, and symbols on money and stamps. He also notes how the media enforces ethnic consciousness by presenting information in terms of the collective—*the* president, *our* economy. At the time I am writing this sentence, a program run by the Canadian government offers one particular—but typical—example of the banal elements of nationalism. It is spending millions of dollars on a contest titled "My Canada, My Inspiration" that asks Canadians

---

3. See also Malešević (2013) and Mosse (1991).

to submit new designs for Canadian coins in celebration of Canada's 150th anniversary. Submissions are supposed to follow one of five themes that emphasize Canadian unity: "Our Passions," "Our Character," "Our Future," "Our Wonders," and "Our Achievements."

And while an ethnic consciousness refocuses ideas of community on the large and abstract, small and concrete micro-dynamics play an important role in sustaining them. Even more, they can prevent social carriers from spreading ethnic consciousness. Regardless of the efforts of states, education, and religion, ethnicity cannot gain salience if family authorities reject it and tell their children and grandchildren to follow suit. This fact helps to explain why efforts to use education to transform Kurds into Turks failed miserably in the 1960s and 1970s. Yet when family members and close friends exemplify banal ethnicity during their everyday activities and relations, their contacts are more likely to accept ethnicity and develop an ethnic consciousness.

Despite using the term "banal," Billig recognizes that the everyday ways in which ethnicity is enacted can be anything but banal in their consequences. By perpetuating and strengthening an ethnic consciousness, banal practices maintain a combustible condition that can explode into violence at any time. The transformation from banal to explosive depends on the social environment, especially growing ethnic inequalities, threats, and competition. Reviewing the literature, psychologist John Duckitt (2003) concludes that "relatively trivial intergroup threats and apparently minor inequalities in power and status may readily become infused with significance and hostility" when ethnicity is salient (583). And when people become more hostile towards Others, ethnic extremists have a much easier time finding support.

States, mass education, and organized religion are all core components of modernity, and this chapter describes how all three play important roles in creating imagined communities of strangers. All three possess organizational and communication technologies that underlie the dissemination of shared ethnic consciousness among large numbers of people and pattern social relations in ways that give meaning to ethnicity and promote shared perceptions, norms, values, and beliefs. While these outcomes have the potential to create unity and thereby limit ethnic violence, the processes that promote ethnic unity are often extremely violent. Moreover, ethnic consciousness is a necessary condition for ethnic violence, as it divides the world into ethnic categories and creates great attachment to ethnicity. In fact, as described in the next chapter, these modernizing processes commonly promote multiple and competing ethnic consciousnesses and thereby provide a fertile environment for ethnic violence.

5

THE ORIGINS OF ETHNIC PLURALISM

France is an exceptional country in a number of ways. To list a few examples, recent surveys find that it leads the world in average annual wine consumption (71 bottles per adult), average annual cheese consumption (59 pounds per capita), and the average annual frequency of intercourse (137 times per adult). With nearly eighty million visits annually, France also receives more tourists than any other country in the world, many of whom come in search of fine wine, good cheese, and romance.[1] The French themselves are not a big tourist draw, however, as a recent survey on the world's rudest tourist destinations gave France top honors. Of greater relevance to this book, France is an exceptionally successful case of nation building and exemplifies the nation-state model as well as any country, so the description of French nation building in the previous chapter—while offering important insight into the origins of ethnic consciousness—does not hold for the majority of countries in the world. Indeed, most countries have populations with multiple and opposing ethnic consciousnesses, and such ethnic pluralism is a necessary condition for ethnic violence. Any effort to explain ethnic violence must therefore consider why only some places turned out like France.

---

1. Although tourist numbers have plummeted since the terrorist attacks in 2014 and 2015.

Explaining Unity and Disunity

Similar to France, both Spain and the United Kingdom were medium-sized composite states that successfully made the transition to directly ruled states and emerged as world powers during the era of state building in early modern Europe. These composite states share many characteristics with empires. Indeed, although smaller in size, they had similar structures as the Danish, Swedish, Hapsburg, Russian, and Ottoman Empires and ruled over peoples speaking diverse languages. Today, we consider France, Spain, and the UK countries instead of empires because their transitions to direct rule proved so successful at integrating their populations into nation-states. Despite their relative success, Spain and the United Kingdom were considerably less successful than France. In the United Kingdom, England was the core region, and the populations in Wales, Scotland, and Ireland were conquered by the English and remained subordinate to them economically, politically, and culturally for hundreds of years. This was especially the case in Ireland, where elites originating from Great Britain dominated the island's political system and economy. The resulting British-Irish divide promoted ethnic violence, first throughout Ireland and then—following Irish independence—in Northern Ireland. Nationalist movements also exist in contemporary Wales and Scotland, the latter of which held a hotly contested referendum on independence in 2014. In Spain, the main communal divisions also involve separatist movements, especially in the Basque and Catalan regions. While the Catalan movement has been peaceful, the Basque movement has been led by ETA, an organization that used terrorist methods for several decades in pursuit of its goal of national independence. Like the United Kingdom, Spanish national divisions were the result of a core region subordinating other regions. Spain differs from the United Kingdom, however, because the regions with strong nationalist movements have historically been among the most economically dynamic in Spain.

Comparing the nation-building processes in France, Spain, and the United Kingdom reveals several differences that help to explain the French state's greater success at popularizing a common national consciousness. One is simply history. France has one of the oldest states in the world and the oldest in Europe, and its boundaries have changed relatively little over the past millennium. Alternatively, modern Spain was only formed in the late fifteenth century with the union of Castile and Aragon. Prior to that, it was divided between multiple autonomous and semiautonomous regions, and Arab Moors ruled most of contemporary Spain for several centuries prior to the country's unification. The United Kingdom was formed even later, with the conquest of Wales in the late thirteenth century, full control over Ireland attained in the mid-sixteenth century, and the final union with Scotland in 1707. In this way, France had a long precedent of nation building relative to Spain and the United Kingdom.

The importance of precedent is threefold. First, the long history of statehood in France promoted a much more unified political elite, including a common court culture among the aristocracy. Alternatively, elites in Spain and the United Kingdom were less unified and commonly opposed nationalization efforts because they remained rooted in the region. Second, alternatives to the state-propagated idea of the French nation were much weaker because France had been unified for much longer. As a result, opponents of French state and nation building had greater difficulty mobilizing alternatives to the French nation-state. Third, France possessed a more directly ruled composite state, something historian John Elliott (1992) refers to as an "accessory union" whereby the territories of the composite state are under the same legal jurisdiction. This more direct form of rule helped to create an institutional environment that reflected and gave meaning to a French national consciousness. Alternatively, in both Spain and the United Kingdom, the composite state was ruled more indirectly,[2] which created a division between periphery and metropole and allowed opponents of Spanish and British nationalism to frame grievances in terms of resistance to English or Castilian domination. In addition, local elites in Spain and the United Kingdom had greater autonomy to resist direct rule and had more to lose with the imposition of direct rule.

Importantly, France incorporated regions bordering Spain relatively late, so the argument of a long history of state and nation building does not hold for them. The modern border between France and Spain effectively split Basque- and Catalan-speaking peoples between the two countries, but the Basque and Catalans have only organized strong nationalist movements on the Spanish side of the border, which raises the question: Why were French Basques and Catalans more likely to accept a core national consciousness than their Spanish counterparts?

Part of the answer concerns the French Revolution and the rigorous implementation of Napoleonic reforms. One outcome of the revolution was a much more centralized and direct form of rule in France. The imposition of this state created several counterrevolutions in different parts of France, but the state successfully contained these movements. As a result, local elites in the Basque and Catalan regions of France were either removed or co-opted into the new

---

2. Elliot (1992) refers to this more decentralized composite monarchy as *aeque principali*, which involved the preservation of local customs and power structures.

French state, and the group that is usually most against state-led nation building was overcome. Notably, Napoleon conquered Spain and implemented similar state-building and centralizing reforms in the Basque and Catalan regions of that country as well. These reforms were much less thorough than in France, however, and the regions retained more autonomy than their counterparts on the French side of the border. Such autonomy, in turn, contributed to the rise of an ethnic consciousness that opposed Spanish nationalism. This is especially the case for the Basque region of Spain.

The Basque region of Spain was never conquered by the Moors and was not part of either Aragon or Castile when they merged to form Spain. Instead, unified Spain conquered the Basque region in the sixteenth century and forcibly incorporated it into the country. Thereafter, Spain granted the Basque region considerable autonomy in recognition of its separate history. This autonomy changed with the Napoleonic reforms, but the French lost control of Spain in 1813, which allowed the Basque region to regain its former autonomy. In the 1830s, the First Carlist Civil War was fought, in part over the autonomy of the Basque region, and the war ended with the Basques retaining their traditional autonomy. After the Second Carlist Civil War twenty years later, the Basque region lost much of its autonomy. But even then, Spanish centralization efforts were weak, with limited state interference and the maintenance of considerable fiscal and administrative autonomy. In the 1930s, the Spanish government agreed to further increase the autonomy of the Basque region, although this ended abruptly with the Spanish Civil War. After the civil war, Franco strongly suppressed any form of Basque autonomy and began the first thorough effort to incorporate the Basque region into the Spanish nation.

Things unraveled very differently in the Basque region of France. Instead of having a back-and-forth struggle over centralization and decentralization, the French implemented direct rule during the French Revolution, and this form of rule never faltered. Thereafter, the central government effectively controlled the Basque region in terms of education, administration, and the economy and used its influence to propagate a French national consciousness, thereby turning Basques into Frenchmen and Frenchwomen.

While a history of political autonomy is a major factor explaining why Basque nationalism was much stronger on the Spanish side of the border, Spanish Catalonia did not have the same autonomy as the Basque region over the past two hundred years (although it did have a long history of autonomy prior to Spanish unification in 1492). Other factors also promoted the Catalan nationalist movement, with education being one of the most influential.

As described in the last chapter, the French state created a unified national education system that forced instructors to teach in French and to present students with curricula crafted to heighten a French national consciousness. Along these lines, mass education in the Catalan region of France was led by the French state and effectively integrated Catalan speakers into the French nation by pushing the French language and teaching a nationalistic curriculum. On the Spanish side of the border, however, the educational system was much more decentralized, and there were more opportunities to propagate alternatives to the Spanish national consciousness. According to political scientist Laia Balcells (2013), Catalan elites in Spain initiated mass education in the region because they were displeased with the central government's slow pace of educational expansion. And because social relations in Catalonia were autonomous from other regions of Spain and because Catalonia had a long and proud history as an independent power prior to the union of Spain, Catalan schools focused on Catalonia instead of Spain. Moreover, the language of instruction was Catalan because it was the dominant regional language. Schools therefore reinforced pre-existing ideas of a Catalan nation instead of integrating students into a Spanish nation, and Franco's subsequent effort to integrate Catalonia by outlawing the use of Catalan in schools and changing the curricula simply backfired.

Ultimately, the comparison of France with Spain highlights a history of regional autonomy and education as two important factors that help to explain the presence of multiple and competing national consciousnesses. In France, consistent and extensive state efforts to nationalize peripheral peoples successfully propagated a French national consciousness. Such efforts succeeded because nationalization efforts were implemented relatively early, systematically, and consistently. In Spain, on the other hand, political and educational autonomy helped to reinforce ethnic difference by accentuating elements of local social relations, empowering local elites, and popularizing alternative national consciousnesses.

Path Dependence, Situationalism, and Ethnic Consciousness

To understand why many Basques and Catalans in Spain are seemingly immune to national assimilation, it is helpful to review an academic debate between primordialists and constructivists on the origins of ethnicity. The earliest scholars of ethnicity generally took a primordialist position and viewed ethnicity as something that was long-standing, unchanging, and almost racial in character. This view is commonly linked to German Romanticism and figures like Johann Gottlieb Fichte and Johann Gottfried Herder, who both viewed ethnicity as natural and having ancient origins. Constructivists, on the other hand, believe there is nothing natural about ethnicity; they view it as a human construct that constantly transforms. In effect, they claim that ethnicity is based on cognition and that cognitive frameworks are constantly transforming and can be manipulated to create new ideas of community. At an extreme, some constructivists claim that cognitive frameworks are so transformative and varied that it is difficult to accurately categorize violence as "ethnic."

Over the past several decades, constructivists have dominated the debate. One reason for this is the inherent racialism of the primordialist position. Moreover, several historical studies document the rise and transformation of ethnicity over time and show that ethnic communities are not natural and unchanging. Both of these are knockout punches, which explains why primordialism lingers on only as a straw man. Yet the constructivist view has its own problems. Most notably, it suggests that ethnicity is constantly constructed and transforming, yet most ethnic frameworks are sticky, that is, they generally transform gradually and with few radical changes (Hale 2004; Jenkins 2008). This stickiness is a real thorn in the side of the extreme constructivist position, which views ethnic transformation as dynamic and with endless possibilities. Instead of scrapping constructivism, this weakness can be addressed by combining constructivism with a temporal concept known as path dependence.

Path dependence suggests that there are crucial periods when major transformations are possible and other periods when major changes are much more difficult (Mahoney 2000). These crucial periods of change—commonly referred to as critical junctures—are made possible by openings that allow for radical change. Once change occurs during the critical juncture, however, the transformations become locked in, making subsequent changes much more difficult. Timing is therefore vitally important for path-dependent processes.

A popular example of path dependence is the QWERTY keyboard, that is, the standard American keyboard on which the first six letters of the upper row are QWERTY (David 1985). The QWERTY layout became popular with the Remington No. 2 typewriter, which was released in 1878 and was the first typewriter to include both upper and lower case letters. At that time, there was no set keyboard. Yet the success of the Remington No. 2 made the QWERTY format the standard format, and other keyboards quickly disappeared because typists who had mastered the QWERTY keyboard did not want to lose time and energy learning a new keyboard. The previous facility of changing the keyboard therefore evaporated, and the QWERTY keyboard became nearly unchangeable.

The formation of an ethnic consciousness appears to follow a path-dependent trajectory, as there are critical periods when an ethnic consciousness can be formed but such a consciousness is much more difficult to transform thereafter. Thus, France was relatively successful at making Basques and Catalans Frenchmen and Frenchwomen because its nationalization efforts preceded the development and proliferation of salient Basque or Catalan ethnic consciousnesses. In Spain, on the other hand, struggles for autonomy in the Basque region and Catalan education reinforced alternative ethnic consciousnesses prior to central government efforts to integrate Basques and Catalans into the Spanish nation, and General Franco's subsequent efforts to turn Basques and Catalans into Spaniards therefore faced strong resistance. Timing is therefore of the utmost importance, with the presence of multiple ethnicities prior to state-led nationalism leading to powerful and persistent divisions.

Path dependence requires mechanisms of reproduction that explain why change is so difficult after the critical juncture. One common mechanism that reproduces ethnic consciousness is cost: The costs of change are relatively low at the critical juncture but much higher afterwards. Cost is the main mechanism underlying the continued use of QWERTY keyboards: Typists invest time and effort learning the QWERTY keyboard and are not willing to incur the costs associated with learning a new one. Along these same lines, major changes in ethnic consciousness and allegiance commonly impose considerable costs, as individuals invest in their communities and receive returns on these investments. One type of cost involves the potential destruction of one's network of social support. For example, if individuals identify with and support ethnicities that are different from those of their friends and family, they might be alienated from their network of social support, which generally comes with enormous costs. A more specific example involves language. Languages commonly define ethnicity, and people make enormous investments in their languages. The acceptance of an alternative ethnic identity based on a language other than one's mother tongue, in turn, has the potential to nullify such investments and create disincentives to assimilate.

A power mechanism also helps explain the stickiness of ethnicity. Powerful interests frequently have a stake in the status quo and exercise their power to prevent change. Once an ethnic consciousness is popularized and social relations are patterned by ethnicity, communal elites receive considerable status, power, and resources due to their position as ethnic leaders. Elites therefore have an interest in the maintenance of the community, which causes them to enforce ethnic consciousness among coethnics and use their influence to obstruct major changes in ethnicity that might threaten their positions.

The socialization mechanism is a third example and is in all likelihood the most influential mechanism limiting changes in ethnic consciousness. It occurs when socialization imparts cognitive frameworks, norms, and values that perpetuate the status quo. Thus an ethnic consciousness is perpetuated when socializing agents tell children who they are, what community they belong to, and the importance of being a member of this community. There are numerous socializing agents involved in this process, including education, the state, and religion. While these three play important roles in perpetuating ethnic consciousness through socialization, they usually play a more important role during the critical juncture. The family, on the other hand, is especially influential at reproducing ethnic consciousness among subsequent generations because it has the most legitimacy in terms of identity: Who better to know who you are than the people who gave birth to you and raised you as a member of their family? In this way, it is difficult to convince people that they are from a particular ethnic community when their family has socialized them to think otherwise (and will punish them if they disagree).

Orson Welles once stated in an interview, "Everything about me is a contradiction, and so is everything about everybody else. We are made out of oppositions" (Estrin 2002, 141). Something similar could be said about ethnicity, as it usually has characteristics that seem antithetical. The stickiness of ethnicity, for example, gives it a primordial character, suggesting that it is timeless and unchanging. But in reality, constructivists rightly note that ethnicity is a social construct and constantly changes (albeit usually incrementally). The stickiness of ethnicity also creates the impression that people always see the world through ethnic lenses, but the truth is very different. As the situational school of anthropology and self-categorization theory in psychology highlight, everyone in the world holds multiple collective identities, and the strength of each identity at any given time depends on the social context in which people find themselves (Galaty 1982; Moerman 1965; Turner et al. 1994; Waters 1990).

A great variety of situations increase the salience and influence of ethnic consciousness. As discussed in the previous chapter, many seemingly "banal" elements of everyday life prod people to recognize ethnicity on a regular basis, such as sports events, songs, memorials, holidays, specialty foods, and novels (Billig 1995). These mundane prompts help to maintain ethnic consciousness among large segments of the population. Similarly, ethnically patterned social relations continually enforce and give salience to ethnic consciousness. Most notably, ethnic structures create interests, exert power, and socialize, thereby providing mechanisms of reproduction. Certain situations, however, produce a much more dramatic and explosive increase in the salience of ethnicity, effectively triggering ethnic consciousness. Examples include ethnic rituals and processions, experiencing ethnic discrimination, and crises that threaten ethnic communities.

The situational character of ethnicity means that ethnic violence can sometimes re-emerge after a period of relative peace and take people by surprise. For example, renowned sociologist Anthony Smith (1986b) described the system of ethnic federalism in the former Yugoslavia as a model to be emulated, but extreme ethnic violence engulfed Yugoslavia only a few years later. Smith was not the only expert who failed to foresee the country's future of ethnic violence. Despite severe ethnic violence as recently as the Second World War, communism in Yugoslavia emphasized class, and ethnic tensions were relatively low. One sign of the limited strength of ethnicity was intermarriage, which increased throughout communist rule (Burg and Shoup 1999). Shortly before the violence, therefore, ethnic consciousness does not appear to have been overly powerful. In hindsight, however, communism clearly did not eliminate ethnic consciousness. The banal elements of ethnicity were present and helped to maintain ethnic frameworks, ethnic segregation persisted, and communism actually institutionalized a system of ethnic federalism that reified ethnicity and the principle of ethnic self-rule. The fall of the Iron Curtain unleashed political uncertainty and competition, both of which promoted the crumbling of the state along ethnic lines and pushed politicians to frame the political crisis in terms of ethnicity and mobilize their constituencies to fight for the well-being of their respective ethnic communities (Gagnon 2004). In this way, a crisis caused relatively banal ethnicity to transform into hot ethnicity, and the latter reinvigorated ethnic consciousness and contributed to severe ethnic violence.

Notably, dramatic fluctuations in the salience of ethnicity are not unique to the former Yugoslavia. As mentioned previously, a variety of analyses offer evidence that severe crises commonly transform banal ethnicity into burning hot ethnicity (Brustein 2003; Hale 2004; Hogg and Mullin 1999; Turner 2007b). Political scientist Scott Straus (2004), for example, documents how ethnic relations were relatively peaceful in pregenocide Rwanda and that ethnicity was relatively banal despite popular prejudice against Tutsis. Severe political crises caused by the Tutsi-led Rwandan Patriotic Front's invasion of Rwanda and the subsequent assassination of Rwanda's president, however, made ethnicity and ethnic difference much more salient.

Ethnic Pluralism in Imperial States

The former Yugoslavia had been ruled by the Austro-Hungarian and Ottoman Empires and only gained independence after both empires began to fall apart. As historian Dominic Lieven (1999) notes, these and other large empires disintegrated because they had a particularly difficult time unifying their populations and stymying competing nationalist movements. Indeed, relative to the smaller composite states like France, Spain, and the United Kingdom, ethnic diversity proved a more powerful disintegrative force in large empires.

Several factors obstructed the construction of a shared national consciousness in large empires. Most importantly, large imperial states ruled over enormous and diverse populations. These empires also adopted nationalist policies relatively late and after alternative ethnic consciousnesses had begun to trickle in and spread among minority peoples. In addition, the geographic size of these empires forced leaders to recognize local communities and grant them considerable autonomy, which contributed to a more localized ethnic consciousness that subsequently impeded nation-building efforts. Finally, the large empires rarely used education as a means of propagating national consciousness. Instead, they usually left local communities to provide their own education, and, like Spanish Catalonia, this contributed to a peripheral ethnic consciousness that opposed the nation-building efforts of imperial states.

The Ottoman Empire highlights the difficult task of building a common national consciousness within a large and diverse empire. It was one of the largest and most enduring empires that have ever existed, lasting some six hundred years and at its peak controlling much of North Africa, Anatolia, the Middle East, and southeastern Europe. In order to control this vast empire, the political leaders implemented a form of indirect rule whereby local regions were granted considerable autonomy from Istanbul. Indirect rule was a necessity because limited organizational, transportation, and communication technologies inhibited more direct forms of rule over such a vast territory. Importantly, there were both political and cultural elements of regional autonomy within the Ottoman Empire. Politically, the Ottomans employed the *timar* system, whereby local elites were empowered to collect taxes in return for passing on a steady flow of revenue to Istanbul, maintaining peace and stability, and helping to raise an army. Culturally, the Ottomans employed the *millet* system, which granted religious communities the right of self-rule within the empire. Most notably, they were allowed to maintain social order in their own communities and provided services to their religious communities, with education being a notable example. Both policing and services required resources, and the millets were therefore given the right to collect revenue from the members of their religious community.

The combination of the *timar* and *millet* systems proved an effective system of rule for hundreds of years, and it allowed the Ottomans to maintain control over such a varied and dispersed empire and establish itself as a world power. By the nineteenth century, however, the populations of several regions—especially in the Balkans—mobilized against Ottoman rule to demand greater autonomy. Diverse factors contributed to these movements: Indirect rule strengthened local ethnic consciousness, European rivals encouraged subnational movements, and an overriding Ottoman national framework was absent, especially in the Christian-dominated areas. Moreover, intense geopolitical competition pushed Ottoman rulers to modernize the state beginning in the late nineteenth century, and this included efforts to build a more direct form of rule. These reforms further strengthened independence movements by increasing state interference in local politics, which intensified resentment among communities who had previously enjoyed greater autonomy and had begun to think of themselves as a nation.

In addition to encouraging subnational movements, western European countries also contributed to the proliferation of ethnic consciousness among Ottoman minorities in a less active way. Many Ottoman minorities—especially Christians—moved to western Europe, observed nationalist movements, became nationalists, and subsequently spread nationalist ideas back in the Ottoman Empire. Albania offers one of several examples. Prior to the emergence of an Albanian nationalist movement in the early nineteenth century, Albanians lacked an ethnic consciousness and accepted their position within the Ottoman Empire. At that time, however, an influential nationalist literature began to emerge and spread among Albanian elites. Most of this literature was produced by Albanians who lived in Italy, Greece, Romania, and Istanbul. Angelo Masci (1758–1821), for example, lived in Naples, where he was influenced by Italian nationalism, and he wrote the first nationalist historiography of Albania, depicting Albanians as a unified people with a long and proud history extending back thousands of years. The proliferation of ethnicity from early modernizers to later modernizers in this and other ways is one important reason why the timing of state-led nation-building efforts is so important and why belated efforts to build a cohesive nation out of diverse peoples—such as that of the Ottoman state's late-nineteenth-century Tanzimat reforms—have had so little success. In this way, the proliferation of an alternative ethnic consciousness effectively ended the critical-juncture period during which states could successfully impose a new national consciousness. That being said, such a critical juncture might never have existed because—different from the French composite state—Ottoman rule institutionalized local autonomy and cultural difference. Education played an important role in the latter.

Similar to Spanish Catalonia, communally controlled schools created and reinforced non-Ottoman ethnic consciousness prior to the disintegration of the Ottoman Empire. Through education, people were taught by their communal leaders that they were something other than Ottoman, and growing ethnic consciousness motivated anti-Ottoman movements once the Ottoman Empire began efforts to create a nation-state. One example that highlights the importance of education is Cyprus.

Cyprus was ruled by the Ottoman Empire for more than three hundred years and possessed a population that was mainly Greek-speaking Orthodox Christian but also included a large minority of Turkish-speaking Muslims. Under the *millet* system, Orthodox Church officials gained considerable power, so much so that they earned the title the "Ethnarchy" and were the local rulers of Ottoman

Cyprus (Persianis 1978, 3). The religious officials were educated in Greece and maintained strong ties with the Greek Orthodox Church, which caused them to see Cyprus as part of a greater Greek civilization. And because the Orthodox Church controlled Greek Cypriot education, Greek Cypriot schools introduced students to powerful ideas of Greek nationalism and imparted a particular Greek perspective by stressing the magnificence of Greek civilization. For this, schools focused their curricula on Greek history and literature, religion, and ancient Greek; and this curricula constantly emphasized the Megali Idea, or Great Idea, which sought to return Greece to its ancient splendor by reincorporating the Greek-speaking population living in adjacent lands (Lange 2012).

As with the Ottoman Empire, ethnic diversity also contributed to the disintegration of the Soviet Union. Relative to the Ottoman Empire, however, the Soviet Empire remained much more intact after its collapse, as Russia maintained the overwhelming majority of the territory and population of the former Soviet Union whereas contemporary Turkey makes up only a tiny fraction of the former Ottoman Empire. This was not because of ethnic homogeneity, as ethnic Russians were a minority in the Soviet Union. Relatively speaking, Russia was more successful transforming an empire into a nation-state.

One reason for this relative success is the way the Soviets politicized class and—despite a number of ethnic purges carried out under Stalin—downplayed ethnicity, thereby limiting the strength of non-Russian ethnic consciousness and reducing the likelihood of ethnic movements. In fact, sociologist Liliana Riga (2008) finds that most early communist leaders were ethnic minorities who championed communism as a way to diminish ethnic discrimination and integrate minorities into the polity. Moreover, the Russian Revolution was similar to the French Revolution in that it created a more directly ruled state that offered more limited space for communal autonomy. The regions that ultimately separated from Russia in turn—much of Central Asia, the southern Caucasus, the Baltic states, and the Ukraine—had recent histories of political autonomy.

While these historical factors related to state and nation building are important, political scientist Keith Darden (forthcoming) argues that education does a better job of explaining both the relative unity of the Russian nation as well as the eventual breakaway of some former regions of the Soviet Union. He offers evidence that where Russian was the language of instruction at the onset of mass education, students gained a Russian national consciousness that trumped more localized ethnic consciousness. Alternatively, where mass education occurred in languages other than Russian and under the control of non-Russian authorities, people developed non-Russian ethnic consciousnesses that conflicted with Russian nationalism. These latter regions, in turn, mobilized in pursuit of independence after the collapse of the Soviet Union.

The political quagmire and violence that began in the Ukraine in 2014 is also linked to education. Some Ukrainians were initially educated in Russian, whereas others were initially educated in Ukrainian. The people living in the regions with a history of Russian education commonly self-identify as Russian Ukrainians, but the people living in regions with a history of Ukrainian education usually do not self-identify as Russian and resent past Russian imperialism (Darden forthcoming). Russian authorities recognized the link between education, language, and nationalism relatively early on; an 1876 memorandum on Russian control of the Ukraine claimed that "nothing divides people as much as differences in speech and writing. Permitting the creation of a special literature for the common people in the Ukrainian dialect would signify collaborating in the alienation of Ukraine from the rest of Russia" (Lieven 1999, 185).

Overseas Colonialism, Missionaries, and Ethnic Diversity

The peripheral regions of the Ottoman and Russian Empires are examples of internal colonialism whereby foreign powers conquered regions and attempted to integrate them into the imperial metropole. Overseas colonialism differed from internal colonialism because the colonial powers did not try to integrate territories and peoples into the metropole. Instead, the colonial powers simply controlled them for the political and economic well-being of the metropole and treated the peoples living in the overseas colonies as nonnationals. Whereas internal colonialism was the dominant form of conquest and control up until the sixteenth century, overseas colonialism became the dominant form of foreign conquest and control thereafter. In fact, the overwhelming majority of contemporary countries—including nearly all countries in Africa, the Americas, Asia, Oceania, and the Middle East—are former overseas colonies of England, France, Portugal, Spain, and other more minor overseas colonizers.

Most former overseas colonies have multiple and salient ethnic divisions. For many overseas colonies, such ethnic pluralism has precolonial origins, as diverse peoples inhabited the regions prior to colonial conquest and rule. Overseas colonialism also shaped diversity in important ways. For one, colonial powers commonly delineated borders based on rivers or lines of latitude and longitude, and such borders paid little attention to pre-existing communities. As a result, the colonies were composed of arbitrary combinations of people and commonly split communities among multiple colonies. In addition, overseas colonialism frequently caused the movement of millions of peoples to the colonies. The most notable example of this is European settlers to the Americas, Australia and New

Zealand, South Africa, Kenya, Algeria, and elsewhere. Millions of slaves were also sent to a number of colonies, especially those in the New World. Finally, millions of indentured laborers migrated to the colonies, usually to work on plantations. Most of these laborers originated from the Indian subcontinent, but many also came from China, Portugal, and elsewhere.

While some degree of diversity is necessary for ethnic violence, ethnic difference can only motivate violence when ethnicity is salient, that is, when people possess an ethnic consciousness. In addition to affecting diversity, overseas colonialism promoted ethnic consciousness. Rwanda, Burundi, and Burma highlight different ways through which colonialism did so.

Colonialism and Competing Ethnicities in Rwanda and Burundi

Prior to the colonization of Rwanda and Burundi, "Hutu" and "Tutsi" were status categories whereby the wealthy and powerful were Tutsi and the masses were Hutu (Mamdani 2001). Under this system, fortunate Hutus became Tutsi, and unfortunate Tutsis were demoted to Hutu status. Shortly after taking over the region, colonial administrators racialized the categories by declaring Tutsis racially superior and the natural rulers of Hutus. Anthropologist Mahmood Mamdani (2001) describes how the colonizers combined eugenics with the Bible to explain and justify social stratification. They claimed that Tutsis were the descendants of Ham, the son of Noah, and whose son Cain was damned by Noah after Ham laughed at his father for passing out naked after a postdiluvian drinking binge (see Gen. 9:20–27). Alternatively, the colonial officials and missionaries believed Hutus were miscreants, completely outside of God's chosen community. Colonialism therefore created a three-tier religiously inspired stratification system whereby the blessed descendants of Noah (the Belgians) were on top, the damned descendants of Noah (the Tutsis) were in the middle, and the group without any ties to the chosen people (the Hutus) were on the bottom.

The colonizers made their racial ideas a reality and created Hutu and Tutsi ethnicities in a variety of ways. Among the most elementary was by simply categorizing people as Tutsi or Hutu. The colonial government gathered data on the "race" of all Rwandans and Burundians for official censuses, and they marked the race of colonial subjects on official ID cards. Because these racial categories were colonial constructs, the act of categorization was arbitrary and based primarily on physical appearance, status, and cattle ownership. Yet through official categorization, the Belgian colonial administration made these differences rigid and permanent, two characteristics that patterned social relations and gave meaning and significance to the categories. Rwanda and Burundi are not the only cases where communal categories helped institutionalize competing ethnic consciousnesses. Political scientists Evan Lieberman and Prerna Singh (2012) find that colonial censuses institutionalized ethnic difference in ways that commonly promoted ethnic violence. Through an analysis of southern Africa, they find that ethnic civil war has been much more common in places where colonial censuses recognized ethnic difference.

Colonial education was one way through which racial categories structured social relations in Rwanda and Burundi. The great majority of students—especially at higher levels—were Tutsi even though Tutsis were only a small minority of the population (King 2015; Linden 1977; Mbonimana 1978, 1995). As a consequence, Tutsis had access to white-collar jobs while Hutus were stuck as laborers. Even more than promoting communal inequality, schools taught curricula describing Tutsis as racially superior and the rightful rulers of Rwanda, which gave a moral element to ethnic divisions (King 2015; Linden 1977).

Institutional discrimination also occurred in the colonial government and contributed to ethnically patterned power relations. The Belgians employed a system of indirect rule that used chiefs as local intermediaries, and they only allowed Tutsis to serve as chiefs. These Tutsi intermediaries helped to maintain order, implement policy, and collect taxes. With the forceful backing of the colonial state, many chiefs became despots and exploited Hutus mercilessly. Most notably, they forced Hutus to pay taxes, took their land, and demanded corvée labor. These acts politicized ethnicity and promoted extreme communal inequalities.

These competing Hutu and Tutsi ethnic consciousnesses were influential determinants of subsequent ethnic violence in both Rwanda and Burundi. In the former, the Hutu Revolution removed Tutsis from their elite positions during the final days of colonial rule and established a Hutu-dominated state, and Tutsis became a common target of violence during the postcolonial period, including the 1994 genocide. In Burundi, on the other hand, the Tutsis remained in power after independence. In 1972, some Hutus began a violent yet unsuccessful struggle to topple the Tutsi-led regime, resulting in an ethnic civil war that killed approximately 100,000 people. Twenty years later, democratizing reforms allowed a Hutu to become president for the first time, but Tutsi generals assassinated the president, thereby beginning a second ethnic civil war that killed 300,000 people.

Missionaries and Ethnic Pluralism in Burma

Political scientist David Abernethy (2000) notes that missionaries and colonial administrators commonly collaborated because their goals were usually complementary, and a growing literature offers evidence that missionaries contributed to many of the effects commonly attributed to colonialism (Woodberry 2012; Lankina and Getachew 2012). We see close and complementary relations in Rwanda and Burundi, as missionaries worked hand-in-hand with colonial administrators in ways that strengthened the salience of ethnic divisions. Most notably, missionaries accepted and helped to propagate the Hamitic myth through their schools, gave Tutsis privileged access to missionary schools, and supported the privileged social positions of Tutsis until the final years of colonialism (King 2015).

This collaborative relationship between colonizers and missionaries was even more evident in Burma (also known as Myanmar). As of 2016, Burma is the location of the world's longest running civil war, which began in 1948, has killed more than 100,000 people, and pits a state that is dominated by ethnic Burmans—known as Bamars—against an organized military opposition from members of a minority community—the Karens—who seek to create an independent Karen homeland. Other minority peoples have also participated in several other ethnic civil wars during this period, making Burma one of the most war-torn countries on the face of the planet since its colonial independence in 1948. In order to understand the causes of this conflict, one needs to consider the historical processes through which colonialists and missionaries shaped the contours, salience, and popularity of ethnicity among minority peoples.

Burma was a powerful kingdom at the turn of the nineteenth century and controlled lands that roughly coincide with its present borders. Similar to composite states in Europe, a core region controlled peripheral polities by granting them considerable autonomy. British colonial conquest was a violent and piecemeal affair, occurring through three different wars of conquest in 1826, 1852, and 1885. The British ruled over the core area of the former Burmese kingdom through direct rule but implemented indirect rule in the former tributary states. Such indirect rule made possible considerable political autonomy and allowed minority communities to maintain a customary system of law. After the onset of colonial rule, these communities had strong relations with the British colonizers, as they collaborated with the British and their members made up most of the colonial military. Alternatively, Bamars had antagonistic relations with the British—who ruled them directly—and were largely excluded from positions of authority. This mixture of direct and indirect rule and preferential treatment toward minorities solidified ethnic differences and contributed to violence between Bamars and minorities, with Bamars trying to keep minorities in subordinate positions and minorities fighting to maintain autonomy.

A Karen ethnic consciousness also gained considerable salience during the colonial period. Different from the northern hill tribes, however, Karens were ruled directly and therefore were not granted self-rule. American Baptist missionaries made up for their lack of political autonomy, however, and played a vital role in shaping, strengthening, and proliferating a Karen ethnic consciousness.

Missionaries coined the term "Karen" during the colonial period to refer to diverse peoples who spoke a variety of languages and dialects (Jørgensen 1997, vi). Despite the absence or extreme weakness of a Karen consciousness, the missionaries wore ethnic lenses and believed that the Karens were a distinct "race" and "nation" even when the Karens did not. At the same time, the missionaries saw the Karen "nation" as primitive and needing assistance to gain the attributes of an "advanced" and "modern" nation. As one prominent missionary remarked in the late nineteenth century, "From a loose aggregation of clans we shall weld them into a nation yet" (Smeaton 1920, 19). Another missionary noted the success of their nation-building endeavors: "These scattered tribes were becoming a united people. Instead of each clan acting for itself, they proposed to unite; and this was undoubtedly the legitimate result of the new life from the Deliverer. Satan divides and destroys. Jesus unites and saves" (Bunker 1902, 237).

Several missionaries worked hard to unify Karens. Only a few years after the establishment of the Karen missions, American Baptists made the first Karen flag and gave it to the Karens to represent their community (Mason 1862, 267). They also encouraged Karens to organize a national association promoting Karen unity and looking out for the well-being of the community. Moreover, missionaries standardized three Karen languages and helped build a common linguistic base on which to build an imagined community. As one British official remarked, "No people can long survive the extinction of their language.... The missionaries, headed by the great Judson, have rescued the Karen language from oblivion and given it a certain permanency by reducing it to writing in the Burmese character" (Smeaton 1920, 219–20).

Although missionaries were delighted that their linguistic work helped to build a Karen ethnic community, the main reason for their standardization of Karen languages was something very different: It made the gospel much more accessible to the Karens. To allow Karens to read the scripture, in turn, American Baptist missionaries also made an enormous effort to educate Karens through the establishment of schools wherever they worked. Karens flocked to these missionary schools and became among the most educated communities in colonial Burma. This education was in one of the three Karen languages used by missionaries, meaning that Karens learned standard dialects shared by many others and made investments in these languages.

Through missionary education, Karens went from being illiterate to being the most educated segment of the Burmese population. Mass literacy, in turn, gave Karens access to literary depictions of the Karen community, something that Benedict Anderson (1983) describes as playing a fundamental role in building a strong and widespread ethnic consciousness. Indeed, the Baptist missionary press was established shortly after the beginning of the mission and was prolific, printing tens of millions of pages of material in the Karen languages. These writings depicted Karens as a coherent community with ancient roots instead of the diverse collection of people that they were. For example, the missionaries established a vernacular newspaper in 1842, which reviewed the current events affecting Karens and continually depicted Karens as a primordial community. One article from 1855 presents a myth that not only exemplifies Anderson's claims about literature and ethnic consciousness but presents the core elements of his theory. It describes how the losing of books (i.e., the loss of literacy) caused the demise of the Karen "nation" and prophesies that the return of books will reunite the Karen nation once again:

> Brethren, I wish to speak to you plainly concerning one thing. It is not true that the Karen nation had no books. The elders of past ages said, one generation to another,—'children and grandchildren, the Karens had books, perfect like other nations.' But they did not take care of their books, and therefore lost them. When they lost their books they lost their knowledge of God; and when they lost their knowledge of God, they could no longer live in peace with each other. The younger brother became an enemy, the elder brother a foe. The more they lived in hostility, the more degraded they became; the more degraded they became, the shorter the period of life; the shorter the period of life, the more they did evil; the more they did evil, the more severe were the judgments of God, afflicting them and more with sickness and death. But the elders left one promise. They said—'Though the Karen nation has deteriorated and increased in wickedness, yet love and compassion will come to them again; when love and compassion come to them again, if they observe and do, they will fraternize again into populous communities; when they fraternize again into populous communities, they will love each other and improve physically and morally.' (Mason 1860 75–76)

By the early twentieth century, articles in the newspaper did more than describe the Karen nation as real; they actively sought to increase a sense of Karen consciousness. An article from 1916 offers one example. Titled "The Karen Language and Karen Loyalty," it describes how language is the basis of Karen identity and demands respect for it as well as for all Karens (American Baptist Historical Society 2015).

As the previous examples highlight, missionaries and the missionary press also played an important role in popularizing ethnic myths that supported a Karen consciousness. American missionaries were extremely interested in Karen customs and culture, as knowledge of both proved vital to evangelical success. Dr. Francis Mason (1870), who helped translate the Bible into Karen, also collected and published Karen myths and traditions. On this, he writes, "The Karens had no books, but I found they had an abundance of traditions, and I went to work collecting all I could find of every description. I pretty well exhausted the Tavoy Karens from one end of the province to the other, for whenever I found a man who knew something that others did not, I had it written down on the spot" (276–77). Among the many myths of Karen origins Mason gathered, he interpreted and popularized one particular version that describes Karens as originating from the Gobi Desert and migrating to Burma thousands of years ago, and this myth became an important part of the Karen myth-symbol complex. By giving the myth a scientific character and describing the origins of the Karen community in concrete terms, this myth strengthened an ethnic consciousness (Rajah 2002).

In addition to the ideal bases of community, missionaries also shaped the more physical foundations on which a Karen consciousness could flourish by promoting interactions among Karens from all over colonial Burma. One way this occurred was through schools, especially secondary schools that brought together Karens from different regions. In addition, churches emerged as a central social institution and allowed Karens to interact with one another. As one colonial official described, "The local church takes the place of the clan-unit, or village. These churches are federally united into associations or missions, which look up to the missionary as their leader. These associations take the place of the confederacies of clans" (Smeaton 1920, 196). Missionaries and their converts organized regular meetings bringing pastors and other Christians together to talk about local and regional affairs, and annual meetings for all Karen Christians brought the leaders of the Karen community together to discuss church governance for the entire community. Such meetings played an important role making the imagined Karen community seem real, especially since the little contact between Karen clans that existed prior to the arrival of the missionaries was often conflictual. One British official noted and clearly described the unifying effects of the meetings, writing, "Opportunities are thus given for the Karens to have friendly and social gatherings, which serve to cement a better understanding among the different tribes, who for many years were jealous and suspicious of each other" (McMahon 1876, 255).

Importantly, missionary influence varied greatly among Karens, and anthropologists find that only a minority of contemporary Karens possesses a strong, overarching Karen consciousness (Buadaeng 2007; Jørgensen 1997). If missionaries were the main cause of ethnic consciousness, we would expect that the strongest Karen nationalists were most influenced by the missions, and this is exactly what the evidence suggests. Specifically, missionaries standardized and put into writing three different Karen languages: Sgaw, P'wo, and Pau. Of these three, missionaries had much more influence on the Sgaw. And although Christian Sgaw Karens are a tiny minority of all Karens (approximately 15 percent), they have almost without exception been the leaders of the Karen nationalist movement, whereas non-Christian and non-Sgaw-speaking Karens commonly oppose the nationalist movement (Harriden 2002; Stern 1968).

Karens are also the largest ethnic minority in northern Thailand, and Thai Karens offer another insightful contrast with Sgaw Karens in Burma. Although Thai Karens continue to face considerable discrimination from the Thai government (including forced relocation), they have not developed a strong Karen consciousness conflicting with Thai nationalism. Instead, anthropologists find that they usually possess dual identities that are equal parts Thai and Karen (Buadaeng 2007). Limited Protestant missionary influence helps to explain this difference.

Protestant missionaries interacted with Thai Karens beginning in the middle to late nineteenth century, but such missionary influence was limited. By the 1920s, for example, only one missionary text had been published in the Karen language, and missionaries did not offer any vernacular education to Karens (McFarland 1928, 33–34). By the time missionaries gained greater influence among Thai Karens in the 1950s, the Thai state had already expanded and gained a strong presence in regions where Karens resided. This began in the 1880s with major centralizing political reforms implemented by King Chulalongkorn, and subsequent governments continued these reforms. The Thai state established public schools and actually made education compulsory in 1921 (although this was largely unenforced). The curricula in the government schools ignored the existence of Karens and imparted the Thai nationalist position, and missionary schools were forced to follow the curricula of Thai schools (McFarland 1928, 36). Thus, whereas missionary schools and presses in Burma helped incorporate Karen victimization into the myth-symbol complex, this did not happen on the Thai side of the border, and political and educational institutions actually taught Karens that they were part of a great Thai nation.

Faced with this situation, missionaries who began working among the Thai Karens in the 1950s acted very differently than missionaries in Burma (Buadaeng 2007). Because Thai Karens commonly knew Thai and because the Karen language uses the Burmese script, missionaries did not teach Karen languages in Thailand, and most Thai Karens are unable to read it today. Moreover, because Karens had access to government schools, most missionaries did not open their own schools. Instead, they simply focused their educational efforts on offering financial support and student housing to Karen students who attended government schools. The educational policy of missionaries among Thai Karens therefore simply increased access to an educational system that promoted the Thai language and Thai nationalism.

To summarize, this chapter reviews a variety of cases from around the world to explore the origins of ethnic pluralism. It suggests that few states conform closely to the nation-state model because their populations have multiple and competing ethnic consciousnesses. There is no single determinant of such ethnic pluralism, and all ethnically diverse countries emerge in their own unique ways. Yet the cases analyzed in this chapter highlight how modernization commonly leads to ethnic pluralism, with states and education playing particularly influential roles. More specifically, histories of political autonomy and ethnicized education promote ethnic pluralism, with local political elites and schools being the main social carriers of ethnicity. The influence of both, however, depends on timing. Ethnicity has path-dependent characteristics, and attempts to transform ethnic consciousness after alternatives have already been popularized face great difficulties and commonly spark ethnic violence.

6

EMOTIONAL PREJUDICE AND ETHNIC OBLIGATIONS
Motives of Ethnic Violence

In cases of murder, establishing motive is a central task for prosecutors, but this activity is highly conjectural because one cannot get inside the heads of people to read their minds. And even if this were possible, factors motivating murder are frequently complex, and the motives described by admitted murderers are commonly ex post facto rationalizations that are oversimplified or erroneous. Indeed, we often do not know all the intricate factors that motivate our actions, although our brains—which strive for order and understanding—trick us into thinking that we do, thereby allowing us to convincingly fabricate explanations.

When analyzing ethnic violence, one must also consider motive. In fact, analyses of ethnic violence necessarily explore motive because ethnic violence is defined by motivation: It is violence that is *motivated* in different ways and to different extents by ethnic difference. Even more than in cases of murder, establishing motive in episodes of ethnic violence is extremely difficult because tens, hundreds, or even thousands of people are commonly involved and because each participant has different sets of motives. Moreover, it is usually impossible to track down all individuals who participate in ethnic violence to ask them about their motives, and such interviews might be worthless because people who participate in ethnic violence are commonly unwilling to divulge their secrets. Finally, even open and honest responses from participants must be questioned because of ex post facto rationalization.

Some might therefore conclude that it is impossible to understand the motivations pushing individuals to participate in ethnic violence, but this assessment is overly pessimistic. Like prosecutors of murder, researchers of ethnic violence can gain insight into motive by analyzing the violent events themselves and the circumstances leading up to the violence. If a man kills someone who molested his daughter, prosecutors can argue that the motive was anger over and revenge for his daughter's suffering. Along these same lines, if members of ethnic community A attack individuals from ethnic community B after a woman from community A was raped by a man from community B, this is evidence that anger over and revenge for the rape motivated the violence. In addition, researchers of ethnic violence have an important advantage over prosecutors of murder because participants in violent movements usually publicize their motives openly in an effort to mobilize support. Yes, many individuals participate in ethnic violence for reasons other than those popularized by leaders and vocal participants (Kalyvas 2006), but the popularized motives that frame movements are influential and should not be trivialized. Such motives are of primary importance because they play a vital role inciting and mobilizing violence.

The literature on ethnic violence and contentious collective action points to a variety of influential motives. In an extensive analysis, sociologist Maurice Pinard (2011) pinpoints interests, emotion-inducing grievances and threats, and obligations as three common and influential motives. These motives conform to three of Max Weber's (1968 [1921]) ideal types of social action: acting on personal interests is an example of instrumental-rational action, emotions underlie affective action, and obligations promote value-rational action.[1] As Weber notes, it is impossible to know for sure why people act the way they do, and almost all individual actions are simultaneously shaped by multiple motives. In an effort to overcome these problems and create a sociology based on social action, he devises ideal types, analytic tools that are abstractions of reality and that help the researcher identify and compare recurring features in the social world to gauge their causal impact.

In this chapter, I use instrumental, emotional, and obligatory motives as ideal types and consider their impact on ethnic violence. While downplaying the importance of instrumental motives, the analysis offers evidence that emotions and obligations are very influential motives for ethnic violence and that modernity promotes each in two main ways. First, emotions and obligations are most likely to motivate ethnic violence when people possess an ethnic consciousness, and the latter is a common outcome of modernity. Second, modernity promotes powerful institutions that are able to spread emotions throughout populations

---

1. Given the rarity of ethnic violence, Weber's fourth ideal type—habitual action—is not an influential motivator of ethnic violence.

and enforce obligations, and such institutions are especially likely to contribute to ethnic violence when institutional elites possess a strong ethnic consciousness.

Interests and Ethnic Violence

The instrumentalist position suggests that people choose to participate in ethnic violence when it is in their personal interest to do so. That is, individuals calculate the costs and benefits of participating in ethnic violence and decide to participate when the personal benefits of action outweigh the costs. Common examples include actors deciding to eliminate communal competitors to gain power and resources, politicians trying to maximize votes by purposefully mobilizing their communities to take up arms against Others, and individuals choosing to attack communal rivals either to prevent them from attacking first or because militants from their own ethnic community threaten sanctions if they fail to participate.

Without any doubt, instrumental interests can and do motivate ethnic violence in these and other ways. Still, a variety of factors frequently limit the influence of instrumental motives in cases of ethnic violence. First, people cannot accurately calculate the costs and benefits of ethnic violence prior to committing acts of violence, which makes instrumental calculation difficult. Moreover, the cost of participating in ethnic violence can be staggering, including life in prison, retaliatory acts against one's family, and death. Such enormous costs are powerful deterrents to participation, but people still choose to participate in ethnic violence.

Findings in neuroscience and psychology also oppose strong instrumentalist claims. Neuroscientists find that emotions have a much greater impact on human action than rational calculation and that emotions shape actions that seem purely instrumental (Damasio 2005; Haidt 2012). Similarly, violent actions that appear mainly instrumental in orientation are commonly motivated by morals and norms that oblige action (Fiske and Rai 2015; Greene 2013).

The collective action problem also weakens instrumentalist arguments. Economist Mancur Olson (1965) famously recognized that individuals who do not contribute to the provisioning of collective goods—like roads—can still reap the benefits of collective goods once such goods have been created by others, thereby allowing noncontributors to ride for free. It is therefore rational to be a free rider, but rampant free riding impedes the construction of collective goods. Along these lines, most of the perceived benefits of ethnic violence are collective, as the perpetrators of ethnic violence usually seek to increase their community's share of power and resources. Thus, because the costs of directly participating in ethnic violence can be great and because nonparticipants cannot be excluded from the perceived benefits of ethnic violence, participation can be irrational.

Similarly, ethnic violence is a form of collective action and requires motives that affect many people, but personal interests are commonly poor motivators of collective action. Interests are most likely to motivate collective violence when they are collective in nature, that is, when people focus on the interests of their ethnic communities instead of their personal interests. When this is the case, interests motivate many people simultaneously and thereby facilitate collective action. The motivational influence of collective interests, however, requires that people place great value on the collective and that normative obligations to protect the collective are present and enforced to avoid the collective action problem.

Although showing how interests can contribute to ethnic violence, a focus on collective interests departs from the instrumentalist perspective in important ways. Using Max Weber's (1968 [1921]) ideal types, it conforms to value-rational action instead of instrumental-rational action. Whereas instrumental-rational action refers to action that is based simply on cost-benefit calculations for personal gain, value-rational action is guided by values and beliefs, with people calculating how to best pursue their beliefs and values. In the case of ethnic violence, participation can be far from instrumentally rational because participants put their personal well-being in jeopardy; participating in ethnic violence can involve personal sacrifices for the well-being of the community. And it is the extreme value that people place on ethnicity—which is hardly rational—that is of primary importance. Instead of instrumental, it is more accurate to refer to this motive as obligatory, as the latter highlights how concern for community, norms, and values combines with rational calculation to shape action. Before considering obligations, however, we need to consider a motive that seems the polar opposite of instrumental-rational action.

Emotional Prejudice and Ethnic Violence

According to Max Weber (1968 [1921]), affective action is driven by emotional impulses, and emotion is an influential motive for ethnic violence. This claim seems anything but controversial, as violent action is commonly compulsive and driven by anger, hatred, fear, envy, and other emotions. Just think of the people you have witnessed acting violently. More than likely, their faces were beaming with emotion, with eyebrows lowered, eyes glaring, and lips tightened to reveal their teeth. Although the first generation of work on ethnic violence paid considerable attention to emotions, the contemporary literature generally downplays emotions as a motivating force. The growing prominence of the instrumentalist position is one reason for the general disregard of emotional motives, as emotions and rational calculation are—quite erroneously—considered incompatible motives. In addition, many link emotions to arguments of ancient hatreds, which suggest that antipathy toward entire categories of people is passed down from generation to generation. The ancient hatreds argument is critiqued by some who note that emotions fluctuate depending on the social context, by others who link it to primordial views of ethnicity, by others who claim it overemphasizes the inevitability of ethnic violence, and by still others who believe it inaccurately depicts participants of ethnic violence as deranged fanatics. While all these critiques have merit, claims that emotions motivate ethnic violence need not accept the ancient hatreds position.

A variety of works within psychology and the sociology of emotion highlight how emotions motivate violence (Duckitt 2003; Fiske 2002; Kaufman 2015; Petersen 2002). Sociologist Randall Collins' (2008) work on the micro-dynamics of violence describes how "emotional energy" influences nearly all incidents of violence. He finds that emotions like anger, envy, and hatred are usually necessary to overcome social conventions and fear of injury and retaliation, both of which commonly impede violent acts. Similarly, studies find that damage and inactivity in the region of the brain that is centrally involved in regulating emotions promotes violent behavior (DeLisi, Umphress, and Vaughn 2009; Freedman and Hemenway 2000; Sarapata et al. 1998). Specifically, people with damaged prefrontal cortexes are much more likely to act violently because they are unable to control their emotions, which suggests that people experiencing powerful emotions are prone to violent behavior.

Another body of work in psychology suggests that emotional contagion contributes to collective violence (Hatfield, Cacioppo, and Rapson 1994). These analyses offer evidence that emotions spread from one person to another when people interact. If you are interacting with a group of angry people, there is a good chance that you will become angry, and riled-up and emotional groups commonly act out violently. More recent work in neurology on mirror neurons offers biological backing to this social scientific finding (Gallese 2001). Such neurons are activated both when an individual does something and when an individual observes someone else doing the same act. Mirror neurons therefore help explain why laughter and yawning are contagious. While several leading experts believe these neurons promote empathy and therefore have the potential to help limit ethnic violence, mirror neurons cause us to have similar emotional states as those around us, meaning that they can contribute to violence when the people we interact with focus negative emotions on other ethnic communities.

Sociologists who study emotions offer their own complementary take on contagion but focus on the social interactions instead of the anatomy of the human brain. Several find that ritualistic interactions create common emotional states among participants (Collins 2004; Durkheim 1965 [1912]; Goffman 1967). Through interactions that synchronize talk and action, emotional energy grows, shared emotions spread throughout the participants, and group solidarity increases. And as Émile Durkheim (1965 [1912]) notes, these ritual interactions shape human action in important ways, as "the vital energies become hyperexcited, the passions more intense, the sensations more powerful," resulting in what he calls "emotional effervescence" (424). Sociologist Mabel Berezin (2002) notes that states and other organizations commonly organize these rituals to promote "communities of feeling."

Several works within sociology and political science focus more explicitly on ethnic violence and highlight the powerful motivating role of emotions. Political scientists Roger Petersen (2002) and Stuart Kaufman (2001, 2015), for example, find that emotions play important roles in instigating violence. A much larger body of work within sociology and political science acknowledges the important role of emotions but does so only implicitly (Gurr 1993; Horowitz 1985; Sambanis 2001; Wimmer, Cederman, and Min 2009). These works focus on threats and grievances and offer evidence that both are among the most influential determinants of ethnic violence. They highlight the particularly important role of communal threats and grievances—as opposed to individual threats and grievances—and find that inequalities, competition, and threats in the realms of politics, culture, and economics are the principal motivators of many episodes of ethnic violence. Most of these works do not unpack threats and grievances to show that they work through emotion.

Communally Oriented Emotions

While hatred, anger, resentment, jealousy, fear, and other negative emotions can all motivate violence against Others, ethnic violence is most influenced by one particular type of emotion, one that is prejudicial and targets entire categories of Others (Talaska, Fiske, and Chaiken 2008; Leyens et al. 2003). Borrowing a term from psychology, I refer to category-oriented emotions as emotional prejudice. Emotional prejudice contributes to ethnic violence in two influential ways: It creates a powerful motive for ethnic violence and it makes possible many potential targets, as people can attack anyone from the designated outgroup. The sheer number of potential targets increases the chance that aggressors find people to attack, but it also allows aggressors to attack more vulnerable victims who pose less of a retaliatory threat.

Émile Durkheim focuses on consensus and peaceful social relations, but his work is vital to any understanding of emotional prejudice. Most notably, he recognizes that humans are *Homo duplex*, with both an individual-level and a collective consciousness. While hardly eradicating our individuality, a collective consciousness makes us social creatures who are aware of the collective, self-identify with the collective, and are highly concerned for the collective's well-being. As a result, the collective is an important source of powerful emotions; we are happy when the collective triumphs but angry and fearful when it is threatened. Although Durkheim largely ignores it, the flip side of our collective consciousness is an awareness of the Other, a powerful prejudice in favor of the ingroup, and negative sentiments toward Others who are perceived as threatening the ingroup. For example, studies find that people with more salient ethnic identities are at much greater risk of being prejudiced and acting discriminatorily (Duckitt 2003; Mullen, Brown, and Smith 1992; E. Smith 1993). It is therefore the innate sociability described by Durkheim that underlies both the binary propensity and emotional prejudice against entire categories of Others.

Several psychological studies highlight the powerful yet complex link between human emotionality, the binary propensity, and emotional prejudice. One study manipulated the moods of participants and then showed them pictures of one white couple and one racially mixed couple (Forgas and Moylan 1991). Those individuals who were manipulated to have unpleasant moods were more likely to see the mixed couple as less likable than the white couple, but participants who were manipulated to have positive or neutral moods viewed each as equally likable. Another study promoted positive emotions in some subjects but left the emotional state of the remaining participants neutral. The researchers then showed videos of people from an outgroup to the participants (Dovidio et al. 1995). The study found that participants with positive emotion had more positive views of outgroup members and, most interestingly, were more likely to expand their ingroups to include outgroup members. Finally, a variety of studies find that hardship and crises—which promote uncertainty and evoke emotions—strengthen ethnic consciousness and cause people to pay more attention to ethnic difference (Brustein 2003; Hale 2004; Hogg and Mullin 1999; Straus 2004; Turner 2007b).

Modernity and Emotional Prejudice

Emotional prejudice is therefore an influential motivator of ethnic violence and is linked to human groupishness, the cognitive propensity to categorize people into ingroups and outgroups, and human emotionality. Still, emotional prejudice is not universal, and the sort powerful enough to motivate ethnic violence is rare. The binary propensity and human emotionality create a predisposition, but other factors must interact with it to promote emotional prejudice. As described in chapter 1, the social environment provokes emotions, meaning that emotional prejudice depends on social relations. Most notably, the social environment shapes ethnic consciousness, and the latter provides the two basic requirements for emotional prejudice: An ethnic consciousness promotes perceptions of ethnicity and places great value on it. Moreover, the social environment provides threats and grievances that heighten concern for ethnicity and trigger emotional responses. Of great interest to this book, modernity shapes several factors that interact with the binary propensity and human emotionality to promote emotional prejudice.

Above all else, emotional prejudice requires an ethnic consciousness. How can you discriminate against whole communities if you do not perceive ethnicity and categorize people into different ethnic categories? As described in chapters 4 and 5, a variety of modern processes shape the contours and strength of ethnicity. And when salient, an ethnic consciousness promotes emotional prejudice by pushing people to perceive and interpret events in terms of ethnicity. One study, for example, found that people with strong ethnic identities are more likely to believe that discrimination causes undesirable outcomes, and perceptions of discrimination are a potent source of emotional prejudice. For example, when job applicants are interviewed by someone with a different ethnicity and do not get the job, applicants who identify strongly with their ethnicity are much more likely to interpret their failure to get the job as discriminatory and are more angry (Operario and Fiske 2001). Even more, such perceptions of discrimination have the potential to arouse powerful negative emotions against entire categories of people instead of simply targeting the individual who is perceived as acting discriminatorily.

A strong ethnic consciousness also promotes communal comparisons, as people who are concerned about their ethnicity will make comparisons to see how their ethnic community stands relative to others. And such comparisons commonly spark negative emotions that target the entire comparison group. So if you compare your ethnic community against another and if this comparison highlights the relative disadvantage of your community, this comparison will likely elicit negative emotions toward the relatively advantaged community if you identify with and value your ethnicity. Indeed, a large literature points to communal comparisons as influential determinants of ethnic violence, suggesting the need to consider them as a separate factor contributing to emotional prejudice (Greenfeld 1992; Horowitz 1985; Petersen 2002; Sambanis 2001).

Making social comparisons is natural, and all humans do it. Psychologists actually measure the extent to which individuals compare themselves to others, and the issue has inspired an entire research tradition known as social comparison theory (Festinger 1954). Although the extent to which people make social comparisons varies, the fact that nearly everyone makes them suggests that we have a genetic predisposition to compare ourselves with others. One reason people make social comparisons is to get information about ourselves. Through comparison, we are able to gauge our relative wealth, intelligence, generosity, honesty, beauty, etc. There seems to be something more than just a need for self-knowledge, however: We seek knowledge about how we stack up against others, something that is probably linked to an inherent drive for status. Social animals that do not have biologically based divisions of labor are status-oriented and compete for higher-status positions.[2] This is clearly evident with wolves, who compete from the time they are born to ascend the status hierarchy and become alpha males and females. Humans are different from wolves in that sexual reproduction is not limited to alphas, so our status is not as important as it is for wolves. We are still status-oriented, however, because the well-being and reproductive opportunities of humans have been influenced by relative status throughout most of our evolutionary history.[3] As a result, most humans are fixated on status, and social comparisons give us constant information about where we stand relative to others.

In addition to individual-level comparisons, humans make group-level comparisons to assess their community's status relative to others. Communal comparisons might seem innocuous, but they commonly spark negative emotions that promote violence. Several analyses find that ethnic comparisons—that is, comparisons of different ethnic communities—elicit intense negative emotions and that these emotions target the entire reference community. Of all works highlighting how ethnic comparisons promote violence through affective motivation, Donald Horowitz's work has been the most influential. In *Ethnic Groups in Conflict* (1985), he offers evidence from a variety of regions around the world that ethnic comparisons are a driving force behind much ethnic violence. In particular, such comparisons promote different negative emotions against entire ethnic communities. Roger Petersen's *Understanding Ethnic Violence* (2002) offers similar findings. He focuses on ethnic violence in Eastern Europe during the twentieth century and presents evidence that the emotions promoted by ethnic comparisons are the best predictors of ethnic violence. Petersen suggests

---

2. For example, termites have a biologically based status system, as the queen termite is atop the social hierarchy but attained this position because of her biology.

3. Although this has changed since the advent of settled agriculture, with the social environment shaping reproduction in ways that weaken the relationship between status and reproduction (Perusse 1993). In fact, contraception, the costs of raising children, and other factors have caused the relationship between status and number of offspring to flip-flop since industrialization.

that such comparisons promote resentment, or negative emotions caused by perceived injustices against one's group. In effect, comparisons promote resentment, and resentment promotes anger against entire communities. Although Horowitz, Petersen, and others focus primarily on how ethnic comparisons promote anger, such comparisons can promote other negative emotions as well. They can promote fear of communal demise when a rival community appears to be surpassing their ethnic community in terms of power and wealth. Ethnic comparisons can also provoke strong feelings of hatred, as both fear and anger commonly lead to antipathy.

Although all humans make comparisons, modernity increases the prevalence of ethnic comparisons. As already mentioned, modernity increases an awareness and concern for ethnic community, and both push people to make ethnic comparisons and promote more intense emotional reactions to such comparisons. Modernity also increases knowledge of the existence of other ethnicities: Education and the media commonly increase one's awareness of other ethnicities, as does greater geographic mobility and urbanization.

Another important way through which modernity promotes ethnic comparisons is through transformations in status systems (Horowitz 1985). With industrialization and the construction of large bureaucratic states, new jobs are created and new sources of mobility emerge. People also intermingle with individuals from diverse communities in economic and political institutions. Given our tendency to categorize people into ingroups and outgroups and to pay attention to status, many people consider how their ethnic community compares with others in this new status system. That is, people compare their ethnicity to others in terms of educational attainment, share of government officials and bureaucrats, and wealth. In foraging and agricultural systems, the number of educated individuals, government officials and bureaucrats, and economic elites are so low that such comparisons are less meaningful. With modernization, however, many white-collar jobs are available in the public and private sectors, and education explodes, both of which make mobility more attainable and push people to compare how their ethnic community is doing in terms of power, wealth, and education.

Another way modernity promotes emotional prejudice is through its effects on nationalism. According to philosopher and anthropologist Ernest Gellner (1983, 1), nationalism is "a political principle, which holds that the political and the national unit should be congruent." In effect, nationalism supports the nation-state model, whereby each ethnicity is supposed to possess its own state and rule itself. As a principle, nationalism is powerful, but it becomes stronger still when it combines with patriotism and other values and beliefs to form an elaborate ideology.

Many note that nationalism is a modern phenomenon (Anderson 1983; Deutsch 1953; Gellner 1983; Hobsbawm 1992; Kohn 1956; Sand 2010; Weber 1976). The spread of nationalist ideologies throughout populations requires organizational, communication, and transportation technologies, and modernity enhances all three. Modernity also contributes to nationalism because it both depends on and intensifies ethnic consciousness. Finally, modernity promotes powerful states, which are the main social carriers of nationalism.

The nationalist principle suggests that ethnicities should organize a state and rule themselves. Alternatively, it claims that wrongs are committed when a community is unable to rule itself or when pre-existing nation-states are jeopardized by people who are not part of the national community. And when something either impedes or endangers ethnic self-rule, people upholding the nationalist principle experience extremely powerful emotions (Gellner 1983). Specifically, the nationalist principle tells us to place the nation on a pedestal above all other communities and to value ethnic self-rule, and both of these cause us to become upset when our community is unable to live up to the nationalist ideal.

The link between nationalism and emotions is apparent to anyone living in a region with multiple and competing nationalisms. I live in Quebec, and the issue of Quebecois nationalism sparks extreme emotions whenever it is discussed. My wife and her former college roommate, for example, are the best of friends but are unable to discuss the topic without getting in heated debates because they have different ideas of nation, causing the pursuit of nationalism for one to come at the expense of the other's idea of nation. For this reason, nationalism is an issue avoided in Quebec unless you are talking among people who share your views or if you want to start an argument. When I was in my early twenties, I lived in another country with multiple and competing ideas of nation—Belgium—and was also able to observe nationalist emotions firsthand. One day, I was riding in a car with Walloons (French-speaking Belgians) when the driver turned purple with rage, began to swear at a large group of bikers, and veered the car so close to them I was sure he would hit them (thankfully, he did not). I learned later that the bikers were Flemish nationalists who were making their annual procession from Brussels to the border of the French-speaking region of Belgium. The purpose of the bike ride is to proclaim Brussels—a primarily French-speaking city situated inside the Flemish-speaking north—part of the Flemish half of the country, and this symbolic act infuriates many Walloons and pushed at least one to put the lives of the Flemish bikers in harm's way.

Nationalist ideologies also include myth-symbol complexes that can provoke and mobilize emotional prejudice against entire categories of people. As the term implies, myth-symbol complexes are collections of myths and symbols that represent communities in an effort to make abstract and imagined communities of strangers seem real (Kaufman 2001; Mosse 1975; Smith 1986a). Cultural historian Johan Huizinga (1924) was among the first to discuss myth-symbol complexes when he described how medieval Christianity made mystic ideas more concrete. "[H]aving once attributed a real existence to an idea," he writes, "the mind wants to see it alive and can effect this only by personalizing it," and myths and symbols proved very successful at personalizing abstract religions (165). Other actors—especially states and education—subsequently copied these religious techniques to make abstract communities of strangers seem real and alive (Mosse 1975). Returning to a point first raised in chapter 4, familial symbols such as "motherland" and "fatherland" help to make sense of communities of strangers and endow ethnic communities with value and meaning. Flags and anthems are also symbols of communities and are commonly used in rituals to heighten collective awareness of the community. Ethnic myths commonly describe the origins of communities, depict heroes, and merge sacred and secular.

Besides generating a belief in the validity and importance of community and helping people make sense of the abstract communities that nationalism glorifies, sociologist Mabel Berezin (2002, 44) notes that ethnic myth-symbol complexes intensify emotional identity, whereby humans gain a powerful emotional attachment to their community. The flip side of this emotional identity is emotional prejudice, and myth-symbol complexes frequently describe and represent ethnic enemies and in so doing elicit strong negative emotions toward designated Others. In *Modern Hatreds*, Stuart Kaufman (2001) finds that ethnic violence commonly depends on pre-existing myths and symbols that heighten negative emotions against one or more rival communities. Leaders manipulate these myth-symbol complexes to heighten emotions among participants and justify violence against Others. Hutu violence against Tutsis in Rwanda, for example, was promoted by myth-symbol complexes depicting Tutsis as evil intruders who conquered and exploited indigenous Hutus (Kaufman 2015). Such myths heighten antipathy toward entire communities and legitimize violence against them by helping to remove them from the moral community. As Scott Straus (2004) notes, educated Rwandans were more acquainted with this myth-symbol complex, which helps to explain why they reported participating in the violence out of fear and anger. Myth-symbol complexes also promote collective fear against whole communities of Others when they describe the hardships a people have faced throughout history and evoke a need to stop such atrocities from happening again. In the former Yugoslavia, for example, a long-standing myth of Serbian martyrdom at the hands of Muslim invaders at the Battle of Kosovo in 1389 was used to promote collective fear against Bosnian Muslims and Kosovo Albanians and underlay the slogan "Only unity saves the Serbs" (Kaufman 2001, 31). Finally, myth-symbol complexes can spark intense emotions when Others reject and disparage them and thereby symbolically attack the community. Disrespecting flags, for example, commonly sparks emotional outbursts that can and have led to violence.[4]

Ethnic Obligations and Ethnic Violence

Obligations promote patterned action by pushing people to act in ways that benefit a larger collective or ideal. They are a type of value-rational action, as people choose to act in ways that support values and beliefs. Obligations affect a great variety of social relations and are linked to human sociability, the latter of which obliges us to look out for the well-being of our acquaintances and ingroups even when it comes at great personal expense. As discussed in chapter 1, for example, psychologist Henri Tajfel (1970, 1978) discovered that people who are randomly assigned to meaningless groups willingly make individual sacrifices for the benefit of the group.

Analyses of ethnic violence rarely focus on obligations.[5] This disregard is surprising since obligations are so widespread and because they commonly motivate ethnic violence in two influential ways. First, people willingly act on obligations when they perceive them as legitimate and beneficial, meaning that people choose to participate in ethnic violence when they believe it is for the good of the ethnic community and when they value the community. Second, people pressure others to fulfill obligations through a variety of sanctions, ranging from mockery and dirty looks to threats of prison and death. For this second type, people do not willingly choose to participate in ethnic violence but do so because others actively pressure them to act on obligations. Importantly, both self-regulation and social sanctions reinforce one another and work in tandem to make obligations a powerful motivator of action.

As an ideal type, obligatory action rarely occurs in a pure form and usually combines with additional motives, including both instrumental and emotional motives. Considering the first, obligations and coercion motivate action in different ways, but it is almost impossible to separate the two when extreme sanctions enforce obligations. Obligations promote a type of value-rational action whereby values and beliefs motivate action, whereas coercion promotes instrumental-rational action, as people calculate their actions in an effort to avoid costly sanctions. While people can simply act instrumentally to avoid sanctions,

---

4. Northern Ireland offers one example. In December 2012, a decision to only fly the Union Jack on designated days at Belfast City Hall led to protests and riots.

5. Chirot and McCauley (2006) and Fiske and Rai (2015) are two notable exceptions.

individuals who follow externally imposed obligations are usually influenced by both value-rational and instrumental-rational motives: They simultaneously support values and beliefs and want to avoid sanctions. Similarly, individuals impose obligations on others for different combinations of value-rational motives (concern for community) and instrumental motives (personal gain).

Whereas externally enforced obligations overlap with instrumental motives, self-imposed obligations and emotional motives commonly coincide with and reinforce one another. Self-imposed obligations promote action when actors willingly act in ways to protect what they value or believe. When beliefs and values are threatened, however, people holding these values commonly experience anger and fear, and both obligations and emotions contribute to action in such instances. For example, when an ethnic community is threatened by another ethnicity, obligations push people to willingly participate in ethnic violence in order to protect their ethnicity, but communal threats also spark emotional prejudice. Such a combination of obligation and emotion can be a potent motivational force, as obligations legitimize violence and give it a righteous character whereas emotional prejudice inspires people to act on obligations. When combined in this way, obligations and emotional prejudice promote a righteous rage.

One type of obligation is particularly relevant to discussions of ethnic violence, and I refer to it as an *ethnic obligation*. Ethnic obligations direct coethnics to act in ways that are intended to protect the well-being of their ethnicity. Individuals act on ethnic obligations when they have a strong attachment to their ethnicity and value the well-being of their community, which makes ethnic obligations highly dependent on ethnic consciousness. People generally gain an ethnic consciousness through socialization, with parents, peers, and communal authorities emphasizing the importance of ethnicity. Nationalism and other ethnic ideologies commonly play important roles in this process, as they extol the virtues of ethnicity and emphasize the duty to make personal sacrifices for the well-being of ethnicity. While ethnic ideologies make people more willing to follow ethnic obligations, they also strengthen externally imposed obligations by inspiring some to impose obligations on others and by legitimizing sanctions that enforce obligations.

Ethnic obligations can be sanctioned by a variety of actors, including family, peers, religious authorities, ethnic leaders, and politicians. Much of the literature on ethnic violence focuses on the latter two, considering how ethnic and political elites motivate and mobilize ethnic violence by demanding that their constituencies act on ethnic obligations. As ethnic authorities, in turn, people view such demands as legitimate and are therefore more willing to act on obligations. Along these lines, the famous Milgram experiments highlight how normal people willingly follow orders from legitimate authority figures and inflict severe physical punishment on people they neither know nor dislike (Milgram 1974).

Although elites use ethnic obligations to mobilize people to participate in ethnic violence, family and peers are also influential in this regard. In fact, studies in psychology and sociology offer evidence that participants in collective violence are most willing to put their own lives in jeopardy when they feel a sense of duty to their loved ones and cocombatants (Collins 2008; Kalyvas 2006; Malešević 2013; Mann 2005; McCauley 1995). These more personal obligations are rarely ethnic obligations but commonly depend on and interact with ethnic obligations. For example, family members can pressure people to act on ethnic obligations, and a sense of obligation to family can push people to follow ethnic obligations to avoid dishonoring their families. Moreover, ethnic obligations commonly push people to join ethnic organizations, but obligations to and pressure from members of these ethnic organizations might have a greater impact on actual participation in ethnic violence than would obligations to ethnicity.

Despite the omnipresence and naturalness of obligations, ethnic obligations are relatively new and linked to modernity. Most importantly, ethnic obligations depend on ethnic consciousness. Indeed, individuals who see the world through ethnic lenses and have a strong attachment to their ethnicity feel a greater obligation to protect the well-being of their ethnicity and are more responsive to communal sanctions. Moreover, modernity promotes nationalism and other ethnic ideologies, and both play an important role in popularizing ethnic obligations.

As noted in chapter 3, modern mass education commonly introduces nationalist ideologies that impress upon students their *duty* to serve the nation at any price. Nationalist literatures also strengthen feelings of moral obligation, with patriotic novels and journalistic accounts of people making heroic sacrifices for the well-being of the community. The central message of Augustine Fouillée's *La Tour de la France par Deux Enfants* (described in chapter 4), for example, is the importance of duty to homeland. Since the rise of the nation-state model, in turn, states have used a variety of means to popularize nationalist ideologies and instill patriotism and a sense of duty on their citizens. Notably, state efforts to cultivate a sense of obligation toward national community are evident before modernity. As quoted in chapter 4, Cicero tried to inculcate a sense of obligation to the state among citizens more than two thousand years ago. What is new with modernity is both the size of the national community as well as the varied means through which the modern state and other actors create a sense of obligation toward the nation and impose these obligations on the public.

While states instill a sense of obligation that some people willingly accept, the modern state is also able to penetrate social relations, regulate society, and coordinate complex collective action through the use of bureaucratic organizations and communication and transportation technologies. As a result, the modern state possesses the coercive ability to force citizens to follow their national obligations. By themselves, such state-imposed obligations are an effective way of forcing people to protect the community, but they are much more effective at motivating ethnic violence when state pressure to act on obligations is backed by a personal sense of duty to community. This helps to explain why state officials make such an effort to extol the virtues of honor, loyalty, and duty and to honor national heroes who exemplify such qualities. It also helps to explain why states began to offer their citizens more and more valuable resources, usually beginning with those who risked the most in service to the state: soldiers.

Emotional Prejudice and Ethnic Obligations in Action

So far this chapter has described how emotional prejudice and ethnic obligations are influential motivators of ethnic violence, and it has considered how modern social environments increase the presence and strength of both. At this point, it is helpful to explore the impact of emotions and obligations on ethnic violence in particular cases. Genocidal violence in Germany and Rwanda offer two examples.

Emotions and Obligations in the German Genocide

At the time Germany unified in 1871, German nationalism was hardly universally accepted among German-speaking peoples, with Prussian elites and intellectuals being the most nationalistic and facing stiff and often violent resistance to their unification efforts (Greenfeld 1992). After unification, however, the German state actively promoted a German national consciousness and proved very successful at spreading nationalism throughout the population. Indeed, Eugen Weber's (1976) description of state-led nation building in France is applicable to Germany even though civil societal actors played a more important role popularizing nationalism in Germany (Mosse 1975). And while the state and civil society were promoting German nationalism, an extremely competitive international environment facilitated their task by clarifying just what the German nation was and giving the German state and civil society reason to mobilize nationalist sentiments.

A particularly powerful form of German nationalism emerged at this time. As described in chapter 3, education, literature, the arts, and patriotic societies played an important role in strengthening and spreading a German nationalist ideology. As with any nationalist ideology, German political elites had to define what it meant to be German and delineate the origins of the great German nation. For this, they pieced together a myth-symbol complex. The myth of Hermann (also known as Arminius) came to represent the birth of the German nation (Kösters 2009; Mosse 1975). Hermann was a leader of a Germanic tribe who joined forces with other tribes and led a rebellion that successfully defeated three Roman legions in 9 AD. According to the myth, this victory convinced Rome to abandon plans to turn present-day Germany into a Roman province and thereby gave birth to Charlemagne's great Frankish Empire, followed by the German Holy Roman Empire. To give an idea of the importance placed on Hermann within the myth-symbol complex, more than fifty major operas and plays were written on Hermann during the eighteenth and nineteenth centuries. An enormous two-hundred-foot-tall statue of Hermann was also constructed in the mid-nineteenth century. At this time, Hermann came to epitomize the strength of a nation striving to be united, free, and powerful (Bland 2013).

In addition to describing the origins of the German nation, the myth-symbol complex also provided symbols representing the German community, such as oak branches, flames, and flags. For symbols to represent the community, however, German myth-symbol complexes also needed to delineate who was part of the German nation. There were two important bases of membership: language and race. Language was a vital element of the German Romantic movement and is linked to three main figures—Johann Gottfried Herder, Wilhelm von Humboldt, and Johann Gottlieb Fichte. Herder famously equated nation with language when he asked, "Has a nation anything more precious than the language of its fathers?" and described it as the collective treasure of the nation (Oakes 2001, 23). Humboldt (1999, 54) saw language as the spirit of humanity, or, as he put it, "spiritual exhalation" and "the formative organ of thought." Fichte (2008) had similar thoughts and claimed that the German language—and therefore the German nation—was superior because it was pure and did not adopt foreign elements, suggesting that foreign influence maligned the spirit of real, primordial nations.

The German myth-symbol complex's emphasis on race emerged later and highlights the mutability of myth-symbol complexes. It was influenced by the *volkisch* movement, which was inspired by Herder, Fichte, and others (Mosse 1964). This movement was a reaction to major social transformations occurring in nineteenth-century Germany and sought a return to the land. It also celebrated the German community, as *volk* translates best into ethnicity, with overtones of nation and race. As part of the latter, the movement celebrated German folklore and mythology and conceptualized Germans as having a particular origin and history. In effect, one was born German; one could not become German. By the late nineteenth century, the growing popularity of Darwinism reinforced the racial component of *volkisch* thinking and influenced the emergence and growing popularity of eugenics in Germany. With eugenics, the terminology changed from the "German people" to the "Aryan race." Similar to *volkisch* thought, the Aryan race was described as superior yet under threat, which prompted demands to limit reproduction by "inferior" races and the mentally disabled. The Nazis ultimately implemented these ideas. While their efforts to eliminate racial minorities is well-known, their active efforts to sterilize and exterminate disabled "Aryans" is less known but was carried out with equal vigor, with some 200,000 Germans killed through the T-4 euthanasia program between 1940 and 1945.

In addition to making sense of the German nation, the myth-symbol complex pinpointed Others as threats to the glorious German nation. Of all communities, Jews had a central place in the myth-symbol complex, and this helps explain why German nationalism went hand-in-hand with anti-Semitism. Different factors underlay the negative portrayal of Jews in the German myth-symbol complex. For one, Jews were commonly blamed for the death of Jesus, and the German nation was perceived as purely Christian. In addition, legal restrictions had historically prevented Jews from owning land, which effectively kept them from being agriculturalists and pushed them to live in urban areas where many were active in money lending and modern industry. These economic characteristics made Jews a despised target of the *volkisch* movement, which depicted tilling the soil as inherently German and vilified modern urban lifestyles as a force destroying the great German nation. The *volkisch* movement therefore commonly used Jews to symbolize the modern evils it feared and hated.

With the development of a German national consciousness, Germans were more likely to view the world through nationalist lenses and to pay attention to national well-being and grievances. The German defeat in the First World War and the devastating economic crisis that followed caused enormous grievances, both individual and national. The national grievances were a great cause of concern among those Germans with an ethnic consciousness, and they sparked intense emotions, especially anger over hardship and fear over the apparent decline of Germany.

The myth-symbol complex, in turn, helped heighten these emotions and provided Hitler and other Nazi leaders with resources that could be used to recruit and mobilize followers. Hitler clearly recognized the power of myths and symbols and manipulated them skillfully. Seeing how Hitler manipulated symbols to mobilize the German population, psychologist Max Lerner claimed, "The power of these symbols is enormous. Men possess thoughts, but symbols possess men" (Kertzer 1988, 5). Hitler was able to draw on the myth of Hermann to describe how Germans came together to defeat a powerful foreign adversary to form the

First German Reich, and he made emotional appeals to overcome the military defeat that destroyed the Second German Reich and establish the Third and greatest German Reich. Of greater importance to this discussion, Hitler was able to exploit the anti-Semitic elements of the myth-symbol complex to scapegoat Jews as both a threat and a source of German national hardship. The position of Jews within the myth-symbol complex helped the Nazis rally many Germans behind their anti-Semitic declarations and policies. As sociologist Michael Mann (2005, 190) notes, however, popular anti-Semitism in Germany was less powerful during the Weimar period than at the turn of the twentieth century. Influenced by earlier discrimination, many German Jews assimilated and married non-Jews, thereby becoming less visible. Between 1926 and 1930, for example, nearly a quarter of Prussian marriages involving at least one Jew were intermarriages (Lowenstein 2005, 25). In this way, Hitler and other Nazi officials skillfully manipulated a pre-existing myth-symbol complex to reinvigorate anti-Semitism.

Emotions were therefore a powerful motivator of anti-Semitic violence, but they were not the only motive. Some supported and participated in anti-Semitic violence for instrumental reasons, such as doctors who stood to gain from removing Jews from the profession and gaining occupational opportunities for joining the Nazi Party. Yet the instrumental motive was commonly combined with emotional prejudice, with two motives being more powerful than one, such as doctors who were anti-Semitic and stood to gain from Nazi policies.

Obligation also motivated many Germans to support and participate in anti-Semitic violence. Because of the rampant patriotism that was present in the powerful nationalist ideology and was taught in schools, many Germans felt a moral obligation to protect the well-being of the German nation. And because Jews were scapegoated as the cause of national problems, many Germans felt obliged to help their nation defeat an officially designated enemy. Of equal importance, the German state and other actors pressured many people to fulfill their obligations to the nation. This included people like SS Lieutenant Colonel Adolf Eichmann, whom Hannah Arendt (2006) famously described as dutifully following orders.

Although many Germans undoubtedly participated in anti-Semitic violence simply because they followed obligatory orders, emotions commonly reinforced such obligations. David Cesarani (2004) and Bettina Stangneth (2014), for example, offer strong evidence that Eichmann was extremely anti-Semitic and far from an innocent cog in the Nazi machine. Similarly, Michael Mann (2005) describes how those Nazis who were involved in the genocidal killings were driven by a nationalist ideology wedded with imperialism and anti-Semitism. In this way, following orders to implement a policy of ethnic annihilation seems to require more than disinterest and a willingness to follow orders; some degree of emotional prejudice against the people who are supposed to die is also help-ful. More generally, ethnic obligations and emotional prejudice reinforce one another, as obligations legitimize violence and emotional prejudice increases one's willingness to accept violent obligations.

Overall, the case of Germany in the late nineteenth and early twentieth cen-turies highlights how emotional prejudice and ethnic obligations contributed to ethnic violence against Jews. The case shows how a German national conscious-ness created a great concern for the well-being of the nation and how German nationalism obliged people to protect the German nation. When combined with anti-Semitic components of the myth-symbol complex and extreme national hardship, they inspired a virulent nationalist emotional effervescence that tar-geted Jews and imposed obligations on the population to deal with the Jewish "menace."

Emotional Prejudice, Ethnic Obligations, and the Rwandan Genocide

The Rwandan genocide differed from the German genocide in that many more civilians—as many as 200,0000—actively participated in the killings (Straus 2004). Indeed, instead of having a bureaucratic machine to implement genocide, most killings were committed by civilians wielding machetes and axes. Despite this difference, emotional prejudice and ethnic obligations were also dominant motives of ethnic violence in Rwanda.

The emotional prejudice and ethnic obligations that motivated the Rwandan genocide depended on ethnic consciousness and a myth-symbol complex that vilified Tutsis, both of which emerged during the colonial period (see chapter 5). An ethnic consciousness made Hutus concerned about the well-being of their ethnicity, and a myth-symbol complex intensified emotional prejudice by depict-ing Tutsis as vile invaders who exploited Hutus and endangered the well-being of the "real" Rwandan nation (Kaufman 2015; Mamdani 2001; Mann 2005; Straus 2004). The main mobilizers of the violence—state officials, the military, and Hutu militias—manipulated the myth-symbol complex in constant propa-ganda to dehumanize Tutsis and increase antipathy against them. Such xeno-phobic hatred was particularly strong among Hutu militia members, and the influence of this emotion cannot be downplayed because of the central role the militias played in organizing and disseminating the violence. Among civilians, however, two conditions limited the prejudicial hatred of Tutsis. First, ethnic boundaries became increasingly porous in Rwanda during the decades leading up to the genocide, as Tutsis and Hutus shared the same culture, practiced the same religions, lived amongst one another, and frequently intermarried. As a consequence, many Hutus did not pay much attention to ethnic difference (even if they knew the ethnicities of their acquaintances and had prejudicial views against Tutsis). Second, discriminatory policies severely constrained the power and mobility of Tutsis, meaning that ethnic comparisons did not increase resentment among Hutus.

Instead of hatred and resentment, Scott Straus (2004) finds that fear and anger were the main emotions pushing most Hutus to participate in the killings. Fear was caused by the precarious positions in which many Hutus found themselves and the role some Tutsis played in this precariousness: The Tutsi-led Rwandan Patriotic Front instigated a civil war in 1990 and sought to replace Hutu rule with a Tutsi-controlled state (Mann 2005; Straus 2004). The dominant myth-symbol complex, in turn, suggested that Tutsi rule would not only return illegitimate "foreigners" to power but would also result in the enslavement of Hutus, and state propaganda emphasized these elements of the myth-symbol complex (Kaufman 2015). In this context, many Hutus feared their Tutsi neighbors as a third column aiding Tutsi militants. Anger, in turn, contributed to the outburst of genocidal violence. The violence erupted shortly after the president of Rwanda was assassinated, which outraged a large number of Hutus, who then blamed Tutsis for his death.

Ethnic obligations were also a dominant motive in the violence, as the Rwandan state obliged many civilians to participate in killing of Tutsis. Although imposed by state actors, ethnic obligations played out in different ways in different places, with the military, militia members, local officials, family, and peers all pressuring Hutus to act on obligations (Fujii 2009; Straus 2004). Most civilian participants followed obligations because they were imposed by a legitimate state during a time of war and because emotional prejudice made ethnic obligations more acceptable. Some participants also followed obligations because they stood to gain economically by killing their Tutsi neighbors. Finally, the extreme sanctions that the militias meted out against Hutus who refused to participate—including death—convinced many to accept obligations.

7

STATES AND ETHNIC VIOLENCE
Containing Violence or Instigating Unrest?

Although Thomas Hobbes and Jean-Jacques Rousseau were both founding figures of liberal philosophy, they had starkly opposing views of both the state of nature and the nature of states. Hobbes believed that humans are base and violent
and that states are needed to suppress our ugly natures. Rousseau saw our state
of nature as true freedom and believed that states debase and entrap us. Thus
Hobbes saw humans as bad and states as a basis of good, whereas Rousseau saw
the state of nature as the basis of good and states as a source of evil.

Most contemporary sociologists believe both Hobbes and Rousseau make
valid points, as states can be a source of either good or bad. This dual and contradictory character is apparent with ethnic violence. Peaceful regions usually
have states that actively obstruct ethnic violence. Places with large-scale ethnic
violence, on the other hand, usually have states that are either actively involved
in the violence, are implicated in the violence through their failure to contain it,
or spark violence through discriminatory policies. In this way, states can either
promote or deter ethnic violence, and differences in states go a long way in explaining why some places are at greater risk of ethnic violence (Goodwin 2005;
Lange and Balian 2008; Wimmer 2013b).

State Effects on Ethnic Violence

States can promote ethnic violence in a variety of ways. In the most extreme
cases, states actively commit ethnic atrocities. Indeed, many of the most ghastly
episodes of ethnic violence—including nearly all genocides and many ethnic civil

wars—have resulted from state-led attacks on ethnic Others. For example, the German state was the main actor orchestrating genocidal acts against Jews, and the Rwandan state played a central role in the genocidal violence suffered by Tutsis. In these and other episodes of extreme violence, soldiers and police officers sometimes act alone and sometimes cooperate with civilians.

States can also contribute to ethnic violence without directly participating in the killings. State officials sometimes encourage civilians to engage in violence by proclaiming communal rivals enemies of the state and asking citizens to take up arms against them. For this, officials commonly draw on myth-symbol complexes and employ ritual gatherings, both of which intensify emotional prejudice. More than encouragement, states sometimes provide civilian supporters with valuable resources that facilitate violence. For example, states sometimes arm civilians and give them important information that allows them to attack communal rivals with greater efficiency, such as when the Sri Lankan state furnished Sinhalese militants with the addresses of Tamils. Finally, as discussed in the previous chapter, states commonly impose obligations on their populations and use a combination of sticks and carrots to cajole people into participating in ethnic violence against designated enemies.

States can also contribute to ethnic violence in a third, more indirect way. When states are ethnicized, they commonly implement discriminatory policies that negatively affect ethnic rivals. Such discrimination can push subordinate ethnic communities to use violence against either the state, the dominant ethnic community, or both (Wimmer 2013b).

One example showing all types of state involvement is the Rwandan genocide. Most directly, the Rwandan military and militias with close ties to the state instigated the violence and killed many people. Members of the Rwandan state also incited violence by decrying Tutsis as a national menace and encouraging Hutu civilians to take up arms against them. In fact, the state provided civilians with arms to fight Tutsis, gave civilian militias lists of Tutsis, and actively organized and coordinated civilian violence. Thus, while Rwandan civilians committed the majority of the murders, the state influenced civilian participation by prodding, instructing, equipping, obliging, and setting an example. Finally, the postcolonial Rwandan state had discriminated greatly against Tutsis, and this discrimination contributed to antistate violence led by exiled Tutsis. This antistate movement not only promoted an ethnic civil war but was the most important factor contributing to the genocide.

In addition to their direct and indirect effects, states also contribute to ethnic violence through their inaction, with some states creating openings that allow civilians to mobilize ethnic violence. In India, for example, Hindu police officers have frequently watched ethnic violence without lifting a finger to stop it because the perpetrators were from their own community and the victims were Others. Yet ethnic violence does not necessarily require such a gaping political opening. Instead, hesitant and light-handed initial responses to violence can be enough to allow the mobilization of ethnic violence. Violence in Assam offers one example.

Assam is a state in northeast India that has experienced several bouts of ethnic violence over the past half-century, all of which have involved violence between ethnic Assamese and different minority communities. The worst violence occurred between 1979 and 1982, when a social movement attempting to remove Bangladeshis from the voting list eventually led to widespread violence that cost thousands of lives. The movement received tacit support from powerful actors. Most importantly, most politicians, government employees, and police were ethnic Assamese, and the movement pushed the regional state to look out for Assamese interests. The regional state therefore acknowledged the movement's grievances and gave it considerable room to maneuver. Although this support did not prevent the regional state from trying to stop violence against minorities once it erupted, the state had created an opening for the violence to occur, and its efforts to contain the violence were belated, haphazard, and lenient.

As the Rwandan and Assamese cases highlight, states that contribute to ethnic violence through their actions and inactions are usually ethnicized, controlled by and serving the interests of one or more ethnic communities above all others. When states are ethnicized, only individuals from particular ethnic communities are allowed to hold high-level positions. Highly ethnicized states also treat civilians differently depending on ethnicity, with members of certain ethnic communities having superior access to public goods and services. Political scientists Raphaël Franck and Ilia Rainer (2012), for instance, analyze eighteen countries in sub-Saharan Africa and find that the education and health of ethnic communities were strongly affected by changes in the ethnicity of the state leaders, with health and education improving when a member of one's ethnic community comes to power. Of greatest interest to this chapter, highly ethnicized states commonly orchestrate ethnic violence, encourage ethnic violence, provide civilians with resources for ethnic violence, leave gaping openings for ethnic violence to occur, and spark violent backlashes by excluded minorities (Gurr 1993; Horowitz 1985; Lange 2012; Sambanis 2001; Wimmer 2013b).

It is difficult to say just how many states are ethnicized, but formal political discrimination against minority communities offers some insight. Based on data from the Minorities at Risk (Bennett and Davenport 2003) project, more than 20 percent of all states in the world formally discriminated against at least one ethnic minority throughout the 1990s, and many more states discriminated against ethnic minorities for part of the decade. The Ethnic Power Relations dataset offers additional insight into the extent to which states are communalized. It finds that, on average, nearly two-thirds of the world's ethnic communities were excluded from political power between 1946 and 2005 (Wimmer 2013b, 264).

While ethnicized states are popularly berated as discriminatory, they usually conform to the nation-state model, which remains the dominant model of the state in the world today. The nation-state model suggests that all people should have self-rule, with the state controlled by and for the nation. Nothing seems more natural or more normal than this. As described in chapter 5, however, this model is difficult to attain when states control ethnically diverse populations. In such cases, communities commonly compete to control the state, and this struggle produces ethnicized states and ethnic violence. And failure to attain the nation-state model provokes powerful emotions that target entire communities of Others. Along these lines, sociologist Michael Mann (2005) notes that the rise of the nation-state model, which is linked to democratic self-rule, has contributed directly to several episodes of genocide. Similarly, sociologist Andreas Wimmer (2013b) finds that the global proliferation of the nation-state model has promoted political exclusion and discrimination and thus violence and warfare. The rise of the nation-state model and the ethnicized states that result from it are therefore important historical determinants of ethnic violence.

Ethnic violence in Sri Lanka clearly highlights how ethnicized states contribute to ethnic violence (de Silva 1986; Lange 2012; Tambiah 1986). Seventy-five percent of Sri Lankans are ethnic Sinhalese, and Tamils are the largest minority community. After colonial independence in 1948, Sinhalese politicians gained control of the state and promptly ethnicized it. Most notably, state officials proclaimed Sinhalese the sole national language and Buddhism the official state religion, thereby symbolically excluding Tamils—who speak Tamil and are overwhelmingly Hindu—from the nation. Tamils strongly and openly opposed the policies, and many Sinhalese viewed Tamil opposition as an affront to the Sinhalese nation. The resulting resentment pushed some Sinhalese to attack Tamils. In addition to provoking rigorous Tamil opposition to discriminatory policies, the ethnicized state contributed to violence in two additional ways: The state's discriminatory nationalist policies both inspired and legitimized anti-Tamil violence, and its support for anti-Tamil violence created a gaping opening. And because of this exclusion, discrimination, and violence, many Tamils concluded it was necessary to establish their own state and subsequently began a secessionist civil war that lasted from 1983 until 2010 and killed approximately 100,000 people.

While the ethnicization of states is the most important factor explaining why some states promote ethnic violence, nonethnicized states can also contribute to ethnic violence. This situation is most common when states are highly ineffective and unable to mobilize their resources in ways that limit openings for ethnic violence. At an extreme, states break down and leave a political vacuum that offers an extremely fertile environment for ethnic violence. Eastern Europe during the Second World War clearly highlights how state breakdown creates a gaping opening for ethnic violence.

The Second World War was extremely destructive and commonly left large swaths of territory without any functioning state whatsoever. During this period of statelessness or near-statelessness, ethnic violence erupted in several locations (Lowe 2012). Lithuanians attacked Jews, Czechs killed Germans, and Croatians and Serbs butchered one another. Violence between Ukrainians, Poles, and Jews living in the borderlands between Poland and Ukraine offers one of the most horrific examples and shows how a political vacuum—in combination with competing nationalisms—promoted deadly ethnic violence. Even before the Nazis invaded Poland, Germans had contacted the Organization of Ukrainian Nationalists (OUN), asking for support in return for Ukrainian independence. OUN accepted this proposition and subsequently collaborated with the Nazis. Most notably, they helped the Nazis exterminate some 200,000 Jews and, in so doing, learned techniques for slaughtering civilians. When Nazi power in the area began to wane in late 1942, the OUN stopped collaborating with the Nazis and formed their own army, the Ukrainian Insurgent Army. In their continued effort to create a homogeneous Ukrainian nation-state and in the absence of any state, the OUN slaughtered most of the region's remaining Jews as well as ethnic Poles, killing an estimated 90,000 men, women, and children. In response, local Poles organized their own militias and massacred some 20,000 Ukrainian civilians (Lowe 2012, 215–19). After the war, the OUN attacked ethnic Russians and fought against the incorporation of the Ukraine into the Soviet Union, a struggle that polarized Ukrainian-speaking and Russian-speaking Ukrainians and provided historical fodder that contributed to the civil war in the Ukraine in 2014.

Along with Eastern Europe, state collapse during the Second World War also contributed to severe ethnic violence in several European colonies in Asia that were conquered by the Japanese, including Burma, Indonesia, and Malaysia. Ethnic violence in Syria and Iraq offers a more contemporary example linking state breakdown to ethnic violence. With the Syrian civil war, the al-Assad government lost control of large parts of Syria. Similarly, the American invasion of Iraq promoted a civil war and state failure. ISIS militants, in turn, were able to take advantage of the resulting political vacuum to attack religious and ethnic minorities.

States and Variation in Ethnic Violence: Assam vs. Kerala

After reviewing the different ways in which states can promote ethnic violence, and after describing how both the ethnicization of states and state effectiveness help explain why some states contribute to ethnic violence more than others, this section highlights and clarifies the main points through a comparative analysis of ethnic violence in two Indian regions: Assam and Kerala. As described previously, Assam has had several incidents of severe ethnic violence, but Kerala has had relatively peaceful ethnic relations. The relative peace of the latter is surprising because ethnic violence in India is overwhelmingly religious in orientation and Kerala has the most religiously diverse population on the subcontinent, with large populations of Hindus, Muslims, and Christians.

One of the most important factors limiting ethnic violence in Kerala is the absence of openings for ethnic violence. In his analysis of ethnic violence in India, political scientist Steven Wilkinson (2004) finds that state officials in Kerala actively and effectively contain ethnic violence, and deaths resulting from ethnic violence are therefore relatively rare. This finding, however, leads to an even more important question: Why has the Keralan state closed political openings for ethnic violence so tightly?

One reason is that the regional state has the means to do so. Many recognize that Kerala has an extremely effective regional state that has consistently enforced the highest level of rule of law in India and contributed to impressive human development (Debroy, Bhandari, and Banik 2003; Heller 1999, 83–84; Sandbrook et al. 2007). And because of its impressive organizational capacity, the state was able to contain ethnic violence. Yet high state capacity can be used to orchestrate ethnic violence, pointing to a second reason for the Keralan state's successful containment of ethnic violence: State officials wanted to stop violence.

A number of factors push Kerala's politicians and officials to willingly contain ethnic violence. For one, coalitions of parties representing diverse constituencies have controlled postcolonial governments in Kerala because no party has been able to win a majority (Wilkinson 2004). As a result, the governments have not pursued the interests of any one ethnic community, thereby limiting state ethnicization. A number of panethnic movements have also helped to limit ethnicized politics. Most notably, labor, caste, and anticolonial movements kick-started the process of class formation during the first half of the twentieth century, and class—not ethnicity—has been the dominant cleavage in Keralan politics ever since (Heller 1999; Sandbrook et al. 2007, 77–78). These panethnic movements, in turn, reinforced a pre-existing Keralan consciousness based on shared language, history, and region; political scientist Prerna Singh (2011) finds that this overarching consciousness has restrained violent ethnic mobilization.

Assam contrasts starkly with Kerala in these ways. Whereas class divisions have historically been more salient than ethnic divisions in Kerala, ethnicity dominates politics in Assam, and the Assamese state is highly ethnicized. Because of this difference, the state in Kerala is more inclusive, with all communities having access to the formal political arena and being protected by the state, but in Assam non-Assamese have much more limited access to the state and receive more limited protection.

As mentioned previously, however, the Assamese state has tried to limit ethnic violence against minorities. In addition to being limited and belated, these efforts were unsuccessful because the Assamese state is much less effective than its counterpart in Kerala. Two factors have limited state effectiveness in Assam. First, as Max Weber (1968 [1921]) famously notes, high levels of bureaucratization increase the state's ability to implement policies as complex as containing ethnic violence. And whereas Kerala has among the most bureaucratic and effective regional states in India, those in Assam are among the least effective. Although bureaucracy presently has several negative connotations, bureaucracy is an amazing organizational technology that allows a number of separate actors to act as a corporately coherent entity to complete complex tasks that no individual—no matter how Herculean—could possibly accomplish. Bureaucracy is particularly good at this because it creates a clear chain of command, places power in positions rather than in people, and monitors actors, all of which make possible the simultaneous coordination of many actors. Alternatively, nonbureaucratic forms of organization tend to concentrate power in individuals, which makes it difficult to coordinate and monitor state actors.

A second characteristic that affects a state's capacity to limit ethnic violence is infrastructural power, a concept introduced by sociologist Michael Mann (1984) that refers to the physical presence of state infrastructure throughout the territory. State infrastructural power affects the likelihood of ethnic violence for the simple reason that states with a greater physical presence are more likely to perceive ethnic violence in its early phases. In fact, state leaders might even see a growing risk of ethnic violence and step in before it begins. States that leave large swaths of territory unmonitored, on the other hand, have a difficult time stopping ethnic violence before it gets out of control. In Assam, we see a situation where the state has a weak presence in large swaths of territory, whereas the Keralan state has a strong presence throughout nearly all its territory. The greater infrastructural power of the Keralan state is the result of its larger size and greater effectiveness. In addition, the Keralan population is dense and evenly spread throughout a relatively small territory (thirty-three million people in a region the size of Switzerland), and this particular human geography facilitates the expansion of state infrastructural power. Assam, on the other hand, is an oddly shaped territory with many mountains and forests, all of which—in combination with the state's limited organizational capacity—limit the presence and reach of the state.

The Resources Behind Ethnic Violence

Ethnic violence is most common in places with highly ethnicized states because ethnicized states are most likely to either use their enormous resources to mobilize ethnic violence, leave openings for coethnic civilians to mobilize ethnic violence, or both. Ethnic violence is also common in places with highly ineffective states, as this leaves political openings for ethnic violence even when states oppose it. That being said, violence remains possible in places with functioning states that are not ethnicized. Such conditions require that the perpetrators of ethnic violence possess strong motivation and, especially, extensive and diverse mobilizational resources that allow them to avoid state efforts to stymie their actions and mobilize others to participate.

The sociological literature on social movements pays considerable attention to mobilizational resources and notes that five main types of resources are vital to any sort of collective movement, be it violent or nonviolent: organizational, communication, material, human, and cultural resources (Jenkins 1983; McCarthy and Zald 1977). As their name implies, organizational resources include various types of organizations and associations, ranging from book clubs to political parties to unions. Such resources offer pre-existing structures that can be used to engage actors in the movement, make collective decisions, and coordinate actors. Communication resources include all technologies that allow participants to disseminate information. Such information is vital to movements because it makes possible the coordination of activities, helps inform participants about potential dangers facing the movement, and facilitates recruitment. Material resources include the funds and physical goods used to mobilize movements. Monetary resources are an obvious example, as movements require funds for a variety of activities, ranging from paying for participants' food and transportation to bailing incarcerated participants out of jail. Another example is an office or house that offers a safe place for movement participants to meet, strategize, coordinate their activities, or hide. Human resources are the fourth type of mobilizational resource. Simply put, the number of people at the disposal of movement leaders and the skills and the experience of movement participants affect the ability of movement leaders to organize a large collective movement. Finally, cultural resources affect movement mobilization. Cultural resources help frame movements in ways that attract participants and increase public support. For example, the myth-symbol complexes described in chapter 6 are commonly employed by movement leaders to increase popular support and participation.

There are many sources of mobilizational resources, but ethnicized organizations are usually the most important means of mobilizing violent ethnic movements. This is because ethnicized organizations focus on ethnic issues and offer organizational, communication, material, human, and cultural resources. Not surprisingly, then, ethnic violence is usually committed by ethnic organizations, not by ethnic communities (Brubaker 2004; Weinstein 2007; Sinno 2008). The ultimate ethnic organization is an ethnicized state, and the enormous mobilizational resources at the disposal of most states make them mobilizers of ethnic violence par excellence. Although less effective, nonstate organizations can also mobilize ethnic violence and are especially important when states either fail to organize ethnic violence or constrain mobilizational openings. These nonstate ethnic organizations are usually organizations that have represented ethnicities and pursued communal interests in different ways prior to their active role in mobilizing ethnic movements. They include religious, political, literary, and educational associations and organizations.

Another look at Assam helps highlight how ethnic organizations can mobilize large-scale ethnic violence. As described previously, ethnic Assamese mobilized several movements during the 1960s, 1970s, and 1980s in an effort to improve the well-being of Assamese relative to other ethnic minorities. Although these movements always started peacefully and pursued change by pressuring government, movement tactics inevitably intensified and became increasingly aggressive and confrontational, and some movement participants instigated violent outbreaks by attacking members of rival ethnicities.

The Assamese state supported key elements of Assamese nationalism that promoted the violent movements, but it was opposed to ethnic violence and therefore did not provide the ethnic movements with mobilizational resources. The violent ethnic movements, in turn, badly needed mobilizational resources to overcome state opposition, which was belated but eventually limited political openings for ethnic violence. The main organization filling this mobilizational need was an educational association that looked out for the economic and political interests of Assamese students: the All Assamese Students Union (AASU) (see Lange 2012).

The AASU has been one of the largest organizations in Assam since its formation half a century ago. Officially, it protects and pursues student interests, regardless of ethnicity. In reality, its members are almost exclusively ethnic Assamese, and the association plays an active role in state-level politics. The AASU pursues an agenda of ethnic nationalism and continuously pushes the state to protect ethnic Assamese interests. Conforming to its name, however, its members are students, primarily at the university level.

The AASU has been the single most important mobilizer of ethnic politics and violence in Assam (Baruah 1986, 1994; Chhabra 1992, 65–69; Dasgupta 1997, 353–54; Deka 1996; Lange 2012; Sarmah 1999, 43). It mobilized the population to make Assamese the sole state language in the early 1960s, to highlight the relatively advantaged economic position of non-Assamese in the late 1960s, to demand that Assamese be the only language of instruction in higher education in the early 1970s, and to expel immigrants in the late 1970s and early 1980s. As one expert notes, "the explosion of micro-nationalist politics in Assam coincided with the founding and consolidation of this organization" (Baruah 1994, 667). Ethnic mobilization over these issues, in turn, caused enormous damage to property and killed thousands of individuals.

AASU members proved capable of coordinating violent ethnic movements because of the powerful mobilizational resources they controlled. Indeed, the AASU—more than any other organization in Assam other than the state—had the organizational capacity to create a broad-based movement. As elsewhere, institutions of higher education in Assam facilitated the organization of movements by bringing thousands of students together. Moreover, the AASU was able to effectively publicize its position both on campus and beyond because it had access to communication technologies and the media. These communication resources proved particularly influential at spreading and heightening emotional prejudice against non-Assamese, and these outcomes helped recruit people into the movement and motivated violence. Most importantly, the AASU had an "extraordinary organizational base" that enabled it to mobilize a large ethnic movement (Baruah 1994, 667). Indeed, its organizational structure was present throughout the state and reached down to most villages, which allowed AASU leaders to mobilize a large and geographically dispersed movement (Chhabra 1992, 66). As one expert describes:

> The AASU has organized a grassroots movement in towns and villages. Every college and high school has its own Students' Union. The 35-member AASU executive body has representatives from seven districts. . . . They have an extremely interesting and effective method of decision making and implementation of decisions. The executive body discusses the strategy, coordinates with AAGSP [Assam Popular Struggle Association, a political party with strong ties to the AASU] and passes the decisions on to local leaders for implementation. (Das 1982, 66)

One of the AASU's mobilizational resources played a particularly influential and direct role in the most deadly episode of ethnic violence in Assam. The Sweccha Sevak Bahini (SSB) was a paramilitary force organized by the AASU in 1980 to identify foreigners, and it had as many as fifteen thousand volunteers throughout Assam during the Assam Movement (Ahmad 1984). As one source notes, "SSB men are trained . . . to organize a sustained underground movement, to operate firearms, to plan and conduct raids on immigrant areas, to cut off communications to vital spots by burning bridges, snapping telephone lines and setting up road blocks, and to man an efficient communications system that re-lies on squads of 'bicycle telegraph' men who carry SSB and AASU diktats to the remotest villages" (Ahmad 1984, 137).

Although students controlled most of the resources used to mobilize violent ethnic movements in Assam, many nonstudents also participated in the violence. Poor farmers from small villages, for example, were the main perpetrators of the Nellie massacre, which occurred during the Assam Movement and killed as many as two thousand Bangladeshi immigrants (Ahmad 1984, 66; Kimura 2003, 231–32). Yet without the AASU's mobilizational efforts, acts of violence commit-ted by nonstudents likely would not have occurred at all, as the AASU strength-ened emotional motivation by framing Others as threats, provided an opening for anyone to address their grievances, and sought to engage nonstudents in their movement.

Modernity, States, and Ethnic Violence

The previous sections of this chapter focus on how states affect ethnic violence in two basic and important ways. First, ethnic violence involves collective action and must be mobilized, and states affect whether mobilizational resources can be effectively employed to organize ethnic violence. Some states use their own powerful mobilizational resources to kill ethnic rivals, other states provide civil-ians with mobilizational resources and oblige them to attack rival communities, and still other states try to limit the mobilizational resources of ethnic extrem-ists in an effort to contain ethnic violence. Second, states affect mobilizational openings, and the latter shape whether civilians are able to use their resources to mobilize ethnic violence. While some states create gaping openings that allow people to mobilize ethnic violence, others constrain the openings, and still others close them tightly.

So what does this say about modernity and its impact on ethnic violence? Ultimately, this chapter offers mixed evidence. Bureaucratic states are a vital and influential component of modernity, and they can either promote or restrain ethnic violence depending on whether they are ethnicized. Notably, states were much less effective—or even absent—during premodern times, which created gaping openings that made violence possible.[1] At the same time, modernity in-creased the mobilizational resources of states (and other organizations) through

---

1. Although other institutions were present and effectively limited openings.

bureaucratization and the expansion of a variety of technologies, and these resources are necessary for large-scale ethnic violence.[2] Most notably, states and
other bureaucratic organizations provide mobilizational resources that have
made possible the worst episodes of ethnic violence the world has ever seen.

Even more importantly than providing these resources, modernity promoted
the nation-state model, which ethnicized states in ways that predisposed state
actors to mobilize ethnic violence. Modernity promoted nation-states through
its effects on ethnic consciousness, as nation-states are nothing more than an ethnically patterned state: State officials perceive ethnicity and designate their own
community as the national community. Similarly, when minorities acquire an
ethnic consciousness, they commonly demand their own ethnicized state; many
violent ethnic organizations focus on this goal.

The vital impact of the nation-state model on ethnic violence cannot be overstated. Nearly all incidents of ethnic violence discussed in this book were influenced by the nation-state model in one way or another. Nazi genocide was
perpetrated to purify the German nation in pursuit of the nation-state ideal.
Hutu extremists in Rwanda viewed Rwanda as a Hutu nation and attempted to
remove "alien" and "dangerous" Tutsis, and Bamars targeted Karens who threatened the well-being and very existence of the Burmese nation-state. In India, we
see repeated violence against Muslims (and increasingly Christians), who are de-
monized because they do not conform to popular ideas of India as a Hindu-based
nation-state. In Assam, the nation-state model was applied to regional states,
with ethnic Assamese viewing themselves as a nation within multinational India
and asserting claims that the Assamese state should be controlled by and look out
for the interests of ethnic Assamese. Even racial violence in the United States is
related to the nation-state: The KKK and other racial extremists are driven by a
belief that whites are the true nation and that all others must be excluded.

Today, the nation-state model is as strong as ever; one might go so far as to describe it as hegemonic. Most people view the nation-state as both natural and desirable, and they possess cognitive frameworks that push them to view the world
in terms of nation-states. Indeed, country and nation-state are usually conflated
and used interchangeably, and people commonly assume that each country has a
unified national population that is ruled by its state. But nation-states are neither

---

2. Bauman (1989) also suggests that bureaucracy, in addition to providing a mobilizational
means, dehumanizes processes in ways that remove moral objections to atrocities. This view is similar
to Arendt's discussion of the "banality of violence" and has been critiqued by others who recognize
that participants in the Holocaust had motives and were not simply unthinking cogs within a bureaucratic machine (Arendt 2006; Cesarani 2004; Joas 2003).

natural nor normal. As described in chapter 4, communal consciousness was very localized until quite recently, and the nation-state model is relatively new. The first states did not try to homogenize their populations and commonly ruled over diverse populations. It was only over the past few centuries with the advent of direct forms of state rule, the rise of national markets, and the spread of mass education that ideas of a shared national community arose and proliferated throughout entire populations. And it was only at this time that the nation-state ideal began to ascend to the hegemonic position that it now has. This nation-state model promoted the ethnicization of states and inspired nationalist ideologies, which contributed to ethnic violence in important ways.

To conclude, we see that modernity promotes some states that are willing and able to prevent ethnic violence and others that are willing and able to incite it. Since modernity promotes both types of states, modernity is linked to ethnic peace and violence. Still, modernity promotes states and other bureaucratic organizations that provide the mobilizational resources needed for large-scale ethnic violence. Moreover, the nation-state model is a central component of modernity, and this model is one of the most powerful motivators and mobilizers of ethnic violence; we cannot understand ethnic violence without it. While recognizing that both the Rousseauian and the Hobbesian views of the state are valuable, the enormous impact of the nation-state model on ethnic violence suggests that modern states are much more Rousseauian than Hobbesian. That being said, the next chapter shows that the Hobbesian view of the state is extremely important and helps us to understand more recent trends in ethnic violence among early modernizers.

8

FROM WORST TO FIRST

Declining Ethnic Violence in Early Modernizers

"Lies, damn lies, and statistics" is one of many well-known phrases attributed to Mark Twain, and it describes how skillful practitioners can manipulate quantitative data to support weak and faulty arguments. Chapter 2 presented a variety of statistics offering evidence that ethnic violence has become increasingly prevalent over the past two hundred years, a finding that supports the revised modernist position and opposes the classic modernist position. Supporters of the classic modernist position might invoke Twain's phrase to refer to these findings, however, and present the same data in a different light to support their position.

Figure 8.1 reuses the data on ethnic civil wars from Figure 2.1 but presents them in a different way: It shows long-term trends in ethnic violence for both early and late modernizers. Importantly, many ethnic wars that occurred outside Europe and North America were instigated by early modernizers and pitted imperialists against colonized peoples, making them a hybrid category. The figure therefore includes "colonial wars" as a third category designating wars between modernizing colonizers and local peoples. The data show that ethnic civil wars were concentrated in Europe and North America until the 1930s and that the remainder of the wars were mostly anticolonial struggles. By the 1950s, however, noncolonial ethnic wars outside Europe and North America had exploded onto the scene. As shown by the black region on the right-hand side of the figure, noncolonial wars among late modernizers became the dominant type of ethnic warfare, constituting more than 90 percent of all ethnic wars during the 1980s and 1990s. Thus early modernizers were involved in most episodes of ethnic warfare until the Second World War but were rarely involved in ethnic warfare

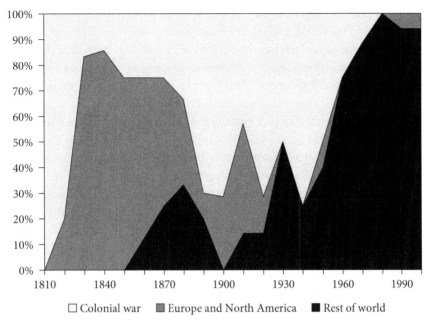

FIGURE 8.1.   Ethnic civil wars by region and type per decade. Source: Wimmer and Min (2006).

afterwards. And at the same time that ethnic violence was declining in the early modernizers, ethnic warfare became much more prevalent in Africa, Asia, and the Middle East.

Since 1950, twenty-two early modernizers located primarily in Western Europe and North America have emerged as global economic and political leaders of the modern world: Australia, Austria, Belgium, Canada, Denmark, Finland, France, Germany, Greece, Ireland, Italy, Japan, Luxembourg, the Netherlands, New Zealand, Norway, Portugal, Spain, Sweden, Switzerland, the United Kingdom, and the United States. A closer look at the data on ethnic violence over the past seventy-five years shows just how peaceful these successful early modernizers have become. Based on the data from Wimmer and Min (2006), only two of the 139 ethnic civil wars that occurred between 1950 and 2009 took place in early modernizers (the Basque secessionist war in Spain and the secessionist war in Northern Ireland), whereas the remaining 144 countries in the world suffered 137 different ethnic civil wars.[1] To put this into perspective, there were only 0.09 ethnic

---

1. These 144 countries include all independent countries with at least 500,000 people in 2013.

civil wars per country among the early modernizers but 0.95 conflicts per country for the rest of the world, making late modernizers more than ten times as likely to suffer an ethnic civil war over the sixty-year period. This discrepancy remains after taking population size into consideration: Averaging data between 1950 and 2009, the early modernizers contained 16.4 percent of the world's population but experienced only 1.4 percent of the world's ethnic civil wars.[2]

The Political Instability Task Force (PITF) (2013), Center for Systemic Peace (CSP) (Marshall 2014), and Minorities at Risk (MAR) (Bennett and Davenport 2003) datasets also show that ethnic violence was relatively rare among early modernizers. The PITF dataset notes eighty ethnic civil wars since the end of the Second World War, and the conflict in Northern Ireland was the only ethnic civil war to occur in any of the twenty-two early modernizers. Thus the early modernizers, which make up 13 percent of the world's countries and 16 percent of the world's population, suffered only 1 percent of the world's ethnic civil wars. The CSP dataset notes 113 cases of armed ethnic warfare after the Second World War, but only two of these occurred in early modernizers.[3] The CSP dataset also provides conservative estimates of the number of deaths caused by ethnic warfare. Given their share of the global population, one would expect the early modernizers to have experienced around 1.3 million deaths from ethnic violence between 1946 and 2013, a figure representing 16 percent of the 7.8 million deaths from ethnic violence that occurred between 1946 and 2013. According to the CSP data, however, only 5,000 people living in early modernizing countries died from ethnic violence, a mere 0.06 percent of the total number of deaths resulting from ethnic violence. The early modernizers therefore had 1/250th the number of deaths from ethnic violence than would have occurred if the deaths had been evenly spread throughout the world's peoples. Clearly, deadly ethnic violence has been a rarity in the early modernizers over the past seventy years, a finding that opposes claims that modernity promotes ethnic violence.[4]

---

2. The figure of 16.4 percent averages the total populations of the twenty-two affluent democracies in 1950, 1955, 1960, 1965, 1970, 1975, 1980, 1985, 1990, 1995, 2000, 2005, and 2010. The data are taken from the World Bank (2014).

3. These two include the conflict in Northern Ireland and violence in Italy over Sardinian secession.

4. The MAR data on ethnic riots and ethnic warfare show similar regional variation, but the data highlight slightly more cases of violence among the early modernizers. For example, MAR finds that thirty-six countries experienced at least one ethnic riot or ethnic war between 2000 and 2006, and two of these were early modernizers. Percentage-wise, 9 percent of early modernizers therefore experienced ethnic violence during this seven-year period, whereas the corresponding figure for the remaining countries was 26 percent. The higher prevalence of ethnic violence among early modernizers—relative to the other datasets—results from MAR's inclusion of low-intensity ethnic

When looking at data over time, the start and end dates can have a large impact on the results, and the cutoff dates of the PITF, CSP, and MAR datasets cause them to miss the long-term patterns evident in the data from Wimmer and Min (2006). This is most definitely the case for the CSP data on deaths from ethnic violence. Whereas nearly all of the 7.8 million people who died from ethnic violence between 1946 and 2013 lived outside Western Europe and North America, German Nazis orchestrated the killings of an equal number of Others during the Second World War alone. Moreover, the lynchings of African Americans and race riots were a regular occurrence before the Second World War, and they killed thousands while keeping the remaining African Americans in a subordinate social position. And indigenous peoples were decimated by white settlers in Australia, Canada, New Zealand, and the United States, often intentionally, causing some to characterize the resulting atrocities as genocidal (Mann 2005). Finally, European colonizers committed horrendous acts of violence against colonized peoples in nonsettler colonies as well. As historian Isabel Hull (2005) describes, German genocidal policy against the Herero in southwest Africa anticipated similar policies in Europe less than four decades later. Similarly, the famous Caribbean poet and politician Aimé Césaire claimed that Hitler exemplified European violence during the first half of the twentieth century, but Europeans vilified him because "he applied to Europe the colonial practices that had previously been applied only to the Arabs of Algeria, the coolies of India and the Negroes of Africa" (Mamdani 2004, 8). Thus, prior to the 1950s, deadly ethnic violence was quite normal in the early modernizers, and Europeans and North Americans committed some of the most barbaric and large-scale acts of ethnic violence the world has ever seen.

We therefore arrive at a paradox: Modernity is linked to ethnic violence, and the earliest and most successful modernizers experienced severe ethnic violence prior to the Second World War; but ethnic violence has been relatively rare among early modernizers over the past seven decades. This paradox is not the result of massaging data until they become damn lies, as Twain suggests. Instead, the seemingly contradictory findings show that the relationship between modernity and ethnic violence is more complicated than the previous chapters describe. Specifically, the previous chapters ignore that the form of modernity

---

violence, and low-intensity violence is much more common in the early modernizers than high-intensity violence. Most notably, all other datasets have a death threshold that must be passed before an incident is categorized as ethnic violence, but MAR does not use a death threshold. For example, the CSP data only categorizes incidents as ethnic warfare if they caused five hundred or more deaths, which the Los Angeles race riots of 1992 did not come anywhere close to attaining. Lacking any death threshold, however, MAR categorized the LA riots as an ethnic riot.

changes over time, and transformations in the form of modernity adjusted its impact on ethnic violence in North America and Western Europe. A look at the relatively peaceful communal relations in post-Nazi Germany offers an insightful place to start exploring what made a former world champion of ethnic violence a contemporary leader of ethnic peace.

Germany: From Genocide to Relative Peace

Relative to the Nazi era, contemporary Germany is an exemplary case of ethnic peace, but the exterminatory nationalism preached by the Nazis continues on a far smaller scale. The neo-Nazi movement grew in the mid-1980s, peaked in the 1990s, and is presently gaining strength once again due to growing anti-immigrant sentiment. At the movement's height in 1992, more than 2,600 acts of neo-Nazi violence and aggression were reported to the police (Kurthen, Bergmann, and Erb 1997, 8). Most of these involved robbery, property damage, and harassment; only 12 percent were attacks on individuals (Kurthen, Bergmann, and Erb 1997, 17). Paralleling trajectories of neo-Nazi violence, support for right-wing parties and extremist organizations also peaked in the early 1990s, with 42,000 members in 1992 (Kurthen, Bergmann, and Erb 1997, 8).

The Nazi and neo-Nazi movements are similar in a variety of ways. A major political goal of neo-Nazis is the legalization of the Nazi Party. Empirical analyses also find that neo-Nazis express ethnocultural and racist ideas of German superiority, are xenophobic, and openly embrace violence as a means of reasserting Aryan dominance (Schubarth 1997, 144). Instead of Jews, however, immigrants—especially Turks and other Muslims—have been their preferred targets.

Despite these similarities, Nazis and neo-Nazis differ in two important ways. Most obviously, contemporary neo-Nazi support and the scale of ethnic violence are minuscule relative to the Nazi era. Second, the Nazi and neo-Nazi movements have very different bases of support. Lower-class individuals with limited education are the main supporters of the neo-Nazi movement, whereas chapter 3 highlights the overrepresentation of educated and upper-class Germans among Nazi supporters in the 1920s and 1930s (Bergmann 1997, 32; Kurthen 1997, 54; Steinmetz 1997). The comparison of the Nazi and neo-Nazi movements therefore raises two intriguing and important questions: Why has support for violent and divisive nationalism diminished since the Second World War? What caused the transformation in the support base of Nazis and neo-Nazis?

One obvious factor that helps explain differences is the general economic situation, which was enormously better at the height of the neo-Nazi movement than in the 1920s and 1930s. In addition, Germany has re-emerged as a global political power and is no longer threatened by its neighbors. As a result of both, Germans have far fewer individual and national grievances and are therefore less likely to embrace nationalist ideology that scapegoats ethnic Others. East Germany is a partial exception in this regard, as former East Germans had much more precarious livelihoods during the early 1990s due to political upheaval and economic difficulty. Former East Germans, in turn, were more likely to participate in the neo-Nazi movement after reunification. Similarly, the less-educated lower classes are a second relatively insecure segment of the population. During the late 1980s and early 1990s, working-class Germans were increasingly squeezed by growing international openness, the destruction of the "moral economy," and competition with immigrants for employment (Steinmetz 1997). Not coincidentally, "lower-class members who are threatened by economic and social change" have filled the ranks of neo-Nazi supporters (Kurthen 1997, 55).

In addition to the greater economic and political stability of contemporary Germany, changes in the content of education also limited ethnic violence and help to explain why level of education is now negatively related to neo-Nazi support. After the Second World War, educational officials in West Germany purged the curricula of divisive nationalism and anti-Semitism, and the new curricula explicitly attempted to decrease prejudice and intolerance and to promote democratic values (Brusten 1997; Oswald 1999, 100). These efforts appear to have succeeded: Studies of political socialization find that schools have increased support for democracy and liberal values, with German teachers actively encouraged open-mindedness and German students strongly supporting democracy (Conradt 1980, 256–58; Torney, Oppenheim, and Farnen 1975). Similarly, sociologist Julian Dierkes (2010) reviews history education in postwar Germany and finds that the educational system in West Germany depicted the country's history as shameful and promoted ideas of regeneration. This helped to weaken and delegitimize xenophobic nationalism and promoted a more inclusive form of German nationalism. In East Germany, on the other hand, education declared capitalism the cause of the Second World War, did not try to counter pre-existing racist narratives, and avoided addressing the issues of anti-Semitism and the Holocaust. Education therefore also contributed to greater support for the neo-Nazi movement in the East.

While education has played an important role in reducing prejudice and expanding ethnic tolerance, other actors have also helped to contain xenophobic nationalism and create an environment in which overt ethnic prejudice and discrimination are no longer acceptable. The state has been the most important of these actors. In addition to pushing educational reforms, the German state has used law, policy, rhetoric, and symbols to limit the presence and acceptability

of ethnic extremism. Underlying all these activities, the state has actively enforced basic rights in ways that contain and delegitimize the neo-Nazi movement. An example highlighting how serious the state takes ethnic extremism
is a one-thousand-page report looking into the murder of ten minorities by a
three-person right-wing extremist cell between 2000 and 2006. The report was
written by members of all political parties, received great public attention and
unanimous support from all political parties in the parliament, condemned the
criminal justice system for failing to stop the racist murders, and made forty-seven
recommendations that could help limit them in the future. Clearly, this is an issue
that is taken with the utmost concern, and this political response highlights an
enormous transformation in German political institutions that only sixty years
previously had committed genocide.

The Quebec Nationalist Movement and Limited Violence in Canada

A comparison of Nazi and postwar Germany highlights how the country transformed from extreme ethnic violence to relative peace. To further explore the
causes of relative peace in early modernizers, one can also analyze the determinants of peaceful relations in early modernizers that possess characteristics
commonly associated with ethnic violence. Canada is a particularly appropriate
case because it has multiple cleavages that could be bases for ethnic violence,
because ethnic communities are mobilized politically, and because some violence
has indeed occurred. This section focuses on conflict resulting from the Quebec
nationalist movement, which gained strength beginning in the 1950s and 1960s.

The Quebec nationalist movement has its roots in the modern social transformations that began in the late nineteenth century and accelerated rapidly
during and after the Second World War. These social transformations include
rapid industrialization and urbanization, mass education, and the growth of an
increasingly powerful subregional state. Coinciding with the modern origins of
the Quebec nationalist movement, those segments of the population that have
been most affected by modernity have dominated the movement since its incep-
tion, especially the modernizing elites and the educated (Cuneo and Curtis 1974;
Hamilton and Pinard 1976; McRoberts and Posgate 1980).

Several factors promoted this particular base of support and leadership. For
one, cultural elites feared the assimilation of Quebecois francophones into the
dominant Anglo-Canadian culture, something that had already happened to
many francophones living outside Quebec. In order to protect Quebecois culture from a similar fate and to allow it to flourish, they desired an independent

Quebecois nation-state. Another important determinant was a linguistic glass ceiling that severely limited the ability of Quebecois francophones to hold elite white-collar positions in the private sector (Clift 1982; Gagnon and Montcalm 1990; Guindon 1964; McRoberts 1975; McRoberts and Posgate 1980). Studies find that anglophones in Quebec held top positions, earned more than francophones, and received greater returns on their education (Shapiro and Stelcner 1987). Similarly, a survey in 1970 found that perceptions of inequality increased with education level (Laczko 1987). Educated francophones were also more likely to report having experienced discrimination at work and to agree that policies were needed to address language-based economic inequalities.

Notably, members of the Front de Libération du Québec (FLQ) were also aggrieved over limited francophone mobility. The FLQ was a revolutionary nationalist organization formed in 1963 that pursued both independence and Marxist economic reforms. Leaders of the FLQ claimed francophones were the white "negroes" of North America and described independence as the only means by which francophones could remove themselves from their marginalized social position. The FLQ was organized in small cells and likely never had more than two hundred members at any time. It orchestrated one hundred bombings and killed seven people. In 1970, the FLQ gained international attention by kidnapping James Richard Cross, the British trade commissioner, and Pierre Laporte, the minister of labour and vice premier of Quebec, subsequently killing Laporte.

Because cultural threat and inequalities are an explosive combination that commonly fuels ethnic violence, the relative peacefulness of the Quebec nationalist movement is surprising. One characteristic of the nationalist movement—with the notable exception of the FLQ—that helps to explain why the movement remained nonviolent is the general absence of radicalism. Indeed, while recognizing the grievances that underlay FLQ violence, the nationalist movement unequivocally denounced the group's tactics. So what explains the dominance of this moderate position?

One important reason for moderation was improved mobility. After the Second World War, the relatively deprived position of francophones improved markedly, which weakened grievances and limited the radicalism of the nationalist movement. Although significant earning differentials existed between francophone and anglophone Quebecois as late as 1970, the gap had already narrowed considerably by that time and disappeared altogether by 1980 (Shapiro and Stelcner 1987). And while the educated francophones were most affected by ethnic inequality in 1970, the economic returns of education were actually greater among francophones than among anglophones by the early 1990s (Lian and Matthews 1998; Vaillancourt, Lemay, and Vaillancourt 2007). The percentage of firms owned by francophones, in turn, increased from 47 percent of total firms in 1961 to 67 percent in 2003 (Vaillancourt, Lemay, and Vaillancourt 2007).

Although economics cannot be ignored, politics played a much greater role in limiting nationalist extremism in Quebec, and it did so in multiple ways. For one, nationalist extremism is commonly a reaction to state coercion, and various Canadian governments respected basic political rights and did not use excessive force as a means of combating the Quebecois nationalist movement. The Canadian state's relative strength curbed state violence in two ways: The capacity to monitor and coordinate state agents allowed the government to control the police and thereby stop unwanted police brutality, and the capacity to effectively regulate social relations limited the need to use coercion. Of equal or greater importance, Canada has a robust democracy that respects the rights of Canadians, and open violence against its citizens would cause any government to lose legitimacy and support.

One example that highlights how limited state violence deterred extremism is, ironically, a rare episode of state coercion: the enactment of the War Measures Act by the Trudeau government in 1970 after the FLQ's kidnappings of Cross and Laporte. After the declaration of the act, the Canadian military had a strong presence in Montreal and coordinated the arrests of 497 people suspected of aiding the FLQ. Many scholars of Quebec politics correctly note that such coercion was excessive given the actual threat posed by the FLQ, and it ultimately strengthened the nationalist movement because force was used against Quebecois citizens. Yet the act was only declared after the premier of Quebec and the mayor of Montreal demanded it, which shows how wary the federal government was of using force. Moreover, nearly all of those detained were quickly released (only 32 were refused bail), and the police and military did not beat or kill anyone. Such restraint allowed the state to use coercive measures to contain violence without provoking a backlash. In other countries with less effective states and more autocratic governments, state coercion would have posed a much higher risk of turning violent—and thereby sparking a violent nationalist backlash—because of a greater willingness among politicians to resort to violence and a much more limited ability to prevent the police and military from using violence.

The lack of formal political discrimination against francophone Canadians after the Second World War is a second important political factor that contained nationalist extremism. Several works find that formal political discrimination creates powerful grievances that motivate ethnic violence (Gurr 1993; Horowitz 1985; Sambanis 2001; Wimmer, Cederman, and Min 2009). Yet in Quebec, not only was formal political discrimination absent, but political reforms at both the federal and provincial levels actually sought to increase the presence of francophones in the public and private sector. The federal government also implemented multicultural policies that reduced the extent to which the state was dominated by and represented anglophone Canadians. With multicultural-ism, the state also formally accepted cultural differences and gave cultural rights to different communities. In this way, the government promoted a more inclu-sive form of Canadian nationalism that helped contain more radical elements of Quebecois nationalism.

Finally, a robust and effective democracy limited ethnic violence by allow-ing disgruntled francophones to address threats and grievances through formal political channels. As a consequence, participants in the nationalist movement have used policy, not violence, to pursue their goals. Canada's federal system of government contributed to this outcome by providing provincial governments with considerable powers and thereby allowing Quebecois politicians to imple-ment policies addressing the grievances and threats that motivated the national-ist movement. Language policy offers one insightful example of how politicians were able to address threats to Quebecois culture in a way that limited extrem-ism. With growing immigration and decreasing birthrates in the 1970s, the per-centage of the population speaking French was declining, and many viewed this situation as a sign that Quebec was in the process of assimilating into Canada's dominant anglophone culture. Shortly thereafter, provincial politicians passed legislation to increase immigrant attendance in French schools, thereby helping to solidify the dominant position of the French language and reducing the type of fears that commonly promote violence.

Although provincial politics played an important role in containing violence by providing formal ways to address grievances, the federal government was also influential. Indeed, without a central government willing to address grievances and threats to minority communities, a federated system of government can actually promote conflict between the center and those regions dominated by ethnic minorities. And the federal government has continually accommodated Quebecois nationalists. Examples include giving Quebec generous equalization payments, making a concerted effort to increase the use of French within the federal government, and—more recently—recognizing Quebec as a distinct na-tion within Canada.

Thus factors related to modernity strengthened the Quebec nationalist movement but did not sufficiently radicalize supporters to promote violence. The economic, social, and political conditions of francophone Quebecois con-tinuously improved—both relatively and absolutely—after the Second World War. This improvement limited grievances that could have sparked emotional prejudice against anglophones. Most importantly, the different levels of govern-ment weakened nationalist extremism by restraining their own use of violence, implementing nondiscriminatory policies (and policies that actually privileged francophones), promoting more inclusive national frameworks, and providing people with formal means to effectively address grievances and concerns. The latter proved particularly important for placating perceptions of cultural threat.

Taken together, these points suggest that timing helped to prevent the Quebecois nationalist movement from turning violent. If the nationalist movement had begun before the government actively protected basic rights, the state would have been much more likely to employ harsh violence to crack down on the movement. And if the nationalist movement had begun at a time when francophone mobility was severely limited, when francophones were unable to address grievances through formal political channels, and when francophones faced greater discrimination, movement leaders would have been more inclined to use violence. A comparison with the Irish nationalist movement seems to support this claim: The Irish nationalist movement began more than a century before the Quebecois movement and was much more violent because the British state was not afraid to use violence at that time, which, in combination with the limited economic and political opportunities of the Irish, radicalized the movement and pushed many nationalists to fight fire with fire.

From Worst to First: An Assessment

Although they are unique cases, a look at Germany and Canada highlights a variety of factors that limited ethnic violence after the Second World War. These factors resulted from the transmutations of modernity, suggesting that the changing forms of modernity helped to counteract its previous effects. Supporting this book's more general findings, these factors restrained violence by shaping the strength and contours of ethnicity, reducing emotional motivation, limiting ethnic obligations, and closing openings for mass violence.

Contemporary Germany and Canada continue to have diverse populations, so recent social transformations did not eliminate ethnic pluralism (despite the best efforts of the Nazis). Still, the boundaries of the national community became less restrictive and more inclusive over the past half-century in both cases. This is most evident in Canada, where the government implemented a multicultural policy that embraced diversity and limited the political exclusion of any community. In Germany, ideas of Aryan-based nationalism were delegitimized and a new and more inclusive German national community emerged. Greater inclusion, in turn, limited ethnic violence by weakening divisions between ingroups and outgroups, something that helps to remove ethnic targets from cognitive radars. Notably, this growing inclusiveness went hand-in-hand with the de-ethnicization of the state: The German state was previously Aryan, and the

Canadian state was previously primarily English, but both have lost much of their ethnic character over the past seventy years. This de-ethnicization of the state is vital for any effort to expand the national community to include previously excluded or marginalized groups.

Other transformations in Germany and Canada helped to reduce emotional prejudice. Growing wealth and prosperity helped contain material grievances in both countries. On the political front, the absence of formal political discrimination against communities, the de-ethnicization of the state, and the ability of ethnic communities to address their grievances through formal political channels all helped to limit emotional motivations for violence. The risk of ethnic violence declines when the grievances of people from all walks of life decline, but the cases highlight the particular importance of elites in this regard. Elites are the most capable of popularizing grievances and mobilizing people to address them, so the weakening of grievances among elites played a particularly influential role in reducing emotional prejudice.

In Germany and Canada, recent social transformations also limited obligations that motivate ethnic violence. Whereas states commonly oblige their citizens to participate in ethnic violence, neither the German state nor its Canadian counterpart imposed violent obligations after the Second World War. Moreover, ethnic obligations depend on broadly accepted norms and social sanctions, but increasing popular support for individual rights and the growing unacceptability of ethnic extremism have undercut norms and sanctions that oblige ethnic violence. Although neo-Nazi organizations and the FLQ sometimes obliged their members to participate in violence, these were exceptions, and the most powerful actors in German and Canadian civil societies have been much more likely to oblige people to refrain from violence.

Last but in no way least, recent modern transformations also helped close openings for ethnic violence. Neither the Canadian nor the German state mobilized ethnic violence after the Second World War. This is an extremely important change, especially when one considers Nazi Germany and previous state-led violence against First Nations Canadians. Even more, the German and Canadian states did their best to prevent civilians from mobilizing ethnic violence.

While showing that recent social transformations have reduced the risk of ethnic violence by weakening the salience of ethnicity, reducing emotional prejudice, eliminating ethnic obligations, and limiting mobilizational opportunities, this analysis highlights three social characteristics that play particularly important roles: robust, rights-based democracy, effective states, and economic prosperity. A rights-based democracy actively protects the political, economic, and cultural rights of its citizens through the legal system and law enforcement. In so doing, a rights-based democracy helps to limit emotional prejudice, ethnic obligations, and the mobilizational resources and openings needed for ethnic violence. More specifically, the enforcement of a rule of law and the protection of basic human rights prevents states from either orchestrating ethnic violence or obliging their citizens to kill Others. It also delegitimizes violence as a form of political action, pushes states to contain violence, allows ethnic communities to address their grievances through formal political channels, and limits formal political discrimination and exclusion. All democracies do not actively protect rights, and democracies do not limit ethnic violence in these ways when they fail to protect rights. In fact, democracies that disregard the rights of citizens likely contribute to ethnic violence by increasing political competition between ethnic communities without forbidding formal political discrimination, delegitimizing violence, and restraining the state's use of violence. The imperfect relationship between democracy and the active enforcement of rights helps to explain why limited democracies (termed anocracies) have particularly high risks of collective violence (Hegre et al. 2001; Snyder 2000).

In addition to the presence of a rights-based democracy, effective states also limited ethnic violence in Germany and Canada over the past half-century. The impact of states on ethnic violence is not independent; it interacts with rights-based democracy, and its suppressing effects depend on the latter. Effective states can either instigate or contain violence, and a rights-based democracy is the most important factor pushing states to contain it. At the same time, the impact of a rights-based democracy on ethnic violence depends greatly on effective states. Not only is a powerful state necessary for a functioning democracy, but effective states are needed to monitor state officials and regulate the general public in ways that protect and enforce rights. In addition, effective states are needed for individuals and communities to address their grievances through formal political channels.

Economic prosperity is the final social characteristic that helped to contain ethnic violence in Germany and Canada. Most notably, general prosperity restrains severe competition and economic grievances that can heighten intercommunal antipathy. More indirectly, robust, rights-based democracy and effective states depend on economic development in various ways.

Of rights-based democracy, effective states, and economic prosperity, the first had the greatest effect on the transition to relatively peaceful ethnic relations. For example, effective states preceded rights-based democracy but only began to limit ethnic violence after the advent of rights-based democracy. Moreover, rights-based democracy reduces the risk of ethnic violence in a greater variety of influential ways: It contributes to more inclusive nationalisms, limits emotional prejudice and ethnic obligations, delegitimizes violence, and severely constrains resources and openings that make ethnic violence possible.

9

MODERNITY AND ETHNIC VIOLENCE IN AFRICA, ASIA, AND LATIN AMERICA

When European colonialists first arrived in the region that is presently Burundi and Rwanda, they were surprised to find a complicated social system in what they considered the heart of darkness. Given European notions of superiority, colonialists still felt the need to introduce "civilization" to the region's peoples. One way was through a program called Social Homes. The program was supported by the colonial government, active in all urban centers, and run by nuns and the wives of colonial officials. Its main objective was to turn African women into "good" wives and mothers. This meant above all else that the women had to confine themselves to the domestic sphere, serve their husbands subserviently, keep a clean home, and know how to hold dinner parties. To impose Victorian womanhood on African women, officials went door-to-door to examine how Africans lived. As one local Rwandan participant reminisced, "They came, passed the whole day at the house. They taught us cleanliness at the house, especially the bed, the children's bed, how to make it, how to cover the bed with bedspreads and checkered sheets" (Hunt 1990, 463). Yes, comfy bedspreads and nicely pressed checkered sheets are just what women living in tropical Africa need to be good wives and mothers!

Social Homes is but one example of the many ways in which the world's earliest modernizers spread their cultures throughout the world. In so doing, the early modernizers promoted global isomorphism, a process whereby particular patterns of social relations proliferated throughout the globe (DiMaggio and Powell 1991). The spread of modernity from Europe and North America to the rest of the world was a major cause of global isomorphism. Most notably, a worldwide system of states emerged, capitalism proliferated, global markets formed, mass education slowly worked its way around the world, and truly world religions arose. Because these elements of modernity shape ethnic consciousness, emotional prejudice, ethnic obligations, and mobilizational resources and openings, global isomorphism contributed to a worldwide expansion of ethnic violence.

Yet the modernities that arose in Africa, Asia, and elsewhere were hardly exact replicas of those in Western Europe and North America. Modernity interacts with and depends on the local social environment, and the social environments present at the onset of modernity varied throughout the world (Bayly 2004). Of equal importance, modernity's agents of proliferation had biases and ulterior motives that caused them to spread forms of modernity that differed markedly from the originals. Two of modernity's most influential social carriers were colonialism and missionaries, and their biases and ulterior motives commonly promoted forms of modernity that provided particularly rich environments for ethnic violence. Most notably, they often institutionalized ethnic diversity and competition before introducing the nation-state model, and this sequence contributed to an explosion of ethnic violence in many parts of the world.

Colonialism and Ethnic Violence

In 2014, open warfare erupted between Israel and Palestinian Hamas. The violence began after a group of Jewish extremists killed a Palestinian youth by burning him alive. Palestinian protests soon erupted, and Hamas shot rockets into Israel, prompting the Israeli government to send their own barrage of missiles and soldiers at the Palestinians living in Gaza. This violence was the latest of a long series of deadly ethnic violence that dated from 1936, when Arab Palestinians attacked Jews during the so-called Arab Revolt. To fully understand the origins of this conflict, however, one needs to go back another two decades.

In what would later be called the Balfour Declaration, British foreign secretary Arthur James Balfour wrote a letter to Baron Rothschild on November 2, 1917, to discuss Great Britain's newly acquired territories in the Middle East. In addition to being a zoologist with more than two hundred different animals named after him, Rothschild was an enormously wealthy banker and an avid Zionist, and it was because of the latter that Balfour contacted Rothschild. In the letter, Balfour (1917) informed Rothschild that British policy would take a pro-Zionist direction, declaring that "His Majesty's government view with favour the establishment in Palestine of a national home for the Jewish people, and will use their best endeavours to facilitate the achievement of this object." After this policy was initiated, many European Jews moved to Palestine, and tension between Jews and

Palestinians began shortly thereafter. Both sides maintained their distance from one another, and the Palestinians feared the Jews were dispossessing them of their lands. Motivated by these and other sentiments, the Palestinian Arabs took up arms in 1936, attacking Jewish settlements and demanding that the British government reverse its pro-Zionist policy.

British colonial policy on Jewish settlement therefore created the conditions that began the seemingly intractable violence between Israelis and Palestinians, and it has caused many to pinpoint colonialism as the ultimate cause of ethnic violence in the region. The ethnic civil war that began in Syria in 2011 was also influenced by colonialism. That civil war pits Alawites—members of a Shia religious sect—against Sunnis, who constitute the large majority of the Syrian population. During the period of French colonial rule, an Arab nationalist movement hindered French control, and colonial officials therefore sought minority communities with whom they could collaborate and from whom they could gain needed support. The Alawites were one such community, and the close relations between the French and the Alawites allowed the Alawites to hold a disproportionate share of administrative and military positions. Alawite influence in the postcolonial military, in turn, allowed General Hafez al-Assad to lead a successful coup in 1970 and surround himself with other Alawites. The end result was an ethnicized state controlled disproportionately by an ethnic minority, a situation that erupted into violence in 2011.

The influential impact of colonialism on ethnic violence is hardly unique to Israel and Syria. Growing bodies of literature in a variety of disciplines all offer evidence that overseas colonialism has had long-term effects on ethnic violence.[1] A review of the literature highlights at least four ways in which colonialism increased the risk of postcolonial violence: by strengthening ethnic divisions, creating ethnic hierarchies, introducing foreign populations, and imposing arbitrary political borders. Of these, introducing alien communities is the primary way in which colonialism contributed to ethnic violence between Palestinians and Jews, whereas French colonialism promoted ethnic violence in Syria by strengthening ethnic divisions and reshuffling ethnic hierarchies.

One insightful work describing how colonialism increased the risk of ethnic violence is political scientist David Abernethy's (2000) *The Dynamics of Global Dominance*. Through a broad historical analysis, he suggests that the Syrian case is more representative of colonialism's impact on ethnic violence than the Israeli case. Because the main imperative of colonialism was to control foreign peoples,

---

1. For a review, see Lange and Dawson (2010) and Lange (2015).

the colonizers commonly resorted to policies of "divide and rule" as a means of shoring up control, and these policies transformed ethnic hierarchies, strengthened ethnic divisions, and heightened ethnic competition.[2]

Abernethy discusses three general strategies of divide and rule. One is *insulation*, whereby the colonial powers keep communities separate from one another to prevent them from uniting to overthrow the proverbial colonial yoke. Colonial powers employing this strategy interact with communities separately and purposefully limit colony-wide representative bodies that unite diverse peoples. The British, for example, created separate administrations for northern, eastern, and western Nigeria as well as northern and southern Sudan and attempted to limit interaction and influence among the different regions, and these insulating practices effectively divided populations and contributed to ethnic-based civil wars in both cases. In colonial India, the British resorted to a different type of insulation when confronted with a growing nationalist movement in the Bengal Presidency: They divided the province into several territories in a strategy to weaken nationalists and strengthen colonial supporters.[3] As Home Secretary Risley wrote, "Bengal united is a power; Bengal divided will pull in several different ways. That is what Congress leaders feel; their apprehensions are perfectly correct and they form one of the great merits of the scheme . . . in this scheme . . . one of our main objects is to split up and thereby weaken a solid body of opponents to our rule" (Darwin 2009, 203–4). Importantly, this policy further insulated Hindus and Muslims and increased intercommunal antagonisms. British colonial policy in Sierra Leone after the Hut Tax Rebellion of 1898 offers a similar example. The rebellion was organized by ten chiefs who controlled the hinterlands of Sierra Leone and ultimately killed approximately a thousand administrators, traders, and missionaries. After mercilessly putting down the resistance, the British subsequently divided the ten chiefdoms into more than 150, a move that weakened the power of any chief and—through insulation—effectively prevented chiefs from collectively resisting colonial rule again. As one historian notes, "after the 1898 rebellion the British Government thought it best to split up these areas into chiefdoms, thus ultimately creating a lot of chiefs. This plan they thought would

---

2. Abernethy (2000) prefers the term "manipulate and rule," claiming that "divide and rule" implies that the colonized were overly naïve and malleable. Because these policies actively strengthened divisions between communities, I use the original term.

3. This policy was partially overturned six years later at the same time that the colonial capital was moved from "disloyal" Calcutta to "loyal" Delhi, which was a completely different way to deal with the Indian nationalists.

finally weaken the powers of any individual chief, as they indirectly planted disunity in the country" (Abraham 1978, 174).

With growing intercommunal intermingling caused by urbanization, colonial powers sometimes resorted to a different sort of insulation that segregated people according to race, religion, and ethnicity. Colonial powers also dealt with anticolonial resistance by ruling urban areas directly but leaving rural areas under the indirect rule of traditional authorities, thereby instituting a bifurcated system of rule. At the same time, indirect rule isolated rural regions from one another because the colonial powers interacted with each traditional authority separately and did not encourage relations between traditional authorities. Of great relevance to this book, insulation via indirect rule shaped the form and salience of ethnicity. As astutely recognized by anthropologist Mahmood Mamdani (2012), in dividing and ruling colonial subjects, indirect rule was a system of "define and rule," whereby insulation crystalized ethnicities by institutionalizing ethnic-based local government. That is, indirect rule used chiefs and other "traditional" authorities as political intermediaries and treated them as rulers of ethnic communities.

Competition is the second divisive colonial strategy described by Abernethy. This strategy pits different communities against one another for jobs, power, and status, and it commonly goes hand-in-hand with insulation. Colonial officials frequently promoted competition through discriminatory policies that gave certain ethnic communities greater opportunities than others. For instance, some communities received greater access to the military, the administration, and education; this advantaged position contributed to intercommunal competition and antipathy. The advantaged position of the Alawites relative to the Sunnis in colonial Syria is one example.

When colonizers moved toward democratic rule, manipulating electoral systems was another way in which they increased competition in an effort to weaken anticolonial movements. Because Hindus dominated the Indian nationalist movement, the British created religious-based electorates to place Muslim politicians on a more equal footing with Hindu politicians (Breuilly 1994). Although effectively preventing electoral competition between Hindus and Muslims, this policy—in combination with other forms of colonial favoritism—allowed Muslim politicians to compete more effectively with Hindu politicians for political influence and thereby obstruct the nationalist efforts of the latter. While weakening the nationalist movement temporarily, the resulting struggle contributed to the division of India into separate Muslim and Hindu states, a move that unleashed extreme ethnic violence that killed more than a million people.

Abernethy's third and final strategy of divide and rule is *stratification*, through which colonial powers gain support from particular communities who possess a privileged position within a rigid, discriminatory, and colonial-imposed status system. In so doing, colonialism strengthens divisions and animosity between elites and nonelites. In colonial Burundi and Rwanda, for example, colonial policy reserved elite positions for Tutsis, thereby excluding Hutus and forcing them into an impoverished and subservient position (Mamdani 2001; Kaufman 2015). In addition to showing how colonialism intentionally strengthened class divisions as a strategy to facilitate colonial control, the Burundi and Rwanda examples highlight how colonial policies shaping stratification had the potential to affect ethnic consciousness. As noted in chapter 5, the Belgian colonial state transformed a former status and political division into an ethnic division by racializing and institutionalizing the Tutsi-Hutu cleavage. Through its use of stratification, the colonial state contributed to the Hutu rebellion during the independence process in Rwanda, the Rwandan genocide three decades later, and several extremely deadly episodes of ethnic violence in postcolonial Burundi.

According to Abernethy (2000), different combinations of insulation, competition, and stratification made possible "a remarkably stable system of [colonial] rule" (286). Of greater relevance to this book, such policies also impeded the construction of a unified and inclusive national consciousness because it patterned social relations in ways that heightened ethnic difference. When colonial authorities sought to divide and rule, they made no effort to unify the colonized into a common nation and frequently did their utmost to divide nationalist movements. At colonial independence, many former colonies therefore possessed populations that were divided by ethnicity and that experienced intense ethnic competition and disfavor. At the same time, colonial officials and postcolonial leaders copied the early modernizers and tried to construct a nation-state at independence. In this way, the desire to control distant lands pushed colonial powers to use techniques that divided peoples, but the colonial powers still imposed the nation-state model on their colonies. And the mismatch between divided societies and the nation-state model created an explosive mix that increased the risk of ethnic violence.

While agreeing with Abernethy that colonialism divided societies in ways that impeded nation building and increased the risk of ethnic violence, others suggest that these colonial effects were commonly unintended. For example, Horowitz (1985) claims that colonial officials sometimes stacked the military with minorities out of a belief that some peoples were better soldiers than others, not because of a desire to create divisions in order to facilitate control. Moreover, he notes that simply categorizing peoples into ethnicities and documenting ethnicity on colonial censuses had the potential to intensify ethnic divisions and competition. Similarly, others describe the colonial state as an "ethnographic" state actively researching, cataloging, and institutionalizing ethnic difference not so much as a means of division but as an attempt to understand and control (Cohn 1987; Wyrtzen 2015).

In support of these claims that colonialism promoted social divisions and conflict, statistical analyses offer evidence that former colonies have experienced a higher risk of ethnic violence than noncolonies (Lange and Dawson 2010). The risk of ethnic violence was particularly high during and shortly after the colonial transition, as different ethnic communities competed intensely for state power and wanted to implement their own views of the nation-state. Not all former colonizers had the same effect, however, and many former colonies have had limited or no ethnic violence. Relative to the French, Portuguese, and Spanish, the risk of ethnic violence has been particularly high in former British colonies (Abernethy 2000; Blanton, Mason, and Athow 2001; Lange and Dawson 2010). Similarly, the citizens in former British colonies are more likely to identify with ethnicity than nation (Ali et al. 2015).

One way British colonialism contributed to ethnic violence was through its effects on ethnic consciousness. More than any other major colonial power, the British colonizers employed indirect rule (Lange 2009). And whereas other colonial officials did use indirect rule in some places, indirect rule in British colonies was more likely to employ multiple units of self-administration and to base each unit on ethnicity, thereby delineating communities and institutionalizing ethnic divisions. At the same time, the British made little effort to build an overlying national identity among their subjects. Not only was this antithetical to their policy of indirect rule, but it also proved a hindrance to continued colonial rule. Importantly, indirect rule also provided communities with powerful organizations that could be used to mobilize ethnic communities.

In strengthening ethnic consciousness, institutionalizing communal diversity, introducing the principle of communal self-rule, and providing communal organizations, the British also intentionally and unintentionally contributed to communal competition. As described previously, the case of India shows how this competition was purposefully introduced to curtail anticolonial movements. More unintentionally, British colonial officials also promoted competition during the transition to independence through democratization. More than any other colonial power, the British made a commitment to setting colonies on a democratic path at independence. While this is laudable, it also unleashed the ethnic competition that previous British policy had helped to build up. Most notably, British officials imposed a nation-state model despite previous colonial policies that heightened divisions and mobilized peoples along ethnic lines, and democratic competition during the independence period unleashed intense communal competition to vanquish ethnic opponents and control the state.

My claims that democracy contributed to ethnic violence by promoting competition seem to oppose the last chapter's claims that robust, rights-based democracy limits ethnic violence, but the form of democracy is key. When democracy is not based on a respect for rights, it can heighten ethnic competition, intensify emotional prejudice, and increase mobilizational resources and openings. And all former British colonies gained independence as limited democracies that did not protect basic rights, which placed them at considerable risk of exacerbating ethnic competition. Thus, the incongruence between divided populations and the nation-state model set the stage for violence once democratic competition ensued.

In addition to India, Nigeria offers a clear example of how divisions, competition, and limited democracy sparked severe ethnic violence in former British colonies. Nigeria is extremely diverse, with more than three hundred distinct languages. During precolonial times, communal consciousness was usually localized (Dike 1956; Usman 2006). British colonial rule, however, divided the region into three separate administrative entities and, in so doing, institutionalized three main ethnic divisions—the Hausa-Fulani in the north, the Igbo in the southeast, and the Yoruba in the southwest. During the buildup to Nigerian independence, all three ethnicities mobilized for democratic elections and sought to control the postcolonial state, and this competition led to several bouts of ethnic violence between Hausas and Igbos and, ultimately, a horrific ethnic civil war over attempts to separate Igboland from Nigeria that killed up to two million civilians.

Although the risk of ethnic violence is particularly high in former British colonies, we cannot forget that ethnic violence is a rare event, and many former British colonies have had overwhelmingly peaceful ethnic relations since independence. Analyses of ethnic violence cannot ignore cases of relative peace because such cases help to highlight the factors that limit violence. When compared to cases that experienced ethnic violence, peaceful cases also help isolate factors that promote violence. Tanzania is one relatively peaceful former British colony that offers both types of insight.

As described previously, the combination of indirect rule and rapid democratization promoted ethnic violence in many former British colonies, and Tanzania was an indirectly ruled British colony that gained independence after democratic reforms. So why didn't this combination promote ethnic violence in Tanzania? Anthropologist Mahmood Mamdani (2012) offers some insight into an answer, noting that Tanzania's first independent prime minister and president, Julius Nyerere, purposefully replaced indirect rule with a system of direct rule. This helped remove the institutional basis for ethnic politics by weakening chiefs, reduced the mobilizational resources controlled by ethnic leaders, and created a unified system of rule. On top of these institutional changes, Nyerere downplayed the importance of ethnicity and emphasized common nationality among a religiously, linguistically, and racially diverse population. As a result of this policy and Nyerere's strong grip on power, democracy did not promote ethnic competition.

A comparative analysis of Tanzania and Kenya by economist Edward Miguel (2004) offers complementary insight. He notes that Tanzania and Kenya were similar in many ways at independence but that only Kenya experienced high levels of ethnic mobilization and violence during the postcolonial period. While Tanzania transformed its system of indirect rule and implemented nationalization efforts in ways that limited ethnic competition and violence, Kenya maintained ethnicized chiefdoms, and the first Kenyan president—and all subsequent presidents—maintained ethnic-based politics. Miguel also shows how educational policy had different effects on ethnic consciousness in the two countries. Whereas Tanzanian education ignored ethnicity and tribes and strengthened a Tanzanian national consciousness, Kenyan education was more decentralized and focused on local history and ethnicity, thereby exacerbating ethnic difference.

Modernity, Missionaries, and Ethnic Violence

In addition to histories of indirect rule and limited democracy, the relative tolerance British officials showed to missionaries increased the risk of ethnic violence in former British colonies. As described in chapter 5, missionaries commonly affected the contours and salience of ethnicity, and an ethnic consciousness causes people to see the world through ethnic lenses, identify with ethnicity, and place great value on ethnicity.

In addition to promoting an ethnic consciousness, missionaries frequently organized the people they worked with to pursue communal interests at the regional and national levels, and these activities politicized ethnicity, promoted ethnic competition, and contributed to threats and grievances. Missionaries frequently attempted to organize communal associations in an effort to give greater voice and power to the peoples with whom they worked and to create the organizational basis that would allow the Christian community to flourish after the departure of the foreign missionaries. In some places, they helped to spearhead the construction of diverse community associations, some of which focused on religious community, some of which focused on region, and some of which focused on linguistic community. Although rarely the goal of the missionaries, these activities commonly led to the pursuit of ethnic interests in national-level politics and sometimes even to demands for ethnic self-rule.

A third way that missionaries contributed to ethnic violence was by transforming ethnic hierarchies. Ethnic consciousness increases concern for the relative status of the community and pushes people to despise and scapegoat other
communities whose members are more advantaged than their own (Horowitz
1985). Throughout large parts of the world, missionaries were the most important source of education, and education was an important means to greater
mobility and communal status. And because many communities facing downward mobility saw missionaries as undesirable and alien and therefore avoided
them, they perceived the greater mobility of the communities influenced by the
missionaries as unjust, which strengthened grievances even further and pushed
people to act on ethnic obligations. In Nigeria, for example, missionaries worked
closely with Igbos but avoided Hausas. The Igbos therefore became much more
educated than the Hausas, and many of the Hausas who attacked Igbos were
motivated—at least in part—by resentment over the much greater education
and mobility of the Igbos and a belief that they needed to protect their community (Abernethy 1969; Paden 1971). Noting the relatively advantaged position of
Igbos, for example, a prominent Hausa-Fulani leader declared that competition
for civil service jobs was "a matter of life and death to us" (Abernethy 1969, 264).

Although all missionaries had the potential to affect ethnic consciousness and
motives of ethnic violence, Protestant missionaries were especially likely to shape
social relations in ways that contributed to ethnic violence. For one, Protestant
missionaries were much more concerned about producing Bibles and educating
in vernacular languages. This was linked to their belief that Christians require no
intermediary between themselves and God and must simply know the Bible in
order to be upstanding followers. Moreover, their interest in literacy, education,
and printing the Bible in vernacular languages caused Protestant missionaries
to establish and run more schools and printing presses, and they taught and
distributed material depicting ethnic communities as real entities. And because
of the much greater emphasis they placed on literacy and education, Protestants
were more likely to transform ethnic hierarchies. Finally, Protestants emphasized
self-rule and used more horizontal organizational structures that included communal associations. Alternatively, Catholic missionaries preferred to use non-
vernacular languages (French, Portuguese, Spanish), were much less interested
in educating the masses, were less likely to run active printing presses, and employed more hierarchical organizations that limited self-rule, all of which limited
the strength of ethnic consciousness and reduced competition and grievances
relative to Protestants.

Notably, these are general differences between Protestants and Catholics, but
several exceptions exist. One common exception occurred when stiff competition with Protestant missionaries forced Catholics to copy Protestant missionary

methods. And when Catholic missionaries copied Protestant techniques, they had similar effects on ethnic violence.

The social context also influenced the impact missionaries had on ethnic violence. For one, the presence of organized religions like Islam, Buddhism, and Hinduism exacerbated the impact of missionaries. In the presence of organized non-Christian religions, indigenous leaders and local peoples were much more likely to vehemently oppose missionaries and resent converts. Such resentment was particularly powerful when missionaries worked with people from minority communities, especially when missionary education helped minorities to work their way up the socioeconomic ladder. And missionaries, in turn, commonly targeted minorities in places with organized religions because they were more likely to convert. In this situation, religion became politicized and nationalist doctrines were more likely to focus on religion and exclude people practicing other religions, and nationalist exclusion is an influential cause of ethnic violence (Wimmer 2013b).

A second social condition affecting missionary influence was colonial status. Most notably, missionary activities relied on state complicity, and overseas colonialism usually created greater openings for missionary activities. Indigenous rulers were more likely than colonial officials to obstruct missionary activities because they viewed missionaries as foreign interlopers who imposed Western religions and paved the way for European colonization. While conflict between colonial officials and missionaries could not be avoided, the recognition that their goals were complementary and that it was in their interests to work together usually minimized conflict and promoted collaborative relations between the two (Abernethy 2000; Porter 2006). Moreover, missionary and colonial effects commonly reinforced one another and contributed to the same ethnic divisions and competition. For example, missionaries in Nigeria promoted regional inequalities in education at the same time as British colonialism institutionalized regional systems of rule, and each reinforced the other and exacerbated conflict between Hausa-Fulani and Igbos (Abernethy 1969).

Although it is difficult to differentiate between British colonial effects and Protestant missionary effects, cross-national statistics highlight a relationship between Protestant missionary influence between 1485 and 1960 and ethnic violence between 1960 and 1999 (Lange 2016). The analysis also shows that the three aforementioned contextual conditions—missionary competition, the presence of non-Christian world religions, and overseas colonialism—increased the risk of ethnic violence. Of these three, the presence of non-Christian world religions appears to have been the most important, suggesting that they were most likely to promote ethnic violence when they faced strong resistance. The processes of particular cases also highlight these effects. The analysis of Burma in chapter 5, for example, shows how missionaries contributed to ethnic violence by promoting a strong ethnic consciousness among influential segments of the Karen minority and how this contributed to a violent backlash led by Bamar nationalists. As described below, the case also highlights how missionaries contributed to ethnic competition and grievances by organizing Karens, politicizing ethnicity, and re-adjusting ethnic hierarches.

Missionaries and Ethnic Violence in Burma

From the beginning, Baptist missionaries pursued Karen self-rule. The cost of sending missionaries overseas and high death rates were two influential factors pushing the missionaries to embed their movement in the Karen community. In addition, the American Baptist mission in Burma had an ideology extolling the virtues of self-support and communal autonomy (American Baptist Foreign Mission Society 1927; Carpenter 1883). As one missionary wrote in a letter: "After we have given to the country or people an educated ministry, teachers, the Bible, and a literature, the rest must be self-sustaining. Karens must sustain Karens, is a sentiment I have re-iterated to our native preachers here. Churches must sustain themselves, must begin, must learn, and believe and feel that is the law of Christ's kingdom" (Carpenter 1883, 159). By promoting communal autonomy, self-support strengthened nationalist desires for self-rule. Along these lines, one internal document of the American Baptist mission noted, "With the development of this policy there has also developed a healthy spirit of independence and power of initiative among the people" (American Baptist Foreign Mission Society 1923, 8).

More than simply pushing Karens to run communal affairs, missionaries also helped organize Karens to pursue communal interests at higher levels of government, something that ultimately provoked anger and resentment among Bamar nationalists. Most notably, missionaries helped establish the Karen National Association in 1881, which had a stated purpose of promoting Karen unity and looking out for the well-being of the Karen community. By the 1920s, the association became increasingly active in colonial politics and began to fight for greater Karen autonomy. It also infuriated Bamar nationalists by demanding that colonial Burma remain part of India. Eventually, the Karen National Association changed its name to the Karen National Union (KNU) and mobilized the Karen separatist movement. The KNU continues to fight a seven-decade-long civil war against the Burmese state.

While Karen demands for a separate independent homeland fueled the ethnic civil war after colonial independence, demands for an independent Karen homeland only emerged after violent attacks showed that Karens would be forcibly excluded from the Bamar nation. And missionaries also contributed to this earlier violence by mobilizing Karens to pursue ethnic interests and by readjusting ethnic hierarchies. Considering the latter, Baptist missionaries founded hundreds of schools and helped converts run them. By 1913, the Baptists had established an entire system of education, including 9 high schools, 3 teachers colleges, 2 theological seminaries, 2 Bible schools for women, 32 boarding schools, and 686 day schools (American Baptist Foreign Mission Society 1913, 9). Although some Bamars and non-Karen minorities attended missionary schools, Karens constituted the great majority of the student body even though they made up only a fraction of the total population. Relatively high levels of education, in turn, allowed Karens to climb the social ladder and receive many of the best jobs in the administration, the military, and the private sector. For example, Karens held nearly 40 percent of the positions in the military in 1931 despite making up less than 10 percent of the total population (Callahan 2003, 36). As one missionary remarked with notable pride in 1931:

> Risen from a place of servitude and fear without a written language or any chance of growth, they now occupy positions of honour throughout the country, in high Government positions and in places of responsibility and trust in business enterprises of all kinds. A large percentage of teachers of the province, in Government as well as mission schools, are Karens. The positions of trust of various kinds occupied by Karens, are out of all proportion to their numbers as compared with the other races of the country. (American Baptist Foreign Mission Society 1931, 5)

In the very year these words were written, a number of Bamars attacked Karens during the Saya San Rebellion. Bamars targeted Karens because of Bamar resentment over Karen mobility, anger over Karen collaboration with the British, and Karen support for policies that were antithetical to Bamar nationalism.

The above discussion focuses on Protestant missions in Burma because they were the first and most influential missionaries, but Catholic missions also had a presence. Catholics working in Burma had to compete with Protestants, so they quickly adopted Protestant techniques such as providing education, teaching in the vernacular, and running an active printing press. For example, the Missions Étrangères de Paris (MEP), which had missions throughout Asia, worked among the Karens, where they competed with Protestant missionaries and ultimately copied their techniques. The 1889 annual report of MEP activities reviewed all their missions throughout the world and emphasized that MEP schools in Burma were exceptionally good and taught many more nonreligious subjects than MEP missions elsewhere, including history, arithmetic, and Burmese minority languages (Societé des Missions Étrangères 1890, 202). Nothing similar was said for any other MEP mission. Competition explains this exception and suggests that Catholics also contributed to violence in Burma by copying Protestant techniques.

The Burmese case also highlights how overseas colonialism mediated the impact of missionaries. Prior to British colonial rule, Burmese leaders effectively prevented missionaries from working. Although present, the early Baptist mission was geographically confined so it could be supervised and could not actively proselytize; any Buddhist who converted faced the death penalty. After the onset of British rule in 1824, however, missionaries were free to interact with all indigenous peoples and could travel unconstrained in British-controlled territory. Thus the first Karen converted to Christianity four years after the arrival of the British. And beyond simply creating an opening for missionary activities, the British administration gave Christian missionaries in Burma considerable support, including free transportation, protection, and financial assistance for missionary education. Colonial officials gave their support primarily for strategic reasons, as missionary activities helped the British control and administer colonial Burma. The most evident example of missionary assistance occurred during multiple episodes of anticolonial violence, during which a handful of missionaries organized their Karen followers to suppress Burmese efforts to overthrow the colonial government. Because of this support, colonial officials subsequently referred to Christian Karens as the "loyal" Karens. This example shows yet another way missionary effects depended on colonialism: Colonialism created an opening for missionaries to organize subordinate Karens against the Bamar majority.

The transformative effects that missionaries had on ethnic hierarchies in Burma also depended to a large extent on British colonialism. As previously mentioned, missionary education allowed Karens to go from being marginalized and stigmatized to relatively affluent, and this transformation caused enormous resentment among Bamars. Both the mobility of Karens and the resentment of Bamars were partially dependent on the colonial context in two ways. First, a well-developed system of Buddhist education preceded the British, but colonial officials systematically privileged Christian education. As a result, Bamars were disadvantaged, and Karens were privileged. Moreover, colonial officials gave Karens special treatment because of their perceived loyalty and civility, which further heightened Bamar resentment against Karen mobility.

Finally, the presence and strength of Buddhism intensified missionary effects on ethnic violence. At the time of missionary onset, the majority of the population in Burma practiced Buddhism, which was supported and propagated by the precolonial government and an extensive system of Buddhist education. Despite prolonged missionary efforts to convert Buddhists, only a handful converted. When working with non-Buddhist minorities, however, Christian missionaries had much more success, and they subsequently focused their efforts on non-Buddhist peoples. In turn, the conversion of Karens and other minorities to Christianity caused considerable resentment among many Bamars, as they saw Christianity as a foreign and illegitimate religion pushed by the colonial powers. Many also greatly resented the fact that missionary education—in combination with colonial support—allowed Karens to work their way up the socioeconomic ladder to take many of the best jobs. Such religious-based resentment and conflict helped to solidify religion's central place in defining the Bamar nation and made Burmese nationalism more religiously exclusionary and discriminatory, and this made Christian Karens—as well as Royhingya Muslims—a favorite target of Bamar nationalists.

Missionaries and Ethnic Violence in Assam

Ethnic violence in Assam, India, first discussed in chapter 7, offers another example of the impact of missionaries. After beginning their missionary activities in Burma, American Baptist missionaries established their second mission in Assam in 1813. Although the missionaries converted only a handful of Assamese, they established cordial relations with the Assamese and transformed social relations in many ways. Most importantly, they strengthened an Assamese ethnic consciousness and established the nation-state principle in Assam, both of which have contributed to postcolonial ethnic violence.

Assamese is a linguistic-based ethnicity, and the dominant Assamese discourse describes how missionaries revitalized the Assamese language and prevented it from disappearing, thereby saving the Assamese community from certain destruction (Dutta 2005, 11; Misra 1987, 3). Shortly after their arrival, Baptist missionaries quickly translated the Bible into Assamese, wrote the first Assamese dictionary and grammar books, and established the first Assamese press. They also founded the first Assamese journal, *Orunodoi*, which published a wide variety of nonreligious pieces by local intellectuals and was instrumental in starting a literary movement that popularized written Assamese (Dutta 2005, 15; Misra 1987, 67; Sharma 2002, 113–15). The importance of *Orunodoi* is evident in the fact that the word "orunodoi," which means "the dawn," is still used to refer to any magazine or newspaper (Sharma 2002, 115). More than simply expanding Assamese literature, the missionaries created a standardized Assamese language from the multiple dialects that existed prior to the arrival of the missionaries, which helped to create a more unified linguistic community based on the dialect in the region in which they first established their mission.

In addition to simply strengthening ethnic consciousness, missionaries also politicized ethnicity. When Assam entered the British Empire, it was incorporated into the Bengal Presidency, and Bengali became the official language of Assam because colonial officials believed Assamese was a dialect of Bengali. As a result, Bengali was the language of government in Assam, and all public schools were taught in Bengali. Because the Baptist missionaries had invested so heavily in the Assamese language and because their vernacular schools would attract more students if their students had better access to government jobs, the missionaries took it upon themselves to lobby the colonial government to recognize both the distinctiveness of the Assamese language and the existence of an Assamese nation. After considerable effort, the colonial government made Assamese the official language of Assam in 1873, helping to cement Assamese as a distinct language rather than a dying dialect of Bengali (Dutta 2005, 13; Misra 1987, 151–53). According to Gareth Price (1997), "without this protest it seems clear that, over time, the marginal differences [between Assamese and Bengali] would have declined leading to the merging of the two languages" (176). Importantly, it was not simply the lobbying of missionaries that helped maintain the Assamese language. Of equal importance, the missionaries standardized Assamese, revitalized it, and almost single-handedly established a vibrant Assamese press. In so doing, they were able to mobilize Assamese intellectuals behind them and prove to the British that Assamese was distinct from Bengali and that the language was alive and able to flourish in the modern world. And more than just protecting the Assamese language, missionary lobbying also proved instrumental in separating Assam from Bengal in 1874 and instituting the principle of ethnic self-rule.

In terms of subsequent ethnic violence, the influence of missionaries on both language and the political autonomy of Assam cannot be overstated. Over the past half-century, most ethnic violence in Assam has pitted ethnic Assamese against Bengali speakers and has occurred during movements that attempted to assert the dominance of the Assamese. Several episodes of violence were sparked by policies that discriminated against Bengali Assamese. These policies promoted vocal opposition from Bengalis, and ethnic Assamese reacted to this opposition by trying to assert Assamese dominance and keep Bengali power and influence in check.

Missionaries, Colonialism, and Ethnic Peace in Vietnam

In contrast to these cases of British colonialism, Protestant influence, and severe ethnic violence, it is insightful to consider places with none of these traits. Vietnam is one example. According to the Center of Systemic Peace's dataset on political violence, Vietnam experienced neither ethnic violence between civilians nor ethnic civil war between 1946 and 2010. Limited ethnic violence in Vietnam is not the result of an ethnically homogeneous population, as linguistic minorities make up 15 percent of the population. The Vietnamese population is even more diverse in terms of religion and historical origins. And in addition to diversity, ethnic minorities—both linguistic and religious—commonly collaborated with the French colonial forces and the American military, something that could have made them targets of ethnic violence. Ethnic violence in Vietnam was therefore a real possibility.

While several factors contributed to the absence of ethnic violence in Vietnam, a comparison with Burma highlights the importance of both missionary denomination and the identity of the colonizer. Contrary to Burma, Catholic missionaries dominated missionary activities in Vietnam. Catholics first arrived in Vietnam in the early sixteenth century and were relatively successful, converting several hundred thousand Vietnamese by the onset of French colonialism in the second half of the nineteenth century. Alternatively, Protestant missionaries only entered Vietnam in 1911 and were never very influential, as there were sixty times as many Catholic missionaries as Protestants in the 1920s. And because of limited Protestant influence, the Catholic missionaries either did not copy Protestant techniques or did so belatedly. For example, Catholic missionaries did not run an active printing press that dispersed information among the Vietnamese population until the 1920s and 1930s (Garcia 2008, 89; Keith 2012, 121). Moreover, although Catholics ran several schools, a small percentage of Vietnamese went to missionary schools, with only 15,382 students attending missionary schools in 1887 (Keith 2012, 32–33). Moreover, the quality of the missionary education was low, and many schools focused exclusively on the catechism (Keith 2012, 33).

The place of minority languages also differed greatly in Vietnam. Among the Catholic missionary schools, the language of instruction was Vietnamese, French, or Latin, and missionaries did not offer vernacular education to linguistic minorities. Indeed, an 1889 annual report of the main Catholic mission in Vietnam mentioned nothing about minority languages but complained that Vietnamese students were not learning enough Latin (Societé des Missions Étrangères 1890, 123). It was not until the 1920s and 1930s that missionaries began to pay much attention to minority languages, and this change was driven largely by colonial pressure. Growing Vietnamese nationalism pushed the colonial administration to work more closely with minority communities, who were perceived as more loyal to the colonial regime (Salemink 2003, 139). Thus, missionaries only began to transcribe most minority languages in the twentieth century, nearly four hundred years after the missionaries' arrival (Missions Étrangères de Paris 1997). And largely because of their failure to use vernacular languages, Catholic missionaries were unsuccessful among minority peoples, with minorities making only 3 percent of all Vietnamese Catholics in 1930, a time when they made up approximately a quarter of the total population (Keith 2012, 18). Thus, one leading missionary writing in the 1940s declared that the inability of the Catholics to make further inroads into Vietnamese society resulted from their failure to work in vernacular languages (Garcia 2008, 80).

The limited impact of missionaries on minority communities in Vietnam had two important consequences. First, it maintained ethnic hierarchies. Low levels of missionary influence among minorities in Vietnam meant that they have remained among the least educated and most isolated peoples in the country. This situation contrasts starkly with Burma, where isolated minorities went from being the least educated—even lacking a written language—to the most educated within a few decades due to missionary influence. And the marginalized position of Vietnamese minorities goes a long way in explaining why there is little hostility against them.

The second important consequence of limited missionary influence among Vietnamese minorities is that missionaries failed to instill a powerful ethnic consciousness among minorities and thereby facilitated the assimilation of minorities into the majority community. Historical evidence suggests that although they are only 15 percent of the total population today, Vietnamese minority communities made up a much larger share of the population in the mid-nineteenth century, but widespread assimilation caused their numbers to decline sharply. Historian Choi Byung Wook (2004), for example, notes that large Khmer and Champa populations lived in southern Vietnam in the early nineteenth century but subsequently disappeared after the government implemented policies to assimilate minorities. At that time, Catholic missionaries had already been present in southern Vietnam for more than three centuries but worked almost exclusively with ethnic Vietnamese. As a consequence, missionaries did not promote vibrant vernacular literatures, vernacular education, and other factors that would have impeded minority assimilation.

The form of French colonial rule also decreased the risk of ethnic violence. Most notably, the British used indirect rule much more than the French, and colonial Vietnam was much more directly ruled than was colonial Burma. And when the French used indirect rule in Vietnam, they retained the precolonial monarchy in ways that promoted national unity, something that contrasts starkly with the multicentered and divisive form of indirect rule used by the British in Burma and elsewhere. Thus, whereas the ethnic minorities living in Burma's forests and mountains were ruled indirectly in ways that institutionalized difference and local self-rule, minorities living in Vietnam's forests and mountains were not ruled through an elaborate system of indirect rule that institutionalized ethnic difference.

And while colonialism and missionaries failed to promote powerful and competing ethnic consciousnesses, the postcolonial state has not been ethnicized and therefore has not enacted policies increasing the salience of ethnicity and exacerbating ethnic competition. Instead, the communist government has downplayed ethnicity and combined Marxism with nationalism to popularize ideas of a class-based Vietnamese nation. As a result, a more encompassing national consciousness impeded the development of salient ethnic divisions.

Ethnic Violence in the Americas

The literature on colonialism and ethnic violence focuses on Africa and Asia and largely ignores Latin America. In the latter, the dominant ethnic divisions are racialized, with peoples tracing their descent from indigenous peoples, European settlers, African slaves, or some combination of the three. During the colonial period, these ethnic divisions were a source of violence. Indeed, the conquest of Latin America was a horribly brutal affair whereby Europeans annihilated as much as 90 percent of all indigenous peoples. While the introduction of Old World diseases did most of the work, European coercion killed many and strained the livelihoods of the indigenous population to such an extent that they were extremely susceptible to diseases. For example, the Spanish and Portuguese enslaved many indigenous peoples, and their extremely harsh working conditions and lack of immunity to European diseases caused most to die within a few years. In fact, slavery was not simply a factor increasing one's susceptibility to disease but must be seen as a particular and nefarious form of ethnic violence. And when indigenous slaves proved unable to provide all the labor that the Latin American settlers demanded, millions of African slaves were imported to take their place. The fate of the African slaves was similar to that of indigenous peoples. In Brazil, for example, the mortality rate of slaves was twice as high as in the United States, resulting in a situation in which slaves were worked to death and then replaced by slaves fresh off the boat (Marx 1998, 57).

Because of this grisly history, it may come as a surprise that Latin America has had relatively peaceful ethnic relations throughout most of its postcolonial history. Statistical analyses controlling for regional variation, for example, find that Latin America has had relatively low levels of ethnic violence over the past seventy years (Cleary 2000; Gurr 1993). Yet relatively peaceful ethnic relations are not the result of ethnic homogeneity. In addition to diversity, there is considerable ethnic inequality, with European settlers and their descendants finding themselves in advantaged positions relative to peoples of indigenous, African, and mixed descent. In fact, Latin America has all the characteristics commonly associated with ethnic violence, making the region's low levels of ethnic violence all the more perplexing (Cleary 2000).

A variety of factors limit ethnic violence in the region, but the most important concerns ethnic consciousness. It would be a wild exaggeration to say that ethnic divisions are nonexistent in Latin America, but ethnic divisions are—relatively speaking—porous. One factor that helps explain this relative weakness is the near hegemonic position that class has played in political mobilization over the past 150 years, which limits the salience of ethnicity. A quick read of the political history of the region highlights that class was the dominant cleavage used to mobilize political support and that ethnicity was largely subsumed and subsequently weakened by the dominance of class. Thus whereas the Shining Path commonly mobilized indigenous peoples against a state that was dominated by people with lighter skin and different cultures, class grievances—not ethnic ones—motivated the movement. This is just one example of many, as a great number of class-based guerrilla movements have been active in the region since the 1950s (Wickham-Crowley 1992).

The centrality of class is therefore an important part of the answer, but it also raises an additional question: Why did class ultimately trump ethnicity in politics, especially in a region that experienced great ethnic violence in the past and continues to experience ethnic inequalities? For an answer to this question, one needs to consider the historical processes that shape ethnic consciousness. Different from the divisive modernizing processes that occurred in former African, Asian, and Middle Eastern colonies, these processes commonly helped smooth over differences and promoted more inclusive national communities.

At the dawn of the age of nationalism, most of Latin America became independent countries and began to develop national ideologies stressing the racially mixed character of the nation, which created a higher-order ethnic category that included whites, indigenous peoples, Afro-Latinos, and mestizos. In Spanish, this mestizo ideology is commonly referred to as *mestizaje*, whereas the Portuguese equivalent in Brazil is *mestiçagem* (Wade 2008). One important reason for the popularity of such ideologies in the region is that so many people—sometimes the majority—were racially mixed. This mixing was the result of restrictions on female migration to the New World, which pushed European men to find non-European partners. In places with large numbers of mestizos and non-Europeans, in turn, the white elites found themselves in a precarious position, as the numerical dominance of non-Europeans threatened their positions. A national ideology portraying the nation as mixed helped mitigate this threat. Moreover, the history of racial mixing throughout much of Latin America made this option palatable, as the barrier between European and non-European was relatively porous.

This ideology of a mestizo nation was influenced by—and subsequently reinforced—a system of communal mobility that did not trap people in hierarchically ordered ethnic categories. Throughout the region, assimilation into the dominant culture effectively whitened nonwhites and allowed indigenous peoples and Afro-Latinos to become mestizos and mestizos to become white. For example, indigenous Mexicans who became Catholic, learned Spanish, and moved to towns or cities became mestizos or even whites. Benito Juarez, a five-term president of Mexico, offers an exceptional example: He was Zapotec and unable to speak Spanish before entering school, but Juarez was whitened via assimilation and ultimately rose to the pinnacle of state power. Non-Europeans and mestizos were actually encouraged to whiten themselves by governments who wanted non-Europeans to accept the dominant culture. Due to these factors, the Latin American population whitened considerably, with more people claiming to be either mestizo or white. In Mexico, for example, more than 54 percent of the population was categorized as indigenous in 1825, but this number was less than 8 percent by 1970 (Wimmer 2002, 144). Similarly, so-called white Brazilians made up only 44 percent of the population in 1890 but 62 percent by 1950 despite higher birth rates among nonwhites (Marx 1998, 163). Notably, the link between porous ethnic boundaries and low violence in Latin America coincides with experimental studies in psychology showing that low-status individuals are less biased against advantaged groups when group boundaries are permeable (Ellemers et al. 1988; Ellemers, van Kippenberg, and Wilkie 1990).

Another historical factor that promoted a more inclusive national community and greater national unity in Latin America was the influence of missionaries. Catholic missionaries had a monopoly on missionary activities in the area for a long time: On average, Catholic missionaries worked in Latin American countries for 350 years before the arrival of Protestant missionaries. And as noted in the previous section, Catholic missionaries were less likely to strengthen ethnic divisions and create grievances. Along these lines, work by Guillermo Trejo (2009) analyzes the impact of contemporary missionary influence on indigenous movements in Mexico and finds that a history of Catholic missionaries deterred indigenous mobilization. With the recent arrival of Protestant missionaries, however, Trejo finds that things have begun to change. Protestant missionary activity in Mexico is strongly associated with indigenous mobilization between 1975 and 2000, and Trejo finds that Protestant missionaries contributed directly to this mobilization by strengthening indigenous identities and offering resources that contributed to communal mobilization. Faced with Protestant competition, Trejo also finds that Catholic missionaries copied Protestant techniques and thereby also began to contribute to indigenous movements.

The influence of missionaries in Latin America was also very different from the influence of missionaries in Africa and Asia because of large-scale European settlement in Latin America. Within settler societies, settlers exerted great influence over missionary work and stopped any missionary activities that opposed the interests of settlers, and empowering nonsettlers was against settler interests. In addition, the presence of white settlers caused missionaries to use European languages instead of vernacular languages and made them much less likely to offer education and services that facilitated upward mobility. As a result, missionary influence helped obstruct ethnic social movements, and this limited settler fears and grievances that commonly motivate ethnic violence.

Thus modernity promoted mestizo ideologies and blurry ethnic boundaries during the early phases of nation building, and both of these reduced the risk of ethnic violence in Latin America by limiting the salience of ethnic divisions and strengthening an inclusive national consciousness. White elites did not stress ethnic difference because they sought support and compliance from other communities, and the mestizo, indigenous, and Afro-Latino communities did not mobilize their communities against ethnic inequality because their middle- and upper-class members became white and because powerful ideologies stressed that the nation was mixed. Missionaries, in turn, helped to integrate subordinate communities into the dominant culture instead of heightening difference. These conditions limited communal closure, weakened ethnic divisions, and obstructed ethnic violence.

Relative to most of Latin America, the United States experienced much more severe ethnic violence, at least up until the 1960s. Ethnic violence in the United States came in two principal forms: lynchings and riots. Although some violence targeted Native Americans, Asians, and Jews, this violence usually pitted white Americans against African Americans, with the latter almost always being the victims. A look at East Jackson, Ohio, helps highlight why the largest settler colony in the Americas had higher levels of ethnic violence.

East Jackson is in the Appalachian foothills in southern Ohio, and nearly all residents of the community consider themselves African American.[4] Most residents of East Jackson, however, are racially mixed, and many have pale complexions, blue eyes, and red hair. Because of the one-drop rule that has dominated the United States since the slave era, however, all individuals of mixed race are classified as African American even if they do not look it. This classification, in turn, has major repercussions on their lives. Most notably, East Jackson is next to Waverly, Ohio, but up until relatively recently people classified as African American were unable to live in Waverly, with prominent signs in the courthouse

---

4. Information from Al Letson's "As Black as We Wish to Be," a radio program aired on NPR. See http://www.prx.org/pieces/85361-pike-county-ohio-as-black-as-we-wish-to-be.

and elsewhere menacingly stating that "niggers" must be out of town by sunset. African Americans were therefore forced to live in impoverished and under-serviced East Jackson, which created a clear and powerful color line that is still visible today (even if the racial categories are not always clear).

The story of East Jackson highlights several stark differences the United States and Latin America. Most importantly, the boundary between whites and nonwhites—that is, the color line—was much more rigorously enforced in the United States over the past 150 years than in Latin America. This is even the case when compared with Latin American countries like Brazil and Venezuela, where large segments of the population are the descendants of former African slaves. A stronger color line, in turn, prevented the rise of an American equivalent to *mestizaje*. Instead, until relatively recently the dominant national ideology of the United States was a nationalism that suggested that white Protestants were the only true Americans, and the one-drop rule maintained clear divisions despite mixed populations. The important divisions between the racial communities, in turn, meant it was important to clearly delineate one's racial category and to prevent people from one category from infiltrating the other. The end result has been the construction of powerful ethnic divisions.

A number of factors caused the color line to be so strong in the United States. Relative to Latin America, there was considerably less racial mixing because many more European women immigrated to the United States, including during the early years of settlement. While this did not stop white men from forcing themselves on their slaves, it limited interracial coupling and stopped white men from either marrying their slaves or raising their racially mixed children as their own, which helped maintain strict racial divisions.

Political scientist Anthony Marx (1998) places greater weight on a different factor. Accepting Karl Deutsch's (1969) famous claims that nations are a group of people united by a hatred of their neighbors, Marx suggests that a common disdain for African Americans helped forge a white nation in the United States. He notes that the United States was an extremely divided nation after the Civil War and offers evidence that African Americans were excluded from the national community in the post-Emancipation period as a means of holding the broken country together. According to this argument, the only way to convince white southerners to accept their defeat was to allow them to maintain a strict racial hierarchy and to promote white Protestant nationalism, which meant that African Americans would be sacrificed for white national unity. Alternatively, the major wars in Latin America were over colonial independence, and these wars brought all races together to fight the Spanish, which created greater unity among diverse populations.

Another determinant of the strong color line in the United States was that African Americans had more limited economic opportunities than nonwhites in Latin America. Because there was a much larger population of poor whites in North America, whites serviced plantations, free blacks were largely excluded from these jobs, and poor whites fought hard to maintain the color line in order to protect their jobs. But in Brazil and other regions with smaller white populations, free Afro-Latinos assumed important roles in the plantation economy, including growing food crops, raising livestock, selling other basic commodities, and catching runaway slaves. By holding these positions, Afro-Latinos provided vital services, which in turn promoted a greater degree of social acceptance and helped weaken the color line (Fredrickson 1997, 88).

Ethnic difference was therefore much more salient in the United States than in Latin America, a difference that had important effects on ethnic violence. Most notably, it underlay the color line and legitimized violence when African Americans overstepped the line by living in white neighborhoods, taking jobs that were supposed to be for whites, or interacting with whites in "inappropriate" ways. The three thousand African American victims of lynchings were commonly targeted for disrespecting the color line. The discriminatory treatment suffered by African Americans, in turn, pushed some of them to resist, which commonly sparked extreme backlashes in the form of race riots against "uppity" African Americans.

The Tulsa race riot of 1921 offers an example of how strong ethnic divisions upheld the color line and legitimized violence against African Americans. The riot is little known today but was large in scale: three hundred people are believed to have lost their lives, and thirty-five city blocks were burnt to the ground, leaving some ten thousand African Americans homeless. The particular circumstances that sparked the riots were similar to those that led to the lynchings in Duluth, Minnesota. A black man named Dick Rowland was erroneously accused of attacking a white woman in an elevator. With the life of Rowland at risk, the sheriff brought him into custody and placed armed men in front of the building to hold off a crowd of some two thousand white men who had gathered for a lynching. Given the prevalence of lynchings around Tulsa at that time, many African Americans were concerned for Rowland's life, and several dozen African American veterans of the First World War collected weapons and offered to reinforce the police guards. Rumors of an armed posse of African Americans spread, and members of the lynch mob viewed the arming of African Americans as an egregious affront to the system of white domination. The inevitable outcome of this series of events was a street battle, and the much larger and better-equipped white contingent soon gained the upper hand. As retribution for resisting white dominance and having the audacity to fight back, many within the white community subsequently tried to remove all African Americans from the city by destroying their neighborhoods. In addition to going door-to-door looting and setting fire to buildings, attackers used six airplanes loaded with incendiary devices to bomb the neighborhood; the planes were also used to shoot unsuspecting African Americans from above.

A comparison of Latin America and the United States therefore shows how differences in ethnic closure affected the strength and contours of ethnicity. In the United States, the heavy enforcement of ethnic boundaries made people extremely aware of ethnic differences and legitimized and even obliged violence against African Americans whenever the boundaries were threatened, and this violence further reinforced ethnic divisions. In Latin America, on the other hand, relatively weak and fluid ethnic boundaries reduced the salience and divisiveness of ethnicity, contributed to an ethnically inclusive nationalism, and limited ethnic violence. This helps to explain why ethnic violence has been relatively rare in Latin America. Yet this comparison also shows that the relative scarcity of ethnic violence in Latin America is a mixed blessing. As the American civil rights movement shows, violence often occurs when subordinate communities mobilize to address inequalities and hardships, and the lack of violence in Latin America—a region with extreme ethnic inequalities—shows that subordinate peoples commonly do not mobilize to improve their livelihoods when fluid ethnic divisions limit the strength of ethnic consciousness (Marx 1998).

Recent indigenous movements suggest that this situation is changing, however. Over the past quarter-century, a number of indigenous movements have emerged and politicized ethnicity by asserting minority rights and publicizing ethnic inequalities. These movements are concentrated in the Latin American countries that have the most limited rights-based democracy, have the least effective states, and are the poorest, which would suggest that they increase the risk of ethnic violence. Yet the legacy of *mestizaje* continues to blur ethnic boundaries and has kept most movements peaceful. As political scientist Raul Madrid (2012) notes, indigenous movements in Latin America have promoted indigenous political parties, but these parties are unlike ethnic parties elsewhere in the world because they are ethnically inclusive and actively court nonindigenous peoples for support, especially lower-class mestizos and whites. In this way, ethnic parties in Latin America neither reify ethnicity nor increase ethnic competition as much as elsewhere, and ethnic violence in Latin America should therefore remain relatively rare in the near future.

After reviewing how colonialism and missionaries contributed to ethnic violence in Africa, Asia, and the Americas, it is time to highlight the significance of these findings. There are two main points to take away, and both deal with the order in which processes unravel. First, the order in which places modernized had effects on the form of modernity. Early modernizers played an important role in spreading modernity to the rest of the world, and their influence promoted new forms of modernity. This chapter highlights how colonialism and missionaries helped proliferate modernity and offers evidence that their ulterior motives—control and conversion—frequently promoted strong ethnic divisions, competition, and grievances. This leads to the second point about order: Colonialism and missionaries commonly promoted national incoherence and ethnic competition prior to introducing the nation-state principle, and this ordering made the creation of unified nation-states a near impossibility in many postcolonial societies. Indeed, in Burma, Rwanda, Burundi, India, Nigeria, and a great number of other former colonies, ethnic divisions became salient, and the nation-state model was imposed at independence. The resulting incongruence promoted widespread ethnic violence after the Second World War, which helps to explain why ethnic violence was skyrocketing in these regions at the same time it was declining in Western Europe and North America.

Not all former colonies have experienced high levels of ethnic violence over the past seven decades, however. Tanzania, Vietnam, and Latin America are three regions with relatively low levels of ethnic violence. These cases also demonstrate the importance of timing but in a different way. Politicians in all three regions implemented nationalist policies before more divisive ethnic consciousnesses became powerful and widespread, and these policies promoted and strengthened an ethnically inclusive national consciousness. Importantly, these policies proved possible in all three regions because colonialism, missionaries, and other actors did not heighten and institutionalize ethnic divisions to the same extent as in Rwanda, Burma, and elsewhere.

10

THE FUTURE OF ETHNIC VIOLENCE

Futurology is a field of study that tries to predict the future. One of its main focuses is new technologies and their potential transformative effects. A number of futurologists, for example, consider how the incorporation of computer technologies into our brains will help us learn anything from European history to Mandarin to advanced algebra by simply downloading information directly into our modified cyber-brains. In turn, futurologists consider the changes that computer-enhanced brains and other new technological developments will have on our societies. Will computer-enhanced brains cause schools to become obsolete? Will one's ability to get a good job depend on possessing a modified brain and downloading the requisite programs and data files?

Although many futurologists are academics, futurology has not made big inroads into academia, and it is extremely difficult to find a university with a futurology department.[1] Futurology's limited presence in academia likely results from a certain mysticism that surrounds it, as one would expect to find courses in futurology at Hogwarts, not Harvard. Still, most futurologists do not make predictions based on tarot cards or crystal balls; they base them on empirical trends and critical assessment, both of which are highly valued by academics. The main reason academics refrain from grandiose prediction is uncertainty: The world is so complicated that it is impossible to make major predictions with

---

1. The University of Houston and the University of Hawaii at Manoa are exceptions.

any confidence. Along these lines, philosopher David Hume (1951) once claimed a doctor cannot forecast the health of patients with any accuracy beyond one or two weeks whereas a politician cannot forecast political trends beyond a year or two (162). Although the predictive power of doctors has improved considerably since Hume made these claims in the eighteenth century, his claims about the social world remain accurate. Predictions about ethnic violence, in turn, are particularly problematic because punctuated crises are usually unpredictable and can transform relatively peaceful relations into ethnic violence almost overnight.

While acknowledging the extremely speculative and uncertain nature of such activities, this concluding chapter dabbles in futurology by using the insights from the previous chapters to make educated guesses about the future of ethnic violence. The chapter also considers potential policy prescriptions that might help to limit the prevalence of ethnic violence. Before both, however, I briefly review the book's major findings.

Modernity and Ethnic Violence: A Summary

Progress is commonly associated with modernity, but this book offers strong and consistent evidence that modernity promoted a dramatic spike in ethnic violence and therefore has a nonprogressive side. It describes how modernity strengthened and proliferated ethnic consciousness, and the latter intensified two motives that commonly inspire ethnic violence: emotional prejudice and ethnic obligations. Even more, modernity enhanced diverse resources that facilitated the mobilization of ethnic violence.

Although the cognitive propensity to categorize people into ingroups and outgroups predisposes humans to have a communal consciousness, few people perceived, valued, identified with, and made sense of ethnicity prior to modernity because the communities that people were conscious of were usually much more concrete and localized. With the rise of modernity, communication and transportation technologies and the proliferation of powerful institutions shaped social relations in ways that contributed to an overarching ethnic consciousness that included many strangers who lived in far-off regions.

The rise and expansion of ethnicity contributed to ethnic violence in different ways. An ethnic framework pushes people to perceive ethnic difference, and ethnic violence is motivated by such difference. When combined with ethnic structures, an ethnic framework promotes an ethnic consciousness, and the latter contributes to emotional prejudice and ethnic obligations, both of which are influential motives of ethnic violence. Emotional prejudice occurs when people target entire categories of people with some combination of anger, resentment, hatred, fear, and jealousy, and ethnic obligations push people to make sacrifices for the betterment of one's ethnic community. Simply put, emotional prejudice and ethnic obligations require salient ethnic divisions, and people become emotional over the well-being of their ethnicity and are most likely to act on ethnic obligations when ethnicity is dear to their hearts.

In addition to ethnic difference and motive, ethnic violence also depends on the ability to mobilize large numbers of people. Modernity, in turn, enhances organizational, communication, and transportation technologies in ways that facilitate the mobilization of ethnic violence. Most importantly, modernity contributes to the ultimate mobilizer of ethnic violence: bureaucratically organized nation-states. Modern bureaucratic states are exceptional in their ability to coordinate the actions of thousands of individuals and implement complex policy. Unfortunately, states commonly use their organizational capacity to mobilize ethnic violence. In fact, the nation-state principle—which holds that each ethnic community should have self-rule—predisposes states to look out for the well-being of their ethnic community and to discriminate against Others. Importantly, ethnicized states also impose ethnic obligations on civilian coethnics, popularize myth-symbol complexes that intensify emotional prejudice, and heighten emotional prejudice among Others through their discriminatory state policies.

Education is another thoroughly modern institution, and *Killing Others* offers evidence that it is second only to states in its effects on ethnic violence. Like states, education is an influential shaper and proliferator of ethnic consciousness. Moreover, education commonly intensifies emotional prejudice by teaching myth-symbol complexes that vilify Others and enforces ethnic obligations by preaching and sometimes enforcing one's duty to protect ethnicity. And education also provides a variety of resources that allow people to mobilize violent ethnic movements.

This book therefore offers strong evidence that modernity lies at the heart of explanations of ethnic violence. But unlike early functionalist claims of a single recurring modernity, this book highlights a variety of modernities and notes that modernity's form is constantly changing. The ever-changing character of modernity is important because it helps to explain how the earliest modernizers transformed from champions of ethnic violence to leaders in ethnic peace. The changing forms of modernity among early modernizers involved the development of robust, rights-based democracy, powerful states, and relative affluence. Together, these factors helped to weaken the nation-state principle, protect human rights, and limit ethnic grievances. Most importantly, rights-based democracy prevented states from actively participating in ethnic violence, forced states to do everything in their power to obstruct ethnic violence, and made xenophobic ethnic extremism unacceptable in the public sphere.

Yet modernity's contemporary form is very different in late modernizers. Not only did these regions modernize in different contexts, but the agents of modernization were different. Most notably, this book offers evidence that colonialism and missionaries were influential social carriers of modernity among most late modernizers, and their particular interests and biases commonly institutionalized ethnic difference and competition while at the same time introducing the nation-state principle. The incongruence between ethnic pluralism and the nation-state, in turn, contributed to a dramatic increase in ethnic violence in former colonies over the past seven decades. The main exception in this regard is Latin America, where more porous ethnic boundaries and early efforts to promote an inclusive national ideology have contributed to relatively low levels of ethnic violence.

Ethnic Violence in the Near Future

One way to make predictions is simply to project present trends into the future. The broad historic trends in ethnic violence presented in chapter 2 show a rise in ethnic violence between the early 1800s and 2000, suggesting that ethnic violence will continue to affect the lives of millions of people annually. At the same time, the data from chapter 8 highlight a dramatic decline in ethnic violence among early modernizers over the past seventy years, so general trends could change directions if late modernizers follow the lead of the early modernizers. Supporting this optimistic interpretation, the data from chapter 2 highlight a reduction in ethnic violence among late modernizers since the 1990s. Based on CSP data, for example, forty-six severe episodes of ethnic violence killed 1.8 million people in the 1990s, but twenty-four episodes of ethnic violence killed 580,000 people in the first decade of the twenty-first century (Marshall 2014). We might therefore be in the midst of a global decline in ethnic violence.

Besides trends, an understanding of the determinants of the phenomenon in question can also inform predictions. Indeed, trends can transform abruptly, and an understanding of the processes underlying the trends offers insight into future trajectories. In this section, I use the insight gained from the previous chapters to do just this. Instead of making predictions of ethnic violence between particular ethnic communities in a specific country, I take a more general approach and assess the risk of ethnic violence among early and late modernizers, beginning with the former. Ultimately, I predict that ethnic violence will continue near present levels over the next decade but should decline slightly thanks to lower levels of violence among late modernizers.

Western Europe and North America: Growing Inclusiveness?

On December 20, 1943, Charles Brown completed his first mission as a pilot of a B-17 bomber, but just barely. His target was near Bremen, Germany, and his plane was badly damaged by German fighter planes during the bombing run. After miraculously pulling out of an unplanned downward spiral that allowed him to escape from the relentless pursuit of several German fighters, he was contemplating how to avoid the air defenses on the German coast when he noticed a German Messerschmitt fighter fast approaching. Franz Stigler was the pilot of the Messerschmitt and one of Germany's best; he needed only one more kill to receive Germany's highest medal of valor. As he approached the B-17, he saw the plane's extensive damage and was amazed it could still fly. He also discovered that the plane was defenseless and that the remaining crew had no hope of surviving Stigler's attack. Although a similar American bomber had killed his brother earlier in the war and although Stigler risked execution for treason if he let the plane go, he recognized the humanity in Brown's terrified eyes and believed that shooting down a defenseless plane was no better than murder. In addition to refusing to attack, Stigler escorted the plane out of German airspace to prevent the German air defenses from downing the plane.

This remarkable story of compassion for one's enemies is recounted in Adam Makos's *A Higher Call* and shows the very opposite of emotional prejudice. Indeed, what we see in Stigler is a breakdown of the division between ingroup and outgroup and a feeling of empathy toward an enemy Other. Although Stigler is remarkable when one considers the horrors of the Second World War, philosopher Peter Singer might view him as simply ahead of his time. In *The Expanding Circle* (2011), Singer claims that increasingly inclusive communal identities have emerged and strengthened in North America and—especially—Western Europe since the end of the Second World War. He argues that ideas of outgroups are in the process of weakening and breaking down, and people increasingly view others as part of an all-inclusive community: humanity. In fact, Singer suggests that this identity might actually expand beyond the human species to include other intelligent mammals like monkeys and dogs. Singer's ideas—at least those pertaining to humans—have been embraced by some scholars who claim that the increasing integration of the world is breaking down national borders and creating more encompassing and cosmopolitan identities (Hobsbawm 1992; Kaldor 2004).

So, is ethnicity in the process of disappearing among early modernizers, making ethnic violence something that will become increasingly rare over the next decades? Although some might interpret the findings of chapter 8 as an affirmative answer to this question, I think the risk of ethnic violence in North America and Western Europe is actually increasing slightly, although large-scale ethnic violence will likely remain rare in the coming decade. More specifically, the maintenance of powerful ethnic divisions and the growing strength of grievances and perceived threats will likely exacerbate ethnic antagonisms, but robust, rights-based democracies buttressed by powerful states and relative affluence should continue to contain ethnic violence.

Over the past seventy years, affluence has helped limit grievances that can lead to ethnic violence. Throughout the past decade, however, most early modernizers have experienced more difficult economic times, and—at the time I am writing these words—such difficulties do not show any sign of subsiding. The recession that began in 2007 has caused a notable dip in national wealth over the past decade and has affected the economic livelihoods of countless individuals, with Greece, Portugal, Spain, and Italy being particularly hard hit. The more recent economic slowdown in China, in turn, suggests that these economic difficulties will persist in the coming years, creating a more nourishing environment for grievances and ethnic scapegoating.

And during periods of economic hardship, economic inequalities become more striking. In the United States, inequalities of wealth and income have been growing so quickly over the past forty years that the top 1 percent owns 40 percent of all national wealth, whereas the bottom 80 percent owns only 7 percent. When such inequality is ethnically patterned, economically marginalized communities are more likely to mobilize to highlight ethnic inequalities. Moreover, white Americans are also affected by economic difficulties and might scapegoat Mexican Americans, African Americans, or other Others for their hardships.

In combination with economic difficulties and growing inequality, high levels of immigration will likely strain ethnic relations even further. While clearly evident in the United States, several factors place Europe at greatest risk of anti-immigrant violence in the coming years. First, Europe has historically been a sending society, not a receiving society, and this has created more rigid ideas of nation that are more firmly rooted in ethnicity and history. In addition, Western European countries have larger and more popular welfare states than Canada and—especially—the United States, and many Europeans believe immigrants pose a threat to the welfare state. Although European welfare states are not disappearing, individual benefits are being scaled back at a time of greater need because of prolonged economic difficulties, past deficits, and aging populations. And because immigrants and certain ethnic minorities are popularly perceived as unfairly taking advantage of welfare benefits, they are at greater risk of being scapegoated. Indeed, several European parties are in favor of the welfare state but want to limit its benefits to "true" members of the nation and to restrain immigration. Finally, the formation of the European Union created a backlash against efforts to expand the ingroup, with nationalists in all countries resisting and resenting such efforts and feeling that their national communities were severely threatened. EU limits on the ability of individual countries to control immigration helped to fuel this nationalist resentment and targeted immigrants with emotional prejudice.

There are also some signs that robust, rights-based democracy is beginning to erode, at least a bit. Right-wing political parties in the United States and throughout Western Europe are raising fears about ethnic threats and proposing discriminatory policies that limit rights as a way to deal with the threats. Hand-in-hand with this rhetoric, we see that candy-coated xenophobia is becoming more and more acceptable in the media and general public. In the United States, conservative leaders are blaming immigrants for hardships and proposing to remove the basic rights of Muslims. An incarceration state that targets African Americans, in turn, continues to infringe on the rights of black men, and African Americans are becoming increasingly active in protests against police brutality. Therefore violence between African Americans and whites, immigrants and nonimmigrants, and Muslims and non-Muslims remains possible.

While all this bodes poorly for the future of ethnic violence among early modernizers, it is easy to get carried away. First, economic hardship is only one source of emotional prejudice, and it is hardly the most influential. Second, despite some risk of backsliding, North America and Western Europe remain rights-based democracies bolstered by powerful states, and there is not a single historical example of a robust, rights-based democracy that reverted to limited forms of democratic rule and subsequently failed to protect basic human rights. The states of early modernizers should therefore continue to actively and effectively contain ethnic violence, soothe grievances, and delegitimize blatant xenophobia. All this should keep ethnic violence under control even if more of the fodder that fuels ethnic violence is accumulating.

Ethnic Violence in Late Modernizers: Declining Ethnic Violence in the Rest?

Given a two-term limit set by the Russian constitution, Vladimir Putin relinquished his position as president of Russia in 2008 to his hand-picked successor, Dmitry Medvedev. Many believe Putin chose Medvedev because Putin could control him and act as the master behind a puppet government. A popular Russian joke suggests that Medvedev's full head of hair also influenced Putin's choice. This joke refers to an unbroken pattern in the hairlines of Russian heads of state that goes back to 1825. In that year, Czar Nicholas I died with very little hair on his head and was succeeded by his brother Alexander II, who had a full head of hair. Bald Alexander III, in turn, succeeded Alexander II, and this bald-hairy pattern of Russian leaders has continued ever since. And by keeping the pattern going with his choice of Medvedev, so the joke goes, Putin was planning ahead for his return to power in 2012.

Few people really believe that hairlines determine Russian politics. Social scientists, however, sometimes use historical patterns to predict the future. For example, modernization theory claims that the first modernizers established a form of development that all subsequent modernizers would inevitably follow, suggesting that we simply need to look at earlier cases to understand later cases. Based on the findings of chapter 8, this logic suggests that all countries in the world should follow the lead of Germany, Canada, and other early moderniz-ers and begin experiencing declines in ethnic violence in the near future. One must be skeptical of the predictive power of pattern-based theories because pre-vious examples do not necessarily predict future cases. Indeed, modernization theory's claims that all regions inevitably modernize in the same way have been debunked, and most experts believe that the different conditions that exist today prevent countries from following the same trajectory as the early modernizers. Because rights-based democracy, effective states, and affluence contributed to the declines in ethnic violence among early modernizers, one can look at trends in all three among later modernizers to assess whether we should expect similar declines.

Figure 10.1 shows the average levels of democracy by region since 1960. In particular, the vertical axis ranges from 10 to -10, with 10 representing a strongly democratic regime, -10 a strongly autocratic regime, and 0 a regime that is equal parts democracy and autocracy. Although these data do not directly measure the extent to which democracy enforces rights, they are relatively good proxies because highly democratic regimes almost always actively protect rights. Based on this figure, there is some room to be optimistic that regions might follow the rights-based democratic trajectory of the early modernizers, as the figure high-lights a process of democratization throughout large regions of the world over the past forty years. This global trend began in Western Europe in the mid-1970s with democratization in Greece, Portugal, and Spain. Shortly thereafter, several countries in Latin America implemented democratizing reforms, and by the late 1980s and early 1990s, there were considerable advances in democracy in all other regions of the world, especially Asia, sub-Saharan Africa, and Eastern Europe. The latter case shows the most extreme transformation, going from au-tocratic to highly democratic in a matter of years.

Based on these trends, many academic experts suggest that continued democ-ratization is inevitable. For example, well-known books by political scientists

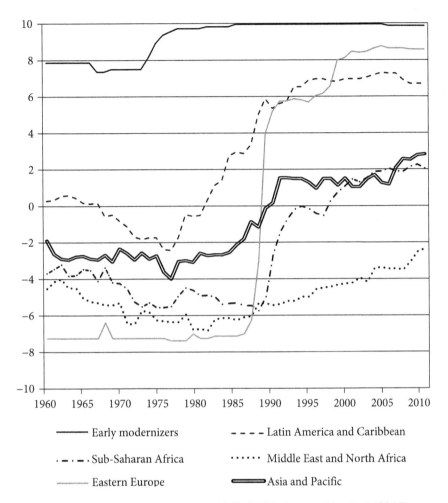

FIGURE 10.1. Democracy by region, 1960–2012. Source: Marshall (2015).

Samuel Huntington (1991) and Francis Fukuyama (1992) offer theoretical reasons for the continuation of this trend. They see authoritarianism as delegitimized with the demise of the Soviet bloc, democracy as the only legitimate form of governance in the world today, and a strong affinity between economic liberalism and democracy. In this way, democratic deepening might presently be reducing the risk of ethnic violence in many parts of the world. Others are more skeptical. Political scientists Grigore Pop-Eleche and Graeme Robertson (2015), for example, note that democratization began to stagnate in the early 1990s and that the number of democratic countries in the world has actually decreased since the beginning of the twenty-first century. And as described in previous chapters, anocracies do not actively and effectively enforce rights and are at a heightened risk of ethnic violence. Pop-Eleche and Robertson claim that this stagnation is the result of structural impediments to democratization that cannot be ignored and that are difficult to address even by leaders who are strongly in favor of democracy. Two of these factors are state effectiveness and economic development, both of which also affect ethnic violence more directly.

Figure 10.2 presents data from the World Bank on state governance. It gives the average scores of three variables—government effectiveness, rule of law, and absence of corruption—by region. The variables measure the standard deviation from the global average, so a positive value shows that a country's score is greater than the global average, and a negative value shows that a country's score is less than the global average. The figure clearly shows that all regions have scores far below those of the world's early modernizers. For all three variables, the scores of the early modernizers are approximately 1.6 standard deviations above the global average, placing the entire region near the 95th percentile globally. These enormously high scores show that the world's most effective

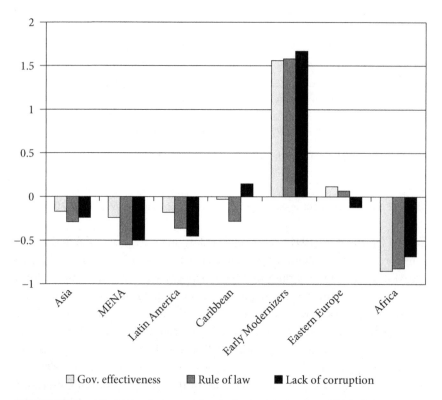

FIGURE 10.2. World Bank governance indicators by region, 2010. Source: World Bank (2012).

states are almost exclusively concentrated among the early modernizers. For all remaining regions of the world, the data show that the average scores are at or below the global average, which limits both future democratization and the ability of governments to contain ethnic violence.

The World Bank has gathered data on state effectiveness since 1996, so one is able to look at trends in state effectiveness over a fifteen-year period. The data show that early modernizers had the highest levels of all three indicators of state effectiveness throughout the period. The indicators have been stable but increasing slightly in East Asia, Latin America, and the Caribbean. Alternatively, the indicators have declined in sub-Saharan Africa, South Asia, and the Middle East and North Africa (MENA), suggesting that state effectiveness in these regions is declining relative to the early modernizers. And there is some evidence that state capacity is declining in absolute terms in several countries. Indeed, a number of contemporary states in Africa and Asia are unable to perform even the most basic actions, including taxation, controlling borders and peoples, and offering goods and services. Political scientists Robert Jackson and Carl Rosberg (1982) claim that extreme examples of these states are simply juridical states, that is, they are recognized by the international community as states but lack the actual organizational components of statehood. According to the Fund For Peace's (2015) Fragile States Index, in 2014, sixteen countries lacked states with the ability to perform even the most basic functions. Starting with the states with the lowest capacities, they include South Sudan, Somalia, Central African Republic, Democratic Republic of Congo, Sudan, Chad, Afghanistan, Yemen, Haiti, Pakistan, Zimbabwe, Guinea, Iraq, Cote d'Ivoire, Syria, and Guinea Bissau. In fact, only 51 of the 178 countries in the Fragile States Index were scored as possessing stable states capable of performing basic functions.

As with state effectiveness, the early modernizers contrast starkly with all other regions in terms of economic development. Figure 10.3 uses data from the World Bank and shows the regional averages of per capita GDP since 1970 in constant 2005 US dollars. The figure clearly shows that all regions of the world were much poorer than the early modernizers in 1970 and that they remain so four decades later. Indeed, the absolute growth in per capita GDP was greatest in the early modernizers, which almost grew off the charts (despite dipping recently). All other regions also grew over the last four decades, but the absolute gap between the early and late modernizers widened considerably. The average per capita GDP in 2012 was only $2,033 in sub-Saharan Africa, $3,879 in Asia and the Pacific, $5,788 in Latin America and the Caribbean, $8,089 in Eastern Europe, and $11,761 in the Middle East and North Africa (MENA), whereas the average per capita GDP of the early modernizers had increased by $22,000 to $40,000 by 2012.

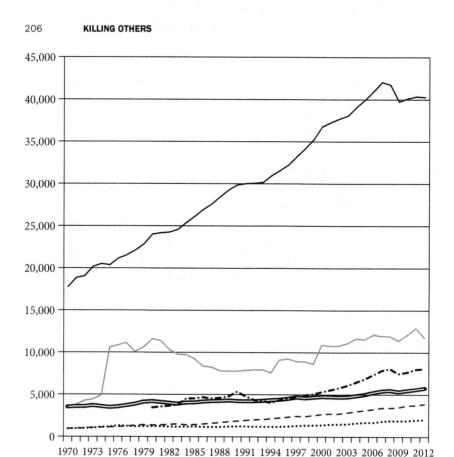

FIGURE 10.3. Per capita GDP (constant 2005 US$) by region, 1970–2012. Source: World Bank (2014).

All in all, the data in Figures 10.1, 10.2, and 10.3 present trends that can be interpreted in different ways and that might not continue into the future. The only clear conclusion one can make is that much of the world does not presently have robust, rights-based democracy, effective states, and abundant wealth and will not likely have them in the near future, which suggests that late modernizers will not inevitably develop the same way as early modernizers and that the risk of ethnic violence will remain relatively high.

That being said, the international environment is changing, and its new form partially compensates for limited rights-based democracy among some late modernizers. International institutions and actors are increasingly influential and have the ability to shape politics in countries throughout the world. Since the peak in ethnic violence in the 1990s, international institutions and actors—ranging from the UN to influential early modernizers to nongovernmental organizations—have played an increasingly important role in pushing states to protect their citizens against ethnic violence. When leaders fail to protect their citizens, they lose international support and legitimacy and commonly incur additional economic and political penalties. And as the cases of Slobodan Milošević and Omar el-Bashir show, leaders of states that actually contribute to ethnic violence risk indictment at the International Court of Justice. As a result of these measures, the international arena is increasingly limiting overt state participation in ethnic violence, and states face growing international pressure to protect human rights. This likely explains some of the decline in ethnic violence since the 1990s and will likely continue to limit extreme ethnic violence in the coming years.

To conclude, the inability of late modernizers to follow the early modernizers' lead in terms of rights-based democracy, effective states, and economic development suggests that the risk of ethnic violence will remain relatively high among late modernizers. Yet growing international pressure from global institutions, early modernizers, and nongovernmental organizations should limit state involvement in ethnic violence and increase state efforts to contain violence. I therefore predict moderate reductions in the risk of ethnic violence over the next decade among late modernizers.

Ways to Limit Ethnic Violence?

So the risk of ethnic violence will likely remain low in North America, Western Europe, and Latin America and should decline slightly but remain relatively high in Africa, Asia, and the Middle East. Yet might there be a way for us to change these trajectories through policy? Can we engineer societies in ways that impede ethnic violence? Although there is no silver bullet that can vanquish ethnic violence, a variety of policy prescriptions might help.

The previous chapters clearly highlight that the nation-state model is linked to ethnic violence. One potential policy option thus involves changing this model in ways that improve ethnic relations. This could involve either changing ideas of nation to create unity or transforming the structural underpinnings of the state to better suit ethnic diversity. Three specific options are multiculturalism, federalism, and consociationalism.

Multiculturalism is a nationalist ideology that embraces and even celebrates diversity. This ideology promotes particular political practices: Multicultural governments treat ethnic communities equally and actively protect the rights of each and every community. Multiculturalism differs markedly from the nationalist ideology surrounding the nation-state model, which usually offers a circumscribed idea of nation and designates Others as nonmembers. And whereas the nation-state model is a powerful motivator of ethnic violence, multiculturalism helps to delegitimize ethnic violence, reduce ethnic grievances, and create a more encompassing national consciousness that unites diverse ethnic communities. Such efforts to create unity out of diversity, in turn, are much more appropriate than overtly assimilationist policies because communities resist and resent forced assimilation.

While acknowledging the potential benefits of multiculturalism, this policy also poses problems. For one, it recognizes difference and can therefore heighten ethnic divisions if a new and a more inclusive nation fails to emerge. And getting people to accept a more inclusive nation is a delicate and long-term task that requires smooth and talented leadership over an extended period of time, and multiculturalism requires the full participation and support of all communities. Most importantly, dominant ethnic communities must be willing to give up their community's special position as the "real" members of the national community and accept a nationalist discourse that presents them as equals to other ethnic communities. Unfortunately, dominant communities rarely give up privileges without a fight. In such a situation, a more realistic option might be something similar to Quebec's version of interculturalism, which recognizes and respects diversity but privileges the core culture by protecting the French language and placing individual rights above group rights.

Whereas multiculturalism tries to create more inclusive ideas of community, another option is to transform the state in a way that makes possible greater ethnic representation and autonomy. The two main options are federalism, which decentralizes power to designated regions, and consociationalism, which formalizes power-sharing arrangements among different ethnic communities. Both offer important means of alleviating ethnic tensions and thereby help to accommodate ethnic pluralism. Most notably, they help transform the nation-state model to better reflect pluri-ethnic realities. In addition, they help weaken the nation-state principle by acknowledging and accommodating ethnic diversity.

As with multiculturalism, however, federalism and consociationalism can also heighten ethnic antagonisms. Both federalism and consociationalism require that the political elites of all communities are motivated to deal with ethnic conflict and make concessions. This requires considerable trust between ethnic communities and their leaders, something that is commonly in short supply. The successful implementation of federalism and consociationalism are also hampered by institutional stasis. That is, once states are created, it is very hard to change their basic structures because several mechanisms—ranging from power to costs to socialization—help to reinforce the structures. And even more than multiculturalism, both federalism and consociationalism institutionalize ethnic difference, something that can severely obstruct national unity over the long term.

In addition to these problems, political scientist Arend Lijphart notes several conditions that are needed for consociationalism: clear communal divisions, a balance of communal power, the presence of an external threat faced by all communities, common loyalty to the state, relative socioeconomic equality among communities, a small population, and a multiparty system with community-based parties (Kerr 2006). The creation of a federal system of government also has particular requirements that make it unviable in many places (McGarry and O'Leary 2005). One necessary condition is the concentration of communities in geographic regions; if communities are dispersed throughout a country, federalism will not increase communal representation and self-rule in any way. The construction of a federal system also requires a radical reorganization of the state. This reorganization, in turn, depends on the pre-existence of a state capable of implementing the reforms (Heller 2001; Lange 2009, 199).

Clearly, multiculturalism, federalism, and consociationalism are not ready-made solutions. That being said, the nation-state model is such an influential determinant of ethnic violence that policy makers trying to limit ethnic violence must consider different variations and combinations of multiculturalism, federalism, and consociationalism and use them as ideals to guide policy. And as with any ideal, officials must implement them in a realistic fashion that takes into consideration local conditions and adjusts the ideals to better match local needs and conditions. Rigid applications of these policies might do more harm than good.

In addition to transforming the nation-state, this book offers evidence that policies promoting robust, rights-based democracy, effective states, and economic development could reduce the risk of ethnic violence. Unfortunately, such policy prescriptions are also difficult to implement. In fact, most regions in the world today are actively pursuing all three, but with only limited success. One clear finding in the social sciences is that unique characteristics allowed all three to emerge in North America and Western Europe, and important structural conditions are needed for other regions to successfully promote economic growth, create rights-based democracy, and strengthen states. It is therefore one thing to say that we should pursue these policies, but it is a completely different thing to successfully implement them. Moreover, while rights-based democracy, economic development, and state building help to limit ethnic violence in the long run, they can be counterproductive in the short run. For example, places rarely go directly from authoritarianism to rights-based democracy, and moving from authoritarianism to limited democracy increases the risk of ethnic violence, thereby creating a Catch-22. Similarly, policy promoting economic growth and state building commonly heighten ethnic divisions and antagonisms.

Much of the difficulty with multiculturalism, federalism, consociationalism, democratization, state building, and economic development is that they are large-scale projects requiring strong leadership, considerable information about local conditions, high levels of governance, social consensus, an abundance of resources, and lots of hard work over an extended period of time. Without all six, such grandiose attempts at social engineering commonly fail. Less grandiose policy prescriptions are therefore more feasible and desirable.

One midlevel policy that can limit ethnic violence involves changing myth-symbol complexes. Because myth-symbol complexes affect ethnic conscious-ness, emotional prejudice, ethnic obligations, and the mobilizational resources that contribute to violence, readjusting myth-symbol complexes can reduce the risk of ethnic violence. Efforts to change myth-symbol complexes should re-place elements that direct negative emotions toward Others with more inclusive myth-symbol complexes that depict Others more favorably. They should also de-scribe past myth-symbol complexes and the reasons for their inappropriateness. Such revisionism is one important means of delegitimizing past myth-symbol complexes and giving people a historical awareness that allows them to critically assess the more intolerant views of previous generations. This is necessary to limit the socializing impact of parents and grandparents who possess emotional prejudice and accept ethnic obligations.

So just how do officials go about changing myth-symbol complexes? While states must also play an important role in revising and propagating myths and symbols that depict the nation in less divisive and more inclusive ways, in most places education is the most effective means of implementing these changes. The previous chapters highlight the socializing power of education, showing how it commonly promotes oppositional identities and emotional prejudice. In the same way, schools can be used to limit ethnic violence by disseminating new information about ethnic origins, key historical events, and the relationship be-tween different ethnicities.

Even if this reform is more viable than larger-scale policies, obstacles and in-herent problems limit the feasibility of transforming myth-symbol complexes in many places. Unfortunately, educational and political reforms that touch on myth-symbol complexes risk mobilizing ethnic extremists in opposition, and this risk is greatest in the places that are most in need of reform. In Cyprus, for ex-ample, different Greek Cypriot organizations lobbied the government to portray Turkish Cypriots more positively, but these efforts mobilized a powerful back-lash that strengthened the position of ethnic extremists. And even if educational curricula changes are formally adopted, they depend on the willingness of instructors to teach the new material, and many will undoubtedly refuse to teach it. The attempted reforms in Greek Cypriot schools were sparked by reforms implemented in Turkish Cypriot schools that portrayed Greek Cypriots in a more positive light. Yet after the reforms, many Turkish Cypriot teachers failed to teach this new message because they were not comfortable with it (Vural 2012). And a few years later, a different government was elected, and Turkish Cypriot schools reverted to their old textbooks depicting Greek Cypriots as an evil threat.

A second midlevel policy addresses ethnic violence through international relations. As noted in the previous section, international actors and institutions can sanction states and charge leaders who are implicated in ethnic violence, pressuring them to contain violence and stopping them from instigating it. To further limit ethnic violence, individual countries and organizations should stop supporting governments involved in ethnic violence, condemn states and leaders who participate in ethnic violence, and give greater support to the International Court's efforts to try leaders implicated in ethnic violence. Through these efforts, the states of late modernizers should become increasingly Hobbesian and less Rousseauian. Thankfully, many international institutions, national governments, and nongovernmental organizations are already pressuring states to respect human rights and stop ethnic violence.

In the end, different policies—if skillfully applied to fit local conditions—could help limit ethnic violence, but all policies face obstacles and have limits, and there is no silver bullet that can eradicate ethnic violence altogether. Our modern environments, which create the fertile conditions that unleash ethnic violence, are simply too difficult to radically alter, and grandiose high-modern policies commonly cause more harm than good (Scott 1998). As Max Weber (2002 [1905]) famously notes, modernity's mechanical foundations have taken on a life of their own and now exert enormous influence over our lives, leaving us little choice but to follow the flow of modernity by paddling our boats with the current at our backs. Yet we are not helpless. Most notably, a better understanding of modernity and ethnic violence allows us to navigate through the rapids and around the debris that lay in our paths. The primary goal of this book is to help to cultivate such an understanding.

References

Abernethy, David. 1969. *The Political Dilemma of Popular Education: An African Case.* Stanford, CA: Stanford University Press.

——. 2000. *The Dynamics of Global Dominance: European Overseas Empires 1415–1980.* New Haven, CT: Yale University Press.

Abraham, Arthur. 1978. *Mende Politics and Government under Colonial Rule.* New York: Oxford University Press.

Abramowitz, Isidore, Hannah Arendt, Abraham Brick, Jessurun Cardozo, Albert Einstein, Herman Eisen, Hayim Fineman, M. Gallen, H. H. Harris, Zelig S. Harris, Sidney Hook, Fred Karush, Bruria Kaufman, Irma L. Lindheim, Nachman Majsel, Seymour Melman, Myer D. Mendelson, Harry M. Orlinsky, Samuel Pitlick, Fritz Rohrlich, Louis P. Roker, Ruth Sager, Itzhak Sankowsky, I. M. Schoenberg, Samuel Shuman, M. Zinger, Irma Wolpe, and Stefan Wolpe. 1948. "New Palestine Party: Visit of Menachen Begin and Aims of Political Movement Discussed." *New York Times*, December 4, 1948. https://archive.org/stream/AlbertEinsteinLetterToTheNewYorkTimes.December41948/Einstein_Letter_NYT_4_Dec_1948#page/n0/mode/2up. Accessed April 2, 2015.

Ahmad, Rafiq. 1984. *The Assam Massacre 1983: A Documentary Record.* Lahore: Centre for South Asian Studies.

Alexander, Thomas, and Beryl Parker. 1929. *The New Education in the German Republic.* New York: John Day Company.

Ali, Merima, Odd-Helge Fjeldstad, Boqian Jiang, and Abdulaziz B. Shifa. 2015. "Colonial Legacy, State-Building and the Salience of Ethnicity in Sub-Saharan Africa." Chr. Michelson Institute. http://www.ictd.ac/ju-download/5-partner-publications/93-colonial-legacy-state-building-and-the-salience-of-ethnicity-in-sub-saharan-africa. Accessed April 12, 2016.

American Baptist Foreign Mission Society. 1913. "The Judson Centennial." Collection 4424, Folder 701-2-6. Division of Rare and Manuscript Collections, Cornell University Library.

——. 1923. "Sgaw Karen Mission." Collection 4424, Folder 705-2-3. Division of Rare and Manuscript Collections, Cornell University Library.

——. 1927. "Report of Devolution Committee of the Burma Mission." Folder 702-4-9. Division of Rare and Manuscript Collections, Cornell University Library.

——. 1931. "The Karen Mission in Burma." Collection 4424, Folder 701-2-7. Division of Rare and Manuscript Collections, Cornell University Library.

American Baptist Historical Society. 2015. "Karen Language and Loyalty." http://judson200.org/index.php/burma-language-exhibit/57-morning-star-articles/195-karen-language-and-loyalty. Accessed September 15, 2015.

Anderson, Benedict. 1983. *Imagined Communities: Reflections on the Origin and Spread of Nationalism.* London: Verso.

Anderson, Eric. 2009. *Inclusive Masculinity: The Changing Nature of Masculinities.* New York: Routledge.

Arendt, Hannah. 1966. *The Origins of Totalitarianism.* New York: Harcourt, Brace, & World.

——. 2006. *Eichmann in Jerusalem: A Report on the Banality of Violence*. New York: Penguin Books.

Balcells, Laia. 2013. "Mass Schooling and Catalan Nationalism." *Nationalism and Ethnic Politics* 19: 467–86.

Balfour, Arthur James. 1917. http://www.ihr.org/jhr/v06/v06p389_John.html. Accessed April 3, 2015.

Banerjee, Sikata. 2012. *Muscular Nationalisms: Gender, Violence, and Empire in India and Ireland, 1914–2004*. New York: New York University Press.

Bannon, Alicia, Edward Miguel, and Daniel Posner. 2004. "Sources of Ethnic Identification in Africa." *Afrobarometer* Working Papers No. 44. http://www.sscnet.ucla.edu/polisci/wgape/papers/5_Bannon.pdf. Accessed April 2, 2015.

Banton, Michael. 1997. *Ethnic and Racial Consciousness*. New York: Longman Publishers.

Barbalet, Jack. 2002. "Introduction: Why Emotions Are Crucial." In *Emotions and Sociology*, edited by Jack Barbalet, 1–9. Malden, MA: Blackwell Publishers.

Bartlett, Robert. 1993. *The Making of Europe: Conquest, Colonization and Cultural Change, 950–1350*. Princeton, NJ: Princeton University Press.

Baruah, Sanjib. 1986. "Immigration, Ethnic Conflict, and Political Turmoil: Assam, 1979–1985." *Asian Survey* 26: 1184–1206.

——. 1994. "'Ethnic' Conflict as State-Society Struggle: The Poetics and Politics of Assamese Micro-Nationalism." *Modern Asian Studies* 28: 649–71.

Bauman, Zygmunt. 1989. *Modernity and the Holocaust*. Ithaca, NY: Cornell University Press.

Bayly, Christopher A. 2004. *The Birth of the Modern World, 1780–1914*. Oxford: Blackwell Publishers.

Behiels, Michael. 1985. *Prelude to Quebec's Quiet Revolution: Liberalism versus Neo-Nationalism, 1945–1960*. Montreal: McGill-Queen's University Press.

Benford, Robert, and David Snow. 2000. "Framing Processes and Social Movements: An Overview and Assessment. *Annual Review of Sociology* 26: 611–39.

Bennett, Scott D., and Christian Davenport. 2003. *Minorities at Risk Project (MARGene v1.0)*. http://www.cidcm.umd.edu/inscr/mar/. Accessed May 1, 2006.

Bergmann, Werner. 1997. "Antisemitism and Xenophobia in Germany since Unification." In *Antisemitism and Xenophobia in Germany After Unification*, edited by Hermann Kurthen, Werner Bergmann, and Reiner Erb, 21–38. New York: Oxford University Press.

Berezin, Mabel. 1997. *Making the Fascist Self: The Political Culture of Interwar Italy*. Ithaca, NY: Cornell University Press.

——. 1999. "Political Belonging: Emotion, Nation and Identity in Fascist Italy." In *State/Culture*, edited by George Steinmetz, 355–77. Ithaca, NY: Cornell University Press.

——. 2002. "Secure States: Towards a Political Sociology of Emotions." In *Emotions and Sociology*, edited by Jack Barbalet, 33–52. Malden, MA: Blackwell Publishers.

Berkowitz, Leonard. 1993. *Aggression: Its Causes, Consequences, and Control*. New York: McGraw-Hill.

Berman, Sherri. 1997. "Civil Society and the Collapse of the Weimar Republic." *World Politics* 49: 401–29.

Berrebi, Claude. 2007. "Evidence about the Link between Education, Poverty, and Terrorism among Palestinians." *Peace Economics, Peace Science, and Public Policy* 13: 1–36.

Billig, Michael. 1995. *Banal Nationalism*. London: Sage Publications.

Blackburn, G.W. 1985. *Education in the Third Reich: A Study of Race and History in Nazi Textbooks*. Albany: State University of New York Press.

Bland, Caroline. 2013. "Hermann's Handmaidens? Male Archetypes and German Nationalism in Nineteenth-Century Women's Writing." *Women's Writing* 20: 567–85.

Blanton, Robert, David Mason, and Brian Athow. 2001. "Colonial Style and Post-Colonial Ethnic Conflict in Africa." *Journal of Peace Research* 38: 473–91.

Blee, Kathleen. 1991. *Women of the Klan: Racism and Gender in the 1920s*. Berkeley: University of California Press.

Bloom, Stephen G. 2005. "Lessons of a Lifetime." *Smithsonian*, September. http://www.smithsonianmag.com/history/lesson-of-a-lifetime-72754306/?no-ist. Accessed June 2, 2016.

Bobo, Lawrence, and Frederick Licari. 1989. "Education and Political Tolerance: Testing the Effects of Cognitive Sophistication and Target Group Affect." *Public Opinion Quarterly* 53: 258–308.

Bombay, Amy, Kimberly Matheson, and Hymie Anisman. 2011. "The Impact of Stressors on Second Generation Indian Residential School Survivors." *Transcultural Psychiatry* 48: 367–91.

Bowker, Lee. 1998. *Masculinities and Violence*. New York: Sage Publishers.

Brass, Paul. 1997. *Theft of an Idol: Text and Context in the Representation of Collective Violence*. Princeton, NJ: Princeton University Press.

Braude, Benjamin. 1997. "The Sons of Noah and the Construction of Ethnic and Geographical Identities in the Medieval and Early Modern Periods." *William and Mary Quarterly* 54: 103–41.

Brehm, Hollie Nyseth. 2013. "Conditions and Courses of Genocide: The Case of 1994 Rwanda." Paper presented at the annual meeting for the American Sociological Association Annual Meetings, New York, August 10–13.

Breuilly, John. 1994. *Nationalism and the State*. Chicago: University of Chicago Press.

Brewer, Marilyne. 1999. "The Psychology of Prejudice: Ingroup Love or Outgroup Hate?" *Journal of Social Issues* 55: 429–44.

Brown, Donald. 1991. *Human Universals*. Philadelphia: Temple University Press.

Brown, Norman. 1984. *Hood, Bonnet, and Little Brown Jug: Texas Politics, 1921–1928*. College Station: Texas A&M University Press.

Brubaker, Rogers. 2004. *Ethnicity Without Groups*. Cambridge, MA: Harvard University Press.

——. 2015. "Religious Dimensions of Political Conflict and Violence." *Sociological Theory* 33: 1–19.

Brubaker, Rogers, and David Laitin. 1998. "Ethnic and Nationalist Violence." *Annual Review of Sociology* 24: 423–52.

Brustein, William. 2003. *Roots of Hate: Anti-Semitism in Europe before the Holocaust*. Cambridge: Cambridge University Press.

Brusten, Manfred. 1997. "Knowledge, Feelings, and Attitudes of German University Students toward the Holocaust." In *Antisemitism and Xenophobia in Germany After Unification*, edited by Hermann Kurthen, Werner Bergmann, and Reiner Erb, 88–109. New York: Oxford University Press.

Buadaeng, Kwanchewan. 2007. "Ethnic Identities of the Karen Peoples in Burma and Thailand." In *Identity Matters: Ethnic and Sectarian Conflict*, edited by James Peacock, Patricia Thorton, and Patrick Inman, 73–97. New York: Berghahn Books.

Bunker, Alonzo. 1902. *Soo Thah: A Tale of the Making of the Karen Nation*. London: Oliphant, Anderson, & Ferrier.

Burbank, Garin. 1971. "Agrarian Radicals and Their Opponents: Political Conflict in Southern Oklahoma." *Journal of American History* 58: 5–23.

Burg, Steven, and Paul Shoup. 1999. *The War in Bosnia-Herzogovina: Ethnic Conflict and International Intervention*. New York: M. E. Sharpe.

Callahan, Mary. 2003. *Making Enemies: War and State Building in Burma*. Ithaca, NY: Cornell University Press.

Campbell, Angus. 1952. "Factors Associated with Attitudes toward Jews." In *Readings in Social Psychology*, edited by T. Newcomb and E. Hartley, 603–12. New York: Henry Holt and Company.

Cardoso, Fernando Henrique, and Enzo Faletto. 1979. *Dependency and Development in Latin America*. Berkeley: University of California Press.

Carpenter, C. H. 1883. *Self-Support, Illustrated in the History of the Bassein Karen Mission*. Boston: Franklin Press.

Cesarani, David. 2004. *Becoming Eichmann: Rethinking the Life, Crimes, and Trial of a "Desk Murderer."* London: Heinemann.

Chandra, Kanchan, ed. 2012. *Constructivist Theories of Ethnic Politics*. New York: Oxford University Press.

Chhabra, K. M. L. 1992. *Assam Challenge*. Delhi: Konark Publishers.

Chickering, Roger. 1984. *We Men Who Feel Most German: A Cultural Study of the Pan-German League, 1886–1914*. Boston: Allen & Unwin.

Chirot, Daniel, and Clark McCauley. 2006. *Why Not Kill Them All: The Logic and Prevention of Mass Political Murder*. Princeton, NJ: Princeton University Press.

Cikara, Mina, Matthew Botvinick, and Susan Fiske. 2011. "Us Versus Them: Social Identity Shapes Neural Responses to Intergroup Competition and Harm." *Psychological Science* 22: 1–8.

Cleary, Matthew. 2000. "Democracy and Indigenous Rebellion in Latin America." *Comparative Political Studies* 33: 1123–53.

Clift, Dominique. 1982. *Quebec Nationalism in Crisis*. Montreal: McGill-Queen's University Press.

Cocoltchos, Christopher. 1992. "The Invisible Empire and the Search for the Orderly Community: The Ku Klux Klan in Anaheim, California." In *The Invisible Empire in the West: Toward a New Historical Appraisal of the Ku Klux Klan of the 1920s*, edited by Shawn Lay, 97–120. Chicago: University of Illinois Press.

Cohn, Bernard. 1987. *An Anthropologist Among the Historians*. Delhi: Oxford University Press.

Collins, Randall. 2004. *Interaction Ritual Chains*. Princeton, NJ: Princeton University Press.

——. 2008. *Violence: A Micro-Sociological Theory*. Princeton, NJ: Princeton University Press.

Connor, Walker. 1994. *Ethnonationalism: The Quest for Understanding*. Princeton, NJ: Princeton University Press.

Conrad, Joseph. 1999 [1899]. *Heart of Darkness and Other Stories*. Cologne: Könemann.

Conradt, David. 1980. "Changing German Political Culture." In *The Civic Culture Revisited*, edited by Gabriel Almond and Sidney Verba, 212–72. Toronto: Little, Brown and Company.

Corrado, Raymond, and Irwin Cohen. 2003. *Mental Health Profiles for a Sample of British Columbia's Survivors of the Canadian Residential School System*. Ottawa: Aboriginal Healing Foundation.

Cottrell, Catherine, and Steven Neuberg. 2005. "Different Emotional Reactions to Different Groups: A Sociofunctional Threat-Based Approach to Prejudice." *Journal of Personality and Social Psychology* 88: 770–89.

Crone, Patricia. 2003. *Pre-Industrial Societies: Anatomy of the Pre-Modern World*. London: Oneworld Publications.

Cuneo, Carl, and James Curtis. 1974. "Quebec Separatism: An Analysis of Determinants within Social-Class Levels." *Canadian Review of Sociology* 11: 1–29.

Damasio, Antonio. 2005. *Descartes' Error: Emotion, Reason, and the Human Brain*. New York: Penguin.

Darden, Keith. Forthcoming. *Resisting Occupation in Eurasia: Mass Schooling and the Creation of Durable National Loyalties*. New York: Cambridge University Press.

Darwin, John. 2009. *The Empire Project: The Rise and Fall of the British World System, 1830–1970*. New York: Cambridge University Press.

Das, Amiya Kumar. 1982. *Assam's Agony: A Socio-Economic and Political Analysis*. New Delhi: Lancers Publishers.

Dasgupta, Jyotirindra. 1997. "Community, Authenticity, and Autonomy: Insurgence and Institutional Development in India's Northeast." *Journal of Asian Studies* 56: 345–70.

David, Paul A. 1985. "Clio and the Economics of QWERTY." *American Economic Review* 75: 332–37.

Debroy, Bibek, Laveesh Bhandari, and Nilanjan Banik. 2003. "How Are the States Doing?" New Delhi: Rajiv Gandhi Institute for Contemporary Studies.

De Dreu, Carsten, Lindred Greer, Michel Handgraaf, Shaul Shalvi, Gerben Van Kleef, Matthijs Baas, Femke Ten Velden, Eric Van Dijk, and Sander Feith. 2010. "The Neuropeptide Oxytocin Regulates Parochial Altruism in Intergroup Conflict Among Humans." *Science* 328: 1408–11.

De Dreu, Carsten, Lindred Greer, Gerben Van Kleef, Shaul Shalvi, and Michel Handgraff. 2011. "Oxytocin Promotes Human Ethnocentrism." *Proceedings of the National Academy of Sciences*: 1–5.

Deka, Meeta. 1996. *Student Movements in Assam*. New Delhi: Vikas Publishing House.

DeLisi, Matt, Zachary Umphress, and Michael Vaughn. 2009. "The Criminology of the Amygdala." *Criminal Justice and Behavior* 36: 1241–52.

de Silva, K. M. 1986. *Managing Ethnic Tensions in Multi-Ethnic Societies: Sri Lanka 1880–1985*. New York: University Press of America.

Deutsch, Karl. 1953. *Nationalism and Social Communication: An Inquiry into the Foundations of Nationality*. New York: Technology Press of the Massachusetts Institute of Technology.

——. 1969. *Nationalism and Its Alternatives*. New York: Knopf.

de Vries, Jan. 1984. *European Urbanization, 1500–1800*. New York: Routledge.

Diamond, Jared. 2012. *The World Until Yesterday: What Can We Learn from Traditional Societies?* New York: Viking Press.

Dierkes, Julian. 2010. *Postwar History Education in Japan and the Germanys: Guilty Lessons*. New York: Routledge.

Dike, Kenneth Onwuka. 1956. *Trade and Politics in the Niger Delta, 1830–1885: An Introduction to the Economic and Political History of Nigeria*. Oxford: Clarendon Press.

DiMaggio, Paul, and Walter Powell, eds. 1991. *The New Institutionalism in Organizational Analysis*. Chicago: University of Chicago Press.

Douglass, Frederick. 1881. "The Color Line." *North American Review* 132: 567–77.

Dovidio, John F., Samuel L. Gaertner, Alice M. Isen, and Robert Lowrance. 1995. "Group Representations and Intergroup Bias: Positive Affect, Similarity, and Group Size." *Personality and Social Psychology Bulletin* 21: 868–77.

Dozier, Rush. 2002. *Why We Hate: Understanding, Curbing, and Eliminating Hate in Ourselves and Our World*. New York: McGraw-Hill.

Drum, Kevin. 2013. "America's Real Criminal Element: Lead." *Mother Jones*, January/
    February. http://www.motherjones.com/environment/2013/01/lead-crime-link-
    gasoline?page-1. Accessed May 5, 2014.
Du Bois, W. E. B. 2014. *W. E. B. Du Bois: Selections from His Writings*. Edited by Bob
    Blaisdell. Mineola, NY: Dover Publications.
Duby, Georges. 1980. *The Three Orders*. Chicago: University Press of Chicago.
Duckitt, John. 2003. "Prejudice and Intergroup Hostility." In *Oxford Handbook of
    Political Psychology*, edited by David Sears, Leonie Huddy, and Robert Jervis,
    559–600. New York: Oxford University Press.
Dunbar, Robin. 1992. "Neocortex Size as a Constraint on Group Size in Primates."
    Journal of Human Evolution 22: 469–93.
Durkheim, Émile. 1965 [1912]. *The Elementary Forms of the Religious Life*. New York:
    Free Press.
———. 1979 [1897]. *Suicide: A Study of Sociology*. New York: Free Press.
———. 1984 [1893]. *The Division of Labor in Society*. New York: Free Press.
Dutta, Uddipan. 2005. *Language Management and Transition of Assamese Identity,
    1826–2005*. Guwahati: Omeo Kumar Das Institute of Social Change and
    Development.
Elias, Brenda, Javier Mignone, Madelyn Hall, Say P. Hong, Lyna Hart, and Jitender
    Sareen. 2012. "Trauma and Suicide Behaviour Histories among a Canadian
    Indigenous Population: An Empirical Exploration of the Potential Role of
    Canada's Residential School System." *Social Science Medicine* 74: 1560–69.
Elias, John. 2013. "Education for Peace and Justice." *Catholic Education: A Journal of
    Inquiry and Practice* 9: 160–77.
Ellemers, Naomi, Ad van Knippenberg, Nanne de Vries, and Henk Wilkie. 1988. "Social
    Identification and Permeability of Group Boundaries." *European Journal of Social
    Psychology* 18: 479–513.
Ellemers, Naomi, Ad van Knippenberg, and Henk Wilkie. 1990. "The Influence of the
    Permeability of Group Boundaries and Stability of Group Status on Strategies of
    Individual Mobility and Social Change." *British Journal of Social Psychology* 29:
    233–46.
Elliott, John H. 1992. "A Europe of Composite Monarchies." *Past and Present* 137:
    48–71.
Ertman, Thomas. 1997. *Birth of the Leviathan: Building States and Regimes in Medieval
    and Early Modern Europe*. New York: Cambridge University Press.
Estrin, Mark ed. 2002. *Orson Welles: Interviews*. Jackson: University Press of Mississippi.
Falter, Jürgen. 1990. "The Two Hindenburg Elections of 1925 and 1932: A Total Reversal
    of Voter Coalitions." *Central European History* 23: 225–41.
Fearon, James, and David Laitin. 2003. "Ethnicity, Insurgency, and Civil War." *American
    Political Science Review* 97: 75–90.
Fedo, Michael. 2000. *The Lynchings in Duluth*. St. Paul: Minnesota Historical Society
    Press.
Ferguson, R. Brian. 2012a. "Pinker's List: Exaggerating Prehistoric War Mortality." In
    *War, Peace, and Human Nature: The Convergence of Evolutionary and Cultural
    Views*, edited by Douglas P. Fry, 112–31. New York: Oxford University Press.
———. 2012b. "The Prehistory of War and Peace in Europe and the Near East." In *War,
    Peace, and Human Nature: The Convergence of Evolutionary and Cultural Views*,
    edited by Douglas P. Fry, 191–240. New York: Oxford University Press.
Festinger, Leon. 1954. "A Theory of Social Comparison Processes." *Human Relations* 7:
    117–40.

Fichte, Johann Gottlieb. 2008. *Addresses to the German Nation*. New York: Cambridge University Press.

Finlay, Graeme. 2011. "The Emergence of Human Distinctiveness: The Genetic Story." In *Rethinking Human Nature: A Multidisciplinary Approach*, edited by Malcolm Jeeves, 107–27. Grand Rapids, MI: William B. Eerdmans.

Fiske, Allan Page, and Tage Shakti Rai. 2015. *Virtuous Violence: Hurting and Killing to Create, Sustain, End, and Honor Social Relations*. New York: Cambridge University Press.

Fiske, Susan. 2002. "What We Know Now about Bias and Intergroup Conflict, the Problem of the Century." *Current Directions in Psychological Science* 11: 123–28.

———. 2009. "From Dehumanization and Objectification to Rehumanization: Neuroimaging Studies on the Building Blocks of Emphathy." *Annals of the New York Acadamy of Sciences* 1167: 31–34.

———. 2011. *Envy Up, Scorn Down: How Comparison Divides Us*. New York: Russell Sage Foundation.

Fiske, Susan, Amy Cudy, and Peter Glick. 2002. "Emotions Up and Down: Intergroup Emotions Result from Perceived Status and Competition." In *From Prejudice to Intergroup Emotions: Differentiated Reactions to Social Groups*, edited by Diane M. Mackie and Eliot R. Smith, 247–64. New York: Psychology Press.

Forgas, Joseph P., and Stephanie Moylan. 1991. "Affective Influences on Stereotype Judgments." *Cognition and Emotion* 5: 379–97.

Franck, Raphaël, and Ilia Rainer. 2012. "Does the Leader's Ethnicity Matter? Ethnic Favoritism, Education, and Health in Sub-Saharan Africa." *American Political Science Review* 106: 294–325.

Fredrickson, George. 1997. *The Comparative Imagination: On the History of Racism, Nationalism, and Social Movements*. Los Angeles: University of California Press.

Freedman, David, and David Hemenway. 2000. "Precursors to Lethal Violence: A Death Row Sample." *Social Science and Medicine* 20: 1757–70.

Friedman, Willa, Michael Kremer, Edward Miguel, and Rebecca Thornton. 2011. "Education as Liberation?" NBER Working Paper No. 16939. http://www.nber.org/papers/w16939. Accessed July 7, 2011.

Fry, Douglas, and Patrik Söderberg. 2013. "Lethal Aggression in Mobile Forager Bands and Implications for the Origins of War." *Science* 341: 270–73.

Fund for Peace. 2015. Fragile States Index 2015. http://fsi.fundforpeace.org. Accessed August 4, 2015.

Fujii, Lee Ann. 2009. *Killing Neighbors: Webs of Violence in Rwanda*. Ithaca, NY: Cornell University Press.

Fukuyama, Francis. 1992. *The End of History and the Last Man*. New York: Free Press.

Gagnon, Alain, and Mary Beth Montcalm. 1990. *Quebec Beyond the Quiet Revolution*. Toronto: Nelson Canada.

Gagnon, V. P. 2004. *The Myth of Ethnic War: Serbia and Croatia in the 1990s*. Ithaca, NY: Cornell University Press.

Galaty, John. 1982. "Being 'Maasai'; Being 'People of Cattle': Ethnic Shifters in East Africa." *American Ethnologist* 9: 1–20.

Gallagher, Hugh Gregory. 1990. *By Trust Betrayed: Patients, Physicians, and the License to Kill in the Third Reich*. New York: Henry Holt and Company.

Gallese, Vittorio. 2001. "The 'Shared Manifold' Hypothesis: From Missor Neurons to Empathy." *Journal of Consciousness Studies* 8: 33–50.

Garcia, Luc. 2008. *Quand les Missionnaires Rencontraient les Vietnamiens (1920–1960)*. Paris: Karthala.

Gat, Azar. 2013. *Nations: The Long History and Deep Roots of Political Ethnicity and Nationalism*. New York: Cambridge University Press.

Gellner, Ernest. 1983. *Nations and Nationalism*. Oxford: Blackwell.

Gerstle, Gary. 2001. *American Crucible: Race and Nation in the Twentieth Century*. Princeton, NJ: Princeton University Press.

Giddens, Anthony, and Christopher Pierson. 1998. *Conversations with Anthony Giddens: Making Sense of Modernity*. Stanford, CA: Stanford University Press.

Gilley, Bruce. 2004. "Against the Concept of Ethnic Conflict." *Third World Quarterly* 25: 1155–66.

Goffman, Erving. 1961. *Asylums: Essays on the Social Situation of Mental Patients and Other Inmates*. New York: Anchor Books.

——. 1967. *Interaction Ritual: Essays on Face-to-Face Behavior*. Garden City, NY: Anchor Books.

Goldberg, Robert A. 1992. "Denver: Queen City of the Colorado Realm." In *The Invisible Empire in the West: Toward a New Historical Appraisal of the Ku Klux Klan of the 1920s*, edited by Shawn Lay, 39–66. Chicago: University of Illinois Press.

Goodwin, Jeff. 2005. "Revolutions and Revolutionary Movements." In *Handbook of Political Sociology: States, Civil Society, and Globalization*, edited by Thomas Janoski, Robert Alford, Alexander Hicks, and Mildred Schwartz, 404–22. New York: Cambridge University Press.

Gracey, Harry. 1975. "Learning the Student Role: Kindergarten as Academic Boot Camp." In *The Sociology of Education: A Source Book*, edited by H. R. Stub, 82–95. Homewood, IL: Dorsey Press.

Greene, Joshua. 2013. *Moral Tribes: Emotion, Reason, and the Gap Between Us and Them*. New York: Penguin Books.

Greenfeld, Liah. 1992. *Nationalism: Five Roads to Modernity*. Cambridge, MA: Harvard University Press.

Guérard, Albert. 1959. *France: A Modern History*. Ann Arbor: University of Michigan Press.

Guindon, Hubert. 1964. "Social Unrest, Social Class, and Quebec's Bureaucratic Revolution." *Queen's Quarterly* 71: 150–62.

Gurr, Ted. 1993. *Minorities at Risk: A Global View of Ethnopolitical Conflict*. Washington, DC: United States Institute of Peace Press.

Gutmann, Matthew. 2003. *Changing Men and Changing Masculinities in Latin America*. Durham, NC: Duke University Press.

Habermas, Jürgen. 1981. "Modernity versus Postmodernity." *New German Critique* 22: 3–14.

Hahn, H. J. 1998. *Education and Society in Germany*. New York: Berg.

Haidt, Jonathan. 2012. *The Righteous Mind: Why Good People Are Divided By Politics and Religion*. New York: Pantheon Books.

Hale, Henry. 2004. "Explaining Ethnicity." *Comparative Political Studies* 37: 458–85.

Hall, John. 1986. *Powers and Liberties: The Causes and Consequences of the Rise of the West*. Berkeley, CA: University of California Press.

Hamilton, Richard. 1982. *Who Voted for Hitler?* Princeton, NJ: Princeton University Press.

Hamilton, Richard, and Maurice Pinard. 1976. "The Bases of Parti Quebecois Support in Recent Quebec Elections." *Canadian Journal of Political Science* 9: 3–26.

Harriden, Jessica. 2002. "'Making a Name for Themselves': Karen Identity and the Politicization of Ethnicity in Burma." *Journal of Burma Studies* 7: 84–144.

Harrington, Evan. 2004. "The Social Psychology of Hatred." *Journal of Hate Studies* 3: 49–82.

Hatfield, Elaine, John Cacioppo, and Richard Rapson. 1994. *Emotional Contagion.* New York: Cambridge University Press.

Hatty, Suzanne. 2000. *Masculinities, Violence and Culture.* New York: Sage Publishers.

Hegre, Håvard, Tanja Ellingsen, Scott Gates, and Nils Petter Gleditsch. 2001. "Toward a Democratic Civil Peace? Democracy, Political Change, and Civil War, 1816–1992." *American Political Science Review* 95: 33–48.

Heilbron, Johan, Lars Magnusson, and Björn Wittrock, eds. 1998. *The Rise of the Social Science and the Formation of Modernity: Conceptual Change in Context, 1750–1850.* Boston: Kluwer Academic Publishers.

Heller, Patrick. 1999. *The Labor of Development: Workers and the Transformation of Capitalism in Kerala, India.* Ithaca, NY: Cornell University Press.

———. 2001. "Moving the State: The Politics of Democratic Decentralization in Kerala, South Africa, and Porto Alegre." *Politics and Society* 29: 121–63.

Hitler, Adolf. 1971 [1925]. *Mein Kampf.* New York: Houghton Mifflin.

Hobbes, Thomas. 1949 [1642]. *De Cive.* New York: Appleton-Century-Crofts.

———. 1957 [1651]. *Leviathan.* New York: Oxford University Press.

Hobsbawm, Eric. 1992. *Nations and Nationalism since 1780.* New York: Cambridge University Press.

Hogg, Michael A., and Barbara A. Mullin. 1999. "Joining Groups to Reduce Uncertainty." In *Social Identity and Social Cognition*, edited by Dominic Abrams and Michael Hogg, 249–79. Malden, MA: Blackwell.

Horowitz, David. 1992. "Order, Solidarity, and Vigilance: The Ku Klux Klan in La Grande, Oregon." In *The Invisible Empire in the West: Toward a New Historical Appraisal of the Ku Klux Klan of the 1920s*, edited by Shawn Lay, 185–215. Chicago: University of Illinois Press.

Horowitz, Donald. 1985. *Ethnic Groups in Conflict.* Berkeley: University of California Press.

———. 2001. *The Deadly Ethnic Riot.* New York: Oxford University Press.

Horsman, Reginald. 1981. *Race and Manifest Destiny: The Origins of American Racial Anglo-Saxonism.* Cambridge, MA: Harvard University Press.

Hroch, Miroslav. 1985. *Social Preconditions of National Revival in Europe: A Comparative Analysis of the Social Composition of Patriotic Groups among the Smaller European Nations.* New York: Cambridge University Press.

Hudson, Nicholas. 1996. "From 'Nation' to 'Race': The Origins of Racial Classification in Eighteenth-Century Thought." *Eighteenth-Century Studies* 29: 247–64.

Huizinga, Johan. 1924. *The Waning of the Middle Ages: A Study of the Forms of Life, Thought and Art in France and the Netherlands in the XIVth and XVth Centuries.* London: E. Arnold.

Hull, Isabel. 2005. *Absolute Destruction: Military Culture and the Practices of War in Imperial Germany.* Ithaca, NY: Cornell University Press.

Human Rights Watch. 2003. *Ill Equipped: US Prisons and Offenders with Mental Illness.* New York: Human Rights Watch.

Humboldt, Wilhelm von. 1999. *On Language.* New York: Cambridge University Press.

Hume, David. 1951. *Theory of Politics.* Edited by Frederick Watkins. Edinburgh: Nelson.

———. 1975 [1738]. *A Treatise of Human Nature.* Edited by L.A. Selby-Bigge. Oxford: Clarendon Press.

Hunt, Nancy Rose. 1990. "Domesticity and Colonialism in Belgian Africa: Usumbura's Foyer Social, 1946–1960." *Signs* 15: 447–74.

Huntington, Samuel. 1991. *The Third Wave: Democratization in the Late Twentieth Century.* Norman: University of Oklahoma Press.

Innis, Harold. 2007. *Empire and Communications.* Toronto: Dundurn Press.

Jackman, Mary R. 1978. "General and Applied Tolerance: Does Education Increase Commitment to Racial Integration?" *American Journal of Political Science* 22: 302–24.

Jackson, Kenneth T. 1967. *The Ku Klux Klan in the City, 1915–1930*. New York: Oxford University Press.

Jackson, Robert H., and Carl Rosberg. 1982. "Why Africa's Weak States Persist: The Empirical and the Juridical in Statehood." *World Politics* 35: 1–24.

Jai, Janet. 2001. "Getting at the Roots of Terrorism." *The Christian Science Monitor*. http://www.csmonitor.com/2001/1210/p7s1-wogi.html. Accessed April 2, 2015.

Jauss, Hans Robert. 1982. *Toward an Aesthetic of Reception*. Minneapolis: University of Minnesota Press.

Jenkins, J. Craig. 1983. "Resource Mobilization Theory and Social Movements." *Annual Review of Sociology* 9: 527–53.

Jenkins, Philip. 1997. *The Extreme Right in Pennsylvania, 1925–1950*. Chapel Hill: University of North Carolina Press.

Jenkins, Richard. 2008. *Rethinking Ethnicity: Arguments and Explorations*. London: Sage Publications.

Joas, Hans. 2003. *War and Modernity*. Malden, MA: Polity Press.

Jørgensen, Anders Baltzer. 1997. "Foreword." In H. I. Marshall, *The Karen People of Burma: A Study of Anthropology and Ethnology*, v–xi. Bangkok: White Lotus.

Kaldor, Mary. 2004. "Nationalism and Globalisation." *Nations and Nationalism* 10: 161–77.

Kalberg, Stephen. 1980. "Max Weber's Types of Rationality: Cornerstones for the Analysis of Rationalization Processes in History." *American Journal of Sociology* 85: 1145–79.

——. 1994. *Max Weber's Comparative-Historical Sociology*. Chicago: University of Chicago Press.

Kalyvas, Stathis. 2006. *The Logic of Violence in Civil War*. New York: Cambridge University Press.

Kater, Michael. 1983. *The Nazi Party: A Social Profile of Members and Leaders, 1919–1945*. Oxford: Basil Blackwell.

——. 1984. "Everyday Antisemitism in Prewar Nazi Germany: The Popular Bases." *Yad Vashem Studies* 16: 129–59.

——. 1986. "The Nazi Physicians' League of 1929: Causes and Consequences." In *The Formation of the Nazi Constituency, 1919–1933*, edited by Thomas Childers, 147–81. Totowa: Barnes.

——. 1987. "Hitler's Early Doctors: Nazi Physicians in Pre-Depression Germany." *Journal of Modern History* 59: 25–52.

——. 1989. *Doctors under Hitler*. Chapel Hill: University of North Carolina Press.

——. 2002. "Criminal Physicians in the Third Reich." In *Medicine and Medical Ethics in Nazi German: Origins, Practices, Legacies*, edited by Francis Nicosia and Jonathan Huener, 77–92. New York: Berghahn Books.

Katz, Jack. 1988. *Seductions of Crime: Moral and Sensual Attractions in Doing Evil*. New York: Basic Books.

Kaufman, Michael. 1987. "The Construction of Masculinity and the Triad of Men's Violence." In *Beyond Patriarchy: Essays by Men on Pleasure, Power, and Change*, edited by Michael Kaufman, 1–29. New York: Oxford University Press.

Kaufman, Stuart. 2001. *Modern Hatreds: The Symbolic Politics of Ethnic War*. Ithaca, NY: Cornell University Press.

——. 2015. *Nationalist Passions*. Ithaca, NY: Cornell University Press.

Kedourie, Elie. 1961. *Nationalism*. London: Hutchinson.

Keeley, Lawrence. 1996. *War Before Civilization: The Myth of the Peaceful Savage*. New York: Oxford University Press.

Keith, Charles. 2012. *Catholic Vietnam: A Church from Empire to Nation*. Berkeley: University of California Press.

Kelly, Raymond. 2000. *Warless Societies and the Origins of War*. Ann Arbor: University of Michigan Press.

Kemper, Theodore. 1978. *A Social Interactional Theory of Emotions*. New York: Wiley.

Kerr, Michael. 2006. *Imposing Power-Sharing: Conflict and Coexistence in Northern Ireland and Lebanon*. Dublin: Irish Academic Press.

Kertzer, David. 1988. *Ritual, Politics, and Power*. New Haven, CT: Yale University Press.

Kimmel, Michael. 2005. *The History of Men: Essays on the History of American and British Masculinities*. Albany: State University of New York Press.

Kimura, Makiko. 2003. "Memories of the Massacre: Violence and Collective Identity in the Narratives on the Nellie Incident." *Asian Ethnicity* 4: 225–39.

King, Elisabeth. 2015. *From Classrooms to Conflict in Rwanda*. New York: Cambridge University Press.

Kohn, Hans. 1956. *The Idea of Nationalism: A Study in Its Origins and Background*. New York: Macmillan Company.

Korsgaard, Ove. 2014. *N.F.S. Grundtvig: As a Political Thinker*. Copenhagen: Djøf Publishing.

———. 2015. "How Grundtvig Became a Nation Builder." In *Building the Nation: N.F.S. Grundtvig and Danish National Identity*, edited by John A. Hall, Ove Korsgaard, and Ove Pedersen, 191–210. Montreal: McGill-Queens University Press.

Koselleck, Reinhart. 2002. *The Practice of Conceptual History: Timing History, Spacing Concepts*. Stanford, CA: Stanford University Press.

Koshar, Rudy. 1990. "Cult of Associations? The Lower Middle Classes in Weimar Germany." In *Splintered Classes: Politics and Lower Middle Classes in Interwar Europe*, edited by Rudy Koshar, 31–54. New York: Holmes and Meier.

Kösters, Klaus. 2009. "The Misappropriated Germanic Leader." *Atlantic Times*, May. http://www.atlantic-times.com/archive_detail.php?recordID=1776. Accessed April 2, 2015.

Kurthen, Hermann. 1997. "Antisemitism and Xenophobia in United Germany: How the Burden of the Past Affects the Present." In *Antisemitism and Xenophobia in Germany after Unification*, edited by Hermann Kurthen, Werner Bergmann, and Reiner Erb, 39–87. New York: Oxford University Press.

Kurthen, Hermann, Werner Bergmann, and Reiner Erb. 1997. "Introduction: Postunification Challenges to Germany Democracy." In *Antisemitism and Xenophobia in Germany after Unification*, edited by Hermann Kurthen, Werner Bergmann, and Reiner Erb, 3–17. New York: Oxford University Press.

Laczko, Leslie. 1987. "Perceived Communal Inequalities in Quebec: A Multidimensional Analysis." *Canadian Journal of Sociology* 12: 83–110.

Lange, Matthew. 2009. *Lineages of Despotism and Development: British Colonialism and State Power*. Chicago: University of Chicago Press.

———. 2012. *Educations in Ethnic Violence: Identity, Educational Bubbles, and Resource Mobilization*. New York: Cambridge University Press.

———. 2015. "State Formation and Transformation in Africa and Asia: The Third Phase of State Expansion." In *Oxford Handbook of Transformations of the State*, edited by Stephan Liebfried, Evelyne Huber, Matthew Lange, Jonah Levy, and John Stephens, 116 30. New York: Oxford University Press.

———. 2016. "Christian Missionaries and Ethnic Violence: A Comparative-Historical Analysis." Paper presented at the annual meetings for the Canadian Sociological Association, Calgary, Alberta, May 30–June 3.

Lange, Matthew, and Hrag Balian. 2008. "Containing Conflict or Instigating Unrest? A Test of the Effects of State Infrastructural Power on Civil Violence." *Studies in Comparative International Development* 43: 314–33.

Lange, Matthew, and Andrew Dawson. 2010. "Education and Ethnic Violence: A Cross-National Time-Series Analysis." *Nationalism and Ethnic Politics* 16: 216–39.

Lankina, Tomila, and Lullit Getachew. 2012. "Mission or Empire, World or Sword? The Human Capital Legacy in Postcolonial Democratic Development." *American Journal of Political Science* 56: 465–83.

Lavergne, Gary. 1997. *A Sniper in the Tower: The Charles Whitman Mass Murder.* Denton: University of Northern Texas Press.

Lay, Shawn, ed. 1992. *The Invisible Empire in the West: Toward a New Historical Appraisal of the Ku Klux Klan of the 1920s.* Chicago: University of Illinois Press.

Leyens, Jacques-Philippe, Brezo Cortes, Stephanie Demoulin, John F. Dovidio, Susan T. Fiske, Ruth Gaunt, Maria-Paola Paladino, Amando Rodriguez-Perez, Ramon Rodriguez-Torres, and Jeroen Vaes. 2003. "Emotional Prejudice, Essentialism, and Nationalism." *European Journal of Social Psychology* 33: 703–17.

Lian, Jason, and David Matthews. 1998. "Does the Vertical Mosaic Still Exist? Ethnicity and Income in Canada, 1991." *Canadian Review of Sociology and Anthropology* 35: 461–81.

Lieberman, Evan S., and Prerna Singh. 2012. "The Institutional Origins of Ethnic Violence." *Comparative Politics* 45: 1–24.

Lieven, Dominic. 1999. "Dilemmas of Empire 1859–1918: Power, Territory, Identity." *Journal of Contemporary History* 34: 163–200.

Linden, Ian. 1977. *Church and Revolution in Rwanda.* Manchester: Manchester University Press.

Lipset, Seymour Martin. 1963. *Political Man: The Social Bases of Politics.* Garden City, NY: Doubleday.

Lipset, Seymour Martin, and Earl Raab. 1970. *The Politics of Unreason: Right-Wing Extremism in America 1790–1970.* New York: Harper and Row.

Loizides, Neophytos. 2009. "Religious Nationalism and Adaptation in Southeast Europe." *Nationalities Papers* 37: 203–27.

Lowe, Keith. 2012. *Savage Continent: Europe in the Aftermath of World War II.* New York: Picador.

Lowenstein, Steven. 2005. "Jewish Intermarriage and Conversion in Germany and Austria." *Modern Judaism* 25: 23–61.

Mackie, Diane M., Thierry Devos, and Eliot R. Smith. 2000. "Intergroup Emotions: Explaining Offensive Action Tendencies in an Intergroup Context." *Journal of Personality and Social Psychology* 79: 602–16.

MacLean, Nancy. 1994. *Behind the Mask of Chivalry: The Making of the Second Ku Klux Klan.* New York: Oxford University Press.

Madrid, Raul. 2012. *The Rise of Ethnic Politics in Latin America.* New York: Cambridge University Press.

Mahoney, James. 2000. "Path Dependence and Historical Sociology." *Theory and Society* 29: 507–48.

Malešević, Siniša. 2004. *The Sociology of Ethnicity.* London: Sage Publications.

———. 2013. *Nation-States and Nationalism.* Malden, MA: Polity Press.

Mamdani, Mahmood. 2001. *When Victims Become Killers: Colonialism, Nativism, and the Genocide in Rwanda.* Princeton, NJ: Princeton University Press.

———. 2004. *Good Muslim, Bad Muslim: America, the Cold War, and the Roots of Terror.* New York: Three Leaves Press.

———. 2012. *Define and Rule: Native as Political Identity*. Cambridge, MA: Harvard University Press.

Mann, Michael. 1984. "The Autonomous Power of the State: Its Origins, Mechanisms and Results." *Archives Européennes de Sociologie* 25: 185–213.

———. 1986. *The Sources of Social Power I: A History of Power from the Beginning to AD 1760*. New York: Cambridge University Press.

———. 2000. "Were the Perpetrators of Genocide 'Ordinary Men' or 'Real Nazis'? Results from Fifteen Hundred Biographies." *Holocaust and Genocide Studies* 14: 331–66.

———. 2005. *The Dark Side of Democracy: Explaining Ethnic Cleansing*. New York: Cambridge University Press.

Manville, Philip Brook. 1990. *The Origins of Citizenship in Ancient Athens*. Princeton, NJ: Princeton University Press.

Marcus, Gary. 2004. *The Birth of the Mind*. New York: Basic Books.

Marean, Curtis. 2015. "The Most Invasive Species of All." *Scientific American* 313: 32–39.

Marshall, Monty. 2014. "Major Episodes of Political Violence." http://www.systemicpeace. org/warlist/warlist.htm. Accessed June 14, 2014.

———. 2015. Polity IV Project: Political Regime Characteristics and Transitions, 1800–2013." http://www.systemicpeace.org/polity/polity4.htm. Accessed January 18, 2015.

Marx, Anthony. 1998. *Making Race and Nation: A Comparison of the United States, South Africa, and Brazil*. New York: Cambridge University Press.

Maryanski, Alexandra, and Jonathan Turner. 1992. *The Social Cage: Human Nature and the Evolution of Society*. Stanford, CA: Sanford University Press.

Mason, Ellen Huntly Bullard. 1862. *Civilizing Mountain Men or Sketches of Mission Work among the Karens*. London: James Nisbet & Co.

Mason, Francis. 1860. *Burmah, Its People and Natural Productions*. London: Trubner and Company.

———. 1870. *The Story of a Working Man's Life: With Sketches of Travel in Europe, Asia, Africa, and America, as Related by Himself*. New York: Oakley, Mason, and Co.

Mbonimana, Gamaliel. 1978. "Christianisation Indirecte et Cristallisation des Clivages Ethniques au Rwanda, 1925–1931." *Enquêtes et Documents d'Histoire Africaine* 3: 125–63.

———. 1995. "Ethnies et Eglise Catholique: Le Remodelage de la Société par l'Ecole Missionnaire, 1900–1931." *Cahiers Centre Sainte-Dominique* 1: 34–44.

McAdam, Doug. 1982. *Political Process and the Development of Black Insurgency, 1930–1970*. Chicago: University of Chicago Press.

McCarthy, John D., and Mayer N. Zald. 1977. "Resource Mobilization and Social Movements: A Partial Theory." *American Journal of Sociology* 82: 1212–41.

McCauley, Clark. 1995. "The Psychology of Terrorism." http://essays.ssrc.org/sept11/ essays/mccauley.htm. Accessed March 9, 2015.

McFarland, George Bradley. 1928. *Historical Sketch of Protestant Missions in Siam, 1828–1910*. Bangkok: Bangkok Times Press.

McGarry, John, and Brendan O'Leary. 2005. "Federation as a Method of Ethnic Conflict-Regulation." In *From Power-Sharing to Democracy: Post-Conflict Institutions in Ethnically Divided Societies*, edited by S. J. R. Noel, 263–96. Toronto: Queens University Press.

McMahon, A. R. 1876. *The Karens of the Golden Chersonese*. London: Harrison and Sons Printers.

McRoberts, Kenneth. 1975. "Mass Acquisition of a Nationalist Ideology: Quebec Prior to the 'Quiet Revolution.'" PhD dissertation, University of Chicago.

McRoberts, Kenneth, and Dale Posgate. 1980. *Quebec: Social Change and Political Crisis.* Toronto: McClelland and Stewart Limited.

McVeigh, Rory. 2009. *The Rise of the Ku Klux Klan: Right-Wing Movements and National Politics.* Minneapolis: University of Minnesota Press.

Miguel, Edward. 2004. "Tribe or Nation? Nation Building and Public Goods in Kenya Versus Tanzania." *World Politics* 56: 327–62.

Milgram, Stanley. 1974. *Obedience to Authority: An Experimental View.* New York: Harper Collins.

Mims, Christopher. 2007. "Strange But True: Testosterone Alone Does Not Cause Violence." *Scientific American.* http://www.scientificamerican.com/article/strange-but-true-testosterone-alone-doesnt-cause-violence/. Accessed March 17, 2015.

Misra, Tilottoma. 1987. *Literature and Society in Assam: A Study of the Assamese Renaissance, 1826–1926.* New Delhi: Omsons Publications.

Missions Étrangères de Paris. 1997. *Missions Étrangères et Langues Orientales: Contribution de la Societé des Missions Étrangères à la Connaissance de 60 Langues d'Asie.* Paris: L'Harmattan.

Moerman, Michael. 1965. "Ethnic Identification in a Complex Civilization: Who are the Lue?" *American Anthropologist* 67: 1215–30.

Mommsen, Hans. 1996. *The Rise and Fall of Weimar Democracy.* Chapel Hill: University of North Carolina Press.

Moore, Leonard. 1997. *Citizen Klansmen: The Ku Klux Klan in Indiana, 1921–1928.* Chapel Hill: University of North Carolina Press.

Mosse, George. 1964. *The Crisis of German Ideology: Intellectual Origins of the Third Reich.* New York: Universal Library.

——. 1975. *The Nationalization of the Masses: Political Symbolism and Mass Movements in Germany from the Napoleonic Wars Through the Third Reich.* New York: Howard Fertig.

——. 1991. *Fallen Soldiers: Reshaping the Memories of the World Wars.* Oxford: Oxford University Press.

Muchembled, Robert. 2012. *A History of Violence.* Malden, MA: Polity Press.

Muhlberger, Detlef. 2003. *The Social Basis of Nazism, 1919–1933.* Cambridge: Cambridge University Press.

Mullen, Brian, Rupert Brown, and Colleen Smith. 1992. "In-Group Bias as a Function of Salience, Relevance and Status: An Integration." *European Journal of Social Psychology* 22: 103–22.

Musgrove, Luke, and Craig McGarty. 2008. "Opinion-Based Group Memberships as a Predictor of Collective Emotional Responses and Support for Pro- and Anti-War Action." *Social Psychology* 39: 37–47.

Oakes, Leigh. 2001. *Language and National Identity: Comparing France and Sweden.* Philadelphia: John Benjamins North America.

Olson, Mancur. 1965. *The Logic of Collective Action: Public Goods and the Theory of Groups.* Cambridge, MA: Harvard University Press.

Operario, Don, and Susan Fiske. 2001. "Ethnic Identity Moderates Perceptions of Prejudice: Judgments of Personal Versus Group Discrimination and Subtle Versus Blatant Bias." *Personality and Social Psychology Bulletin* 27: 550–61.

Oswald, Hans. 1999. "Political Socialization in the New State of Germany." In *Roots of Civic Identity: International Perspectives on Community Service and Activism in Youth,* edited by Miranda Yates and James Youniss, 97–113. New York: Cambridge University Press.

O'Toole, Laura, and Jessica Schiffman, eds. 2007. *Gender Violence: Interdisciplinary Perspectives.* New York: New York University Press.

Otterbein. Keith. 2004. *How War Began*. College Station: Texas A&M University Press.

Paden, John. 1971. "Communal Competition, Conflict and Violence in Kano." In *Nigeria: Modernization and the Politics of Communalism*, edited by Robert Melson and Howard Wolpe, 113–44. East Lansing: Michigan State University Press.

Pape, Robert. 2005. *Dying to Win: The Strategic Logic of Suicide Terrorism*. New York: Random House.

Payne, Keith. 2006. "Weapon Bias: Split Second Decisions and Unintended Stereotyping." *Current Directions in Psychological Science* 15: 287–91.

Persianis, Panayiotis. 1978. *Church and State in Cyprus Education: The Contribution of the Greek Orthodox Church of Cyprus to Cyprus Education During the British Administration (1878–1960)*. Nicosia: Violaris Press.

Perusse, Daniel. 1993. "Cultural and Reproductive Success in Industrial Societies: Testing the Relationship at the Proximate and Ultimate Levels." *Behavioral and Brain Sciences* 16: 267–322.

Petersen, Roger. 2002. *Understanding Ethnic Violence: Fear, Hatred, and Resentment in Twentieth-Century Eastern Europe*. New York: Cambridge University Press.

Piggott, Stuart. 1965. *Ancient Europe: From the Beginning of Agriculture to Classical Antiquity*. Edinburgh: University of Edinburgh Press.

Pinard, Maurice. 2011. *Motivational Dimensions in Social Movements and Contentious Collective Action*. Montreal: McGill-Queen's University Press.

Pinker, Steven. 2011. *The Better Angels of Our Nature: Why Violence Has Declined*. New York: Viking Press.

Political Instability Task Force. 2013. "Internal Wars and Failures of Governance, 1955-Most Recent Year." http://globalpolicy.gmu.edu/political-instability-task-force-home/pitf-problem-set-codebook/. Accessed January 14, 2013.

Pop-Eleches, Grigore, and Graeme Robertson. 2015. "Democratization." In *Oxford Handbook of Transformations of the State*, edited by Stephan Liebfried, Evelyne Huber, Matthew Lange, Jonah Levy, and John Stephens, 779–95. New York: Oxford University Press.

Porter, Andrew. 2006. "Empires of the Mind." In *The Cambridge Illustrated History of the British Empire*, edited by P. J. Marshall, 185–223. New York: Cambridge University Press.

Price, Gareth. 1997. "The Assam Movement and the Construction of Assamese Identity." PhD dissertation, Bristol University.

Proctor, Robert. 1988. *Racial Hygiene: Medicine under the Nazis*. Cambridge, MA: Harvard University Press.

Quillian, Lincoln. 1996. "Group Threat and Regional Change in Attitudes Toward African-Americans." *American Journal of Sociology* 102: 816–60.

Rajah, Ananda. 2002. "A 'Nation of Intent' in Burma: Karen Ethno-Nationalism, Nationalism and Narrations of Nation." *Pacific Review* 15: 517–37.

Riga, Liliana. 2008. "The Ethnic Roots of Class Universalism: Rethinking the Russian Revolutionary Elite." *American Journal of Sociology* 114: 649–705.

Ringer, Fritz. 1967. "Higher Education in Germany in the Nineteenth Century." In *Education and Social Structure: In the Twentieth Century*, edited by Walter Laqueur and George Moss, 123–38. New York: Harper and Row.

Rodney, Walter. 1972. *How Europe Underdeveloped Africa*. London: Bogle-L'Ouverture Publications.

Rostow, Walter. 1960. *The Stages of Economic Growth: A Non-Communist Manifesto*. New York: Cambridge University Press.

Russell, Charles, and Bowman Miller. 1978. "Profile of a Terrorist." In *Contemporary Terrorism: Selected Readings*, edited by John Elliot and Leslie Gibson, 81–95. Gaithersburg, MD: Bureau of Operations and Research.

Rydell, Robert J., Diane J. Mackie, Angela T. Maitner, Heather M. Claypool, Melissa J. Ryan, and Eliot R. Smith. 2008. "Arousal, Processing, and Risk-Taking: Consequences of Intergroup Anger." *Personality and Social Psychology Bulletin* 34: 1141–52.

Salemink, Oscar. 2003. *The Ethnography of Vietnam's Central Highlanders: A Historical Contextualization, 1850–1900.* Honolulu: University of Hawai'i Press.

Sambanis, Nicholas. 2001. "Do Ethnic and Non-Ethnic Civil Wars Have the Same Causes? A Theoretical and Empirical Inquiry (Part 1)." *Journal of Conflict Resolution* 45: 259–82.

Sand, Shlomo. 2010. *The Invention of the Jewish People.* London: Verso.

Sandbrook, Richard, Marc Edelman, Patrick Heller, and Judith Teichman. 2007. *Social Democracy in the Global Periphery: Origins, Challenges, Prospects.* New York: Cambridge University Press.

Sarapata, Michael, Douglas Herrmann, Tom Johnson, and Rose Aycock. 1998. "The Role of Head Injury in Cognitive Functioning, Emotional Adjustment and Criminal Behaviour." *Brain Injury* 12: 821–42.

Sarmah, Alaka. 1999. *Immigration and Assam Politics.* Delhi: Ajanta Books International.

Scheff, Thomas, and Suzanne Retzinger. 1991. *Emotions and Violence: Shame and Rage in Destructive Conflicts.* Lexington, MA: Lexington Books.

Schmidt, Volker. 2006. "Multiple Modernities or Varieties of Modernity?" *Current Sociology* 54: 77–97.

Schubarth, Wilfred. 1997. "Xenophobia among East German Youth." In *Antisemitism and Xenophobia in Germany after Unification,* edited by Hermann Kurthen, Werner Bergmann, and Reiner Erb, 143–58. New York: Oxford University Press.

Scott, James C. 1998. *Seeing Like a State: How Certain Schemes to Improve the Human Condition Have Failed.* New Haven, CT: Yale University Press.

Segal, Lynne. 1990. *Slow Motion: Changing Masculinities, Changing Men.* New Brunswick, NJ: Rutgers University Press.

Selznick, Gertrude, and Stephen Steinberg. 1969. *The Tenacity of Prejudice.* New York: Harper and Row.

Shapiro, D. M., and M. Stelcner. 1987. "Earnings Disparities among Linguistic Groups in Quebec, 1970–1980." *Canadian Public Policy* 13: 97–104.

Sharma, Jayeeta. 2002. "The Making of 'Modern' Assam, 1826–1935." PhD dissertation, Cambridge University.

Simmel, Georg. 1955. *Conflict and the Web of Group Affiliation.* New York: Free Press.

Singer, Peter. 2011. *The Expanding Circle: Ethics, Evolution, and Moral Progress.* Princeton, NJ: Princeton University Press.

Singh, Prerna. 2011. "We-ness and Welfare: A Longitudinal Analysis of Social Development in Kerala, India." *World Development* 39: 282–93.

Sinno, Abdulkader. 2008. *Organizations at War in Afghanistan and Beyond.* Ithaca, NY: Cornell University Press.

Skocpol, Theda. 1979. *States and Social Revolutions: A Comparative Analysis of France, Russia, and China.* New York: Cambridge University Press.

Smeaton, Donald MacKenzie. 1920. *The Loyal Karens of Burma.* London: Kegan Paul, Trench, Trubner & Co. LTD.

Smith, Anthony D. 1986a. *The Ethnic Origin of Nations.* Oxford: Basil Blackwell.

——. 1986b. "State-Making and Nation-Making." In *States in History,* edited by John Hall, 228–63. Oxford: Basil Blackwell.

——. 1993. *National Identity.* Reno: University of Nevada Press.

——. 2003. *Chosen Peoples: Sacred Sources of National Identities.* New York: Oxford University Press.

Smith, Eliot R. 1993. "Social Identity and Social Emotions: Toward New Conceptualizations of Prejudice." In *Affect, Cognition, and Stereotyping: Interactive Processes in Group Perception*, edited by Diane Mackie and David Hamilton, 297–315. San Diego: Academic Press.

Snyder, Jack. 2000. *From Voting to Violence: Democratization and Nationalist Conflict*. New York: W. W. Norton.

Societé des Missions Étrangères. 1890. *Compte Rendu des Travaux de 1889*. Paris: Seminaire des Missions Étrangères.

Spitz, Rene. 1945. "Hospitalism: An Inquiry into the Genesis of Psychiatric Conditions in Early Childhood." *Psychoanalytic Study of the Child* 1: 53–74.

Stangneth, Bettina. 2014. *Eichmann Before Jerusalem: The Unexamined Life of a Mass Murderer*. New York: Knopf Doubleday.

Steinberg, Michael. 1977. *Sabers and Brown Shirts: The German Students' Path to National Socialism, 1918–1935*. Chicago: Chicago University Press.

Steinmetz, George. 1997. "Social Class and the Reemergence of the Radical Right in Contemporary Germany." In *Reworking Class*, edited by John R. Hall, 335–68. Ithaca, NY: Cornell University Press.

Stember, Charles H. 1961. *Education and Attitude Change*. New York: Institute of Human Relations Press.

Stern, Theodore. 1968. "*Ariya* and the Golden Book: A Millenarian Buddhist Sect Among the Karen." *Journal of Asian Studies* 27: 297–328.

Stone, Dan. 1999. "Modernity and Violence: Theoretical Reflections on the Einsatzgruppen." *Journal of Genocide Research* 1: 367–78.

Straus, Scott. 2004. *The Order of Genocide: Race, Power, and War in Rwanda*. Ithaca, NY: Cornell University Press.

Tajfel, Henri. 1970. "Experiments in Intergroup Discrimination." *Scientific American* 223: 96–102.

——. 1974. "Social Identity and Intergroup Behavior." *Social Science Information* 13: 65–93.

——, ed. 1978. *Differentiation Between Social Groups: Studies in the Social Psychology of Intergroup Relations*. London: Academic Press.

Talaska, Cara, Susan Fiske, and Shelly Chaiken. 2008. "Legitimating Racial Discrimination: Emotions, Not Beliefs, Best Predict Discrimination in a Meta-Analysis." *Social Justice Research* 21: 263–96.

Tambiah, Stanley. 1986. *Sri Lanka: Ethnic Fratricide and the Dismantling of Democracy*. Chicago: University of Chicago Press.

Tilly, Charles. 1978. *From Mobilization to Revolution*. New York: Random House.

——. 1985. "War Making and State Making as Organized Crime." In *Bringing the State Back In*, edited by Peter Evans, Dietrich Rueschemeyer, and Theda Skocpol, 169–91. Cambridge: Cambridge University Press.

——. 1992. *Coercion, Capital, and European States, AD 990–1992*. Cambridge, MA: Blackwell.

Tönnies, Ferdinand. 2001 [1887]. *Community and Civil Society*. New York: Cambridge University Press.

Torney, Judith, A. N. Oppenheim, and Russell Farnen. 1975. *Civic Education in Ten Countries: An Empirical Study*. New York: Wiley.

Toy, Eckard V. 1992. "Robe and Gown: The Ku Klux Klan in Eugene, Oregon, During the 1920s." In *The Invisible Empire in the West: Toward a New Historical Appraisal of the Ku Klux Klan of the 1920s*, edited by Shawn Lay, 153–84. Chicago: University of Illinois Press.

Trejo, Guillermo. 2009. "Religious Competition and Ethnic Mobilization in Latin America: Why the Catholic Church Promotes Indigenous Movements in Mexico." *American Political Science Review* 103: 329–42.

Tuch, Steven. 1987. "Urbanism, Region, and Tolerance Revisited: The Case of Racial Prejudice." *American Sociological Review* 52: 504–10.

Turner, John C., Penelope J. Oakes, S. Alexander Haslam, and Craig McGarty. 1994. "Self and Collective: Cognition and Social Context." *Personality and Social Psychology Bulletin* 20: 454–63.

Turner, Jonathan. 2007a. *Human Emotions: A Sociological Theory*. New York: Routledge.

——. 2007b. "Self, Emotions, and Extreme Violence: Extending Symbolic Interactionist Theorizing." *Symbolic Interaction* 30: 270–301.

UNESCO. 1995. "Declaration of Principles on Tolerance." http://www.unesco.org/webworld/peace_library/UNESCO/HRIGHTS/124–129.HTM. Accessed February 21, 2013.

United States Census Bureau. 1920. *Fourteenth Census of the United States (1920) Volume 8–13: Statistics of Population, Occupation, Agriculture, and Manufactures for the District-Compendium for: District of Columbia, Florida, Georgia, Idaho, Illinois, and Indiana* (Washington, DC).

United States Department of Justice. 2011. "Homicide Trends in the United States, 1980–2008." http://www.bjs.gov/content/pub/pdf/htus8008.pdf. Accessed March 19, 2015.

Usman, Yusuf Bala. 2006. *Beyond Fairy Tales: Selected Historical Writing of Yusuf Bala Usman*. Zaria, Nigeria: Abdullahi Smith Centre for Historical Research.

Uwazaninka, Beata. 2006. "Treasure Your Mothers and Fathers." Aegis Trust. http://av.hmd.org.uk/1251984178-78.pdf-. Accessed June 2, 2016.

Vaillancourt, François, Dominique Lemay, and Luc Vaillancourt. 2007. "Laggards No More: The Changed Socioeconomic Status of Francophones in Quebec. No. 103." C. C. Howe Institute.

van Zomeren, Martijn, Russell Spears, and Colin W. Leach. 2008. "Exploring Psychological Mechanisms of Collective Action: Does Relevance of Group Identity Influence How People Cope with Collective Disadvantage?" *British Journal of Social Psychology* 47: 353–72.

Verwimp, Philip. 2005. "An Economic Profile of Peasant Perpetrators of Genocide." *Journal of Development Economics* 77: 297–323.

Viereck, Peter. 2004. *Metapolitics: From Wagner and the German Romantics to Hitler*. Brunswick, NJ: Transaction Publishers.

Voegelin, Eric. 1940. "The Growth of the Race Idea." *Review of Politics* 2: 283–317.

Vural, Yücel. 2012. "Seeking to Transform the Perceptions of Intercommunal Relations: The Turkish-Cypriot Case (2004–2009)." *Nationalism and Ethnic Politics* 18: 406–30.

Wade, Peter. 2008. "Race in Latin America." In *A Companion to Latin American Anthropology*, edited by Deborah Poole, 177–92. Malden, MA: Blackwell Publishing.

Wallerstein, Immanuel. 1976. *The Modern World-System: Capitalist Agriculture and the Origins of the European World-Economy in the Sixteenth Century*. New York: Academic Press.

Walter, Enders, and Todd Sandler. 2006. *The Political Economy of Terrorism*. New York: Cambridge University Press.

Waters, Mary. 1990. *Ethnic Options: Choosing Identities in America*. Berkeley: University of California Press.

Weber, Eugen. 1976. *Peasants into Frenchmen: The Modernization of Rural France, 1870–1914*. Stanford, CA: Stanford University Press.

Weber, Max. 1968 [1921]. *Economy and Society*. New York: Bedminster Press.
——. 2002 [1905]. *The Protestant Ethnic and the Spirit of Capitalism*. New York: Penguin Books.
Weil, Frederick L. 1985. "The Variable Effects of Education on Liberal Attitudes: A Comparative-Historical Analysis of Antisemitism Using Public Opinion in Data." *American Sociological Review* 50: 458–74.
Weinstein, Jeremy. 2007. *Inside Rebellion: The Politics of Insurgent Violence*. New York: Cambridge University Press.
Weiss, John. 1996. *Ideology of Death: Why the Holocaust Happened in Germany*. Chicago: Ivan R. Dee.
——. 2003. *The Politics of Hate: Anti-Semitism, History, and the Holocaust in Modern Europe*. Chicago: Ivan R. Dee.
Weitz, Eric. 2003. *A Century of Genocide: Utopias of Race and Nation*. Princeton, NJ: Princeton University Press.
Weyers, Wolfgang. 1998. *Death of Medicine in Nazi Germany: Dermatology and Dermatopathology under the Swastika*. Edited by A. Bernard Ackerman. Philadelphia: Ardor/Screbendi.
Weymar, Erich. 1961. *Das Selbstverständnis der Deutschen*. Stuttgart: Jahrhundert.
Wickham-Crowley, Timothy. 1992. *Guerrillas and Revolution in Latin America: A Comparative Study of Insurgents and Regimes since 1956*. Princeton, NJ: Princeton University Press.
Wilgoren, Jodi. 2001. "After the Attacks: The Hijackers; A Terrorist Profile Emerges that Confounds the Experts." *New York Times*, September 15.
Wilkinson, Steven. 2004. *Votes and Violence: Electoral Competition and Ethnic Riots in India*. New York: Cambridge University Press.
Willer, Robb, Christabel L. Rogalin, Bridget Conlon, and Michael T. Wojnowicz. 2013. "Overdoing Gender: A Test of the Masculine Overcompensation Thesis." *American Journal of Sociology* 118: 980–1022.
Williams, Leanne M., Belinda J. Liddell, Andrew H. Kemp, Richard A. Bryant, Russell A. Meares, Anthony S. Peduto, and Evian Gordon. 2006. "Amygdala-Prefrontal Dissociation of Subliminal and Spraliminal Fear." *Human Brain Mapping* 27: 652–61.
Wimmer, Andreas. 2002. *Nationalist Exclusion and Ethnic Conflict: Shadows of Modernity*. New York: Cambridge University Press.
——. 2013a. *Ethnic Boundary Making: Institutions, Power, Networks*. New York: Oxford University Press.
——. 2013b. *Waves of War: Nationalism, State Formation, and Ethnic Exclusion in the Modern World*. New York: Cambridge University Press.
Wimmer, Andreas, Lars-Erik Cederman, and Brian Min. 2009. "Ethnic Politics and Armed Conflict: A Configurational Analysis." *American Sociological Review* 74: 316–37.
Wimmer, Andreas, and Brian Min. 2006. "From Empire to Nation-State: Explaining Wars in the Modern World, 1816–2001." *American Sociological Review* 71: 867–97.
Woodberry, Robert. 2012. "The Missionary Roots of Liberal Democracy." *American Political Science Review* 106: 244–74.
Wook, Choi Byung. 2004. *Southern Vietnam under the Reign of Minh Mang: Central Policies and Local Responses*. Ithaca, NY: Cornell University Press.
World Bank. 2012. *World Governance Indicators*. http://info.worldbank.org/governance/wgi/index.aspx#home. Accessed December 27, 2012.
World Bank. 2014. *World Development Indicators On-Line*. http://data.worldbank.org/data-catalog/world-development-indicators. Accessed May 23, 2014.

World Powerlifting Federation. 2015. "Men's and Women's Bench Press Records." http://
wpfpowerlifting.com/records.htm. Accessed April 4, 2015.

Wyrtzen, Jonathan. 2015. *Making Morocco: Colonial Intervention and the Politics of
Identity*. Ithaca, NY: Cornell University Press.

Zernatto, Guido. 1944. "Nation: The History of a Word." *Review of Politics* 6: 351–66.

Ziegler, Herbert. 1989. *Nazi Germany's New Aristocracy: The SS Leadership, 1925–1939*.
Princeton, NJ: Princeton University Press.

Index